# The Scandal of the Century

# The Scandal of the Century
## and Other Writings

Gabriel García Márquez

Translated by Anne McLean
Foreword by Jon Lee Anderson
Edited by Cristóbal Pera

ALFRED A. KNOPF   New York

2019

THIS IS A BORZOI BOOK
PUBLISHED BY ALFRED A. KNOPF

English translation copyright © 2019 by Heirs of
Gabriel García Márquez

Library of Congress Cataloging-in-Publication Data
Names: García Márquez, Gabriel, 1927–2014, author. |
McLean, Anne, [date] translator.
Title: The scandal of the century : and other writings /
Gabriel García Márquez ; translated by Anne McLean.
Description: First edition. | New York : Alfred A. Knopf, 2019. |
Translation of: El escándalo del siglo :
textos en prensa y revistas (1950–1984).
Identifiers: LCCN 2019001736| ISBN 9780525656425 (hardcover : alk. paper) |
ISBN 9780525656432 (E-book)
Subjects: LCSH: García Márquez, Gabriel, 1927–2014—
Translations into English.
Classification: LCC PQ8180.17.A73 A2 2019 | DDC 864/.64—dc23
LC record available at https://lccn.loc.gov/2019001736

Jacket photograph by Ulf Anderson / Getty Images
Jacket design by Carol Devine Carson

Manufactured in the United States of America
First Edition

# Contents

Contents *vii*

# Foreword

The world recognizes Gabriel García Márquez as an extraordinary novelist—the beloved creator of Colonel Aureliano Buendía and of Macondo, of the epic love between Fermina Daza and Florentino Ariza, of the death of Santiago Nasar, and of the colossal, solitary dictator of *The Autumn of the Patriarch*. For all of this, he received the maximum literary recognition possible, a Nobel Prize, and when he did, the Spanish-speaking world rejoiced at the sight of one of their own, "one of the seventeen children of the telegraphist of Aracataca," standing before the Swedish monarchs to receive his distinction.

But García Márquez, or "Gabo"—the affectionate nickname by which he was known in the Hispanic world—was more than a novelist. He is also remembered for having been the friend and confidant of Fidel Castro and Bill Clinton, as well as Julio Cortázar and Carlos Fuentes and his other colleagues of the Boom, and for having been the husband of Mercedes Barcha and the father of two sons, Gonzalo and Rodrigo, and when he died in 2014, multitudes of people thronged to his funeral, which was held in the beautiful palace of Bellas Artes in the capital of Mexico, his longtime country of residence. When Juan Manuel Santos, who was then the president of Colombia, Gabo's birthplace, said that he had been the best Colombian of all time, no one challenged the assertion.

In addition to all of that, Gabo was a journalist. Journalism was, in a sense, his first true love, and, like all first loves, it was the longest lasting. The profession of journalism helped form him as a writer, which is something he recalled forever afterward. His admiration for journalism reached the point where he proclaimed it, on one occasion, with his characteristic generosity, to be "the best job in the world."

Gabo's hyperbole was inspired by a sentiment of genuine respect and affection toward a profession that he made his own at the same time as he took his first steps as a writer. In 1947, his first year at the Universidad Nacional in Bogotá, Gabo's first short stories were published in the daily newspaper *El Espectador*. He already wanted to become a writer, but had entered law school in order to please his father.

IT WAS NOT LONG, however, before Gabo's academic life was interrupted by political violence. The April 1948 assassination of the charismatic Liberal politician Jorge Eliécer Gaitán in Bogotá triggered an outbreak of violent public unrest in the Colombian capital lasting several days. During the chaos, which became remembered as "*el Bogotazo*," Gabo's student residence went up in flames and the university itself was closed indefinitely. It was the beginning of a civil war between the country's two main political parties, the Liberals and their rivals, the Conservatives.

The conflict, which would become known as "*la Violencia*," would last a decade and cost the lives of some 200,000 people. Colombia would never be the same, and nor would the life of Gabo. To continue his studies, he moved to the city of Cartagena de Indias, on the Caribbean coast, and signed up at the university there. He also began to collaborate with a new local daily paper, *El Universal*, and, before long, gave up his studies altogether to devote himself to writing full-time. He soon began writing articles for *El Heraldo*, a newspaper published in the larger, neighboring city of Barranquilla, and he moved there in 1950. These were happy and formative years for Gabo, in which he was surrounded by other young creative personalities—writers, artists, and bohemians—with whom he became friends and who together made up the so-called Group of Barranquilla. While living in a flophouse that doubled as a bordello, Gabo eked out a living as a columnist, writing under the nom de plume "Septimus," and he completed his first novella, *Leaf Storm*.

THIS ANTHOLOGY FOCUSES ON the unique journalistic legacy of Gabriel García Márquez via a selection of fifty of his articles published between 1950 and 1984. The pieces assembled here were selected by Cristóbal Pera, who worked with Gabo as an editor on his memoirs, culling from the exhaustive collection of Gabo's journalism compiled by Jacques Gilard, the late French Hispanist, for his extraordinary five-volume anthology of Gabo's work published in the 1980s.

*The Scandal of the Century* takes us from the early writings of the young, unknown Gabo of his Barranquilla days through nearly four decades, into the mid-1980s, when he was a mature, internationally renowned author. Among other things, this anthology reveals Gabo to have been blessed with abundant talent from the start, as well as an easygoing sense of humor, and a writer whose journalism is barely distinguishable from his fiction. Indeed, in his explanation for this selection, Pera tells us that he chose the works that most revealed Gabo as "the storyteller he was," in which "the seams of reality are stretched by his unstoppable narrative impulse."

In "Topic for a Topical Piece," for instance, Gabo writes about the difficulty of finding an appropriate topic with which to begin a piece. "There are those who turn the lack of a topic into a topic for a journalistic piece. The choice is absurd in a world like ours, where things of imperceptible interest are happening." After reviewing a series of curious stories appearing in the newspapers—including one telling of how the daughter of the Spanish dictator, the "Generalissimo" Francisco Franco, was getting married, and that her bridegroom, his future son-in-law, or *yerno,* was already being referred to as *"el Yernissimo,"* and another incident in which some youths were reported as having been burned for playing with "flying saucers," Gabo makes it clear that it is possible to write an entertaining article, as he has just done, about nothing in particular.

In "An Understandable Mistake," Gabo reveals more than anything else his urge to, as he used to say, *"echar un cuento bien contado"*—spin a good yarn. Adopting a Gothic noir tone, he narrates the circumstances in which a deeply drunk man nearly committed suicide by throwing himself out of his hotel window after seeing fish falling from the sky. In the course of the tale, we see that Gabo has riffed imaginatively on a pair of news items from the city of Cali.

> Cali. April 18. Today, in the early hours of the morning, a stranger jumped out the window of his apartment located on the third floor of a building in the city. The decision seemed to have been due to the nervous excitement produced by alcohol. The injured man is now in the hospital, where his condition does not appear to be serious.

> Cali. April 18. Inhabitants of the capital of the Cauca Valley had an extraordinary surprise today, as they observed in a downtown city street the presence of hundreds of small silvery fish, approximately two inches long, that appeared strewn all over the place.

IN 1954, Gabo returned to Bogotá to work for *El Espectador,* the national newspaper that had published his first short stories. He began by writing movie reviews, but he also penned articles about a wide range of things that caught his interest, everything from popular folklore to his reflections on events that intrigued him. In "Literaturism," he writes of a horrifying murder that occurred in the Colombian interior, in Antioquia. With a tone of admonishment leavened by his customary black humor, Gabo notes, "The news has not earned—at the current exchange rate of the journalistic peso—more than two columns on the regional news page. It is a bloody crime, like any other. With the difference that these days there is nothing extraordinary about it, since as a news item it is too common and as a novel too gruesome. It would be best to recommend [to] real life [that it] exercise a bit more discretion."

In "The Postman Rings a Thousand Times," Gabo demonstrates once again that it is possible to write an interesting story about nothing very much with an exquisite piece about an address in Bogotá where the letters that never reach their destinations end up.

Gabo earned a national reputation with his dramatic 1955 serial, entitled *The Story of a Shipwrecked Sailor,* based on his interviews with Luis Alejandro Velasco, a crewman on the Colombian warship ARC *Caldas* and the sole survivor among seven sailors who were thrown overboard when the vessel lurched suddenly to one side. Gabo's story was a huge success. Published in fourteen installments, the series simultaneously broke sales records for *El Espectador* and sparked controversy when it discredited the official account of events, which had blamed the disaster on a nonexistent storm, and asserted that the ship had, in fact, listed because it was overloaded with contraband cargo brought on board by the officers and crew. To extricate Gabo from the public storm, the paper's editor sent him to Europe to report. It was the first time Gabo had been outside of Colombia.

FOR THE NEXT TWO and a half years, Gabo was *El Espectador*'s roving correspondent, traveling to Paris, Italy, and Vienna, and even to some of the countries of Eastern Europe on the other side of the Iron Curtain. Gabo wrote idiosyncratic pieces about whatever caught his interest—everything from a world leader's summit in Geneva to the ostensible squabbles between two Italian movie celebrity actresses. He wrote another serialized story, as he had done with the *Shipwrecked Sailor,* about the mysterious death of a young Italian woman named Wilma Montesi; the mock-tabloid title of this book has also been borrowed from that story, "The Scandal of the Century." Gabo even wrote, hilariously, about London's famous fog. His prose was fresh, and his chronicles were sharp and laden with irony; he was a great "*mamador de gallo,*" as jokesters are known in Colombia, and the loyal fans he had acquired at home were ready to read anything he wrote.

In one of his dispatches, "H.H. Goes on Vacation," Gabo expands artfully on the pope's habitual drive from the Vatican to his palace of Castel Gandolfo, situated on the outskirts of Rome. In Gabo's hands, the journey becomes a suspenseful epic. "The pope went on vacation. This afternoon, at five o'clock sharp, he settled into his own Mercedes, license plate SCV-7, and drove out through the Holy Office gate, to the Castel Gandolfo Palace, twenty miles from Rome. Two gigantic Swiss Guards saluted him at the gate. One of them, the taller and heftier one, is a blond teenager with a flattened nose, like a boxer's nose, the result of a traffic accident."

The story moves on, imbued with dramatic timing thanks to the trick of adding subtitles to the piece, including one about the high temperature of the day: "Ninety-five degrees in the shade" and another, "Accidents along the way," in which Gabo informs us that His Holiness's ten-minute delay in reaching his palace was caused by a truck blocking the way. The pope's eventual arrival is shared in a confiding tone: "No one in Castel Gandolfo noticed which entrance the pope took into his holiday palace. He entered from the west side, into a garden with an avenue bordered by hundred-year-old trees."

WHEN HE RETURNED to Latin America at the end of 1957, Gabo was recruited by a Colombian friend, Plinio Apuleyo Mendoza, to come and work with him on *Momento,* a magazine published in Caracas, Venezuela. Mendoza had also accompanied Gabo on his journey to the countries of Eastern Europe. Gabo's arrival in Caracas coincided with the onset of a politically convulsive era in Latin America. A short time after he arrived, in January of 1958, came the toppling of the Venezuelan dictator Marcos Pérez Jiménez. It was the first popular overthrow of a dictator in a period when Latin America was governed almost exclusively by despots. What Gabo lived through in Venezuela's volatile atmosphere over the next year sparked a political awakening in him.

Gabo returned briefly to Barranquilla to marry Mercedes Barcha, a beautiful young woman from the Magdalena River town of Magangué

with whom he had fallen in love several years before, during his Barranquilla period. They returned to Caracas together. When Gabo's
friend Mendoza left *Momento* after a disagreement with the magazine's
owner, Gabo quit in solidarity and began writing for other publications
as a freelancer. Two of his pieces from that time, "Only Twelve Hours
to Save Him" and "Caracas Without Water," which are included here,
are classics of Gabo's emerging literary style, in which his narration
involves a detailed reconstruction of real-life dramas, conveyed with a
suspense that is almost Hitchcockian, and focuses on a riddle that is
only revealed at the story's end.

IN JANUARY OF 1959, two weeks after Fidel Castro's rebel army over-
threw dictator Fulgencio Batista and seized power in Cuba, Gabo and
Mendoza managed to travel to the island onboard a beat-up old plane
that had been flown to Caracas by the triumphant "*barbudos*," as the
bearded rebels were known, to bring journalists back with them. For
Gabo, the trip marked the beginning of a relationship with Cuba, and
its revolution, that would last the rest of his life. About this first Cuban
experience, he wrote memorably in "I Can't Think of Any Title."

In his text, Gabo situated the nascent revolution in the political
context of the moment via a genial vignette about the Cuban poet
Nicolás Guillén, whom he had known in Paris when both of them were
lodged in the same seedy hotel in the Latin Quarter a few years before:

> [E]ven in the cruelest times of winter, Nicolás Guillén maintained
> in Paris the very Cuban custom of rising (without a rooster) at the
> crowing of the first roosters, and of reading the newspapers as he
> sipped his coffee lulled by the sweet wind of the sugar mills and
> the counterpoint of guitars in the clamorous dawns of Camagüey.
> Then he opened the window of his balcony, also as he would in
> Camagüey, and woke up the whole street by shouting the news
> from Latin America translated from French into Cuban slang.
> [. . .] So one morning Nicolás Guillén opened his window and
> shouted a single piece of news:

"The man has fallen!"

There was a commotion in the sleeping street because each of us believed the man who had fallen was his. The Argentinians thought it was Juan Domingo Perón, the Paraguayans thought it was Alfredo Stroessner [. . .], the Guatemalans thought it was Castillo Armas, the Dominicans thought it was Rafael Leónidas Trujillo, and the Cubans thought it was Fulgencio Batista. It was Perón, actually. Later, talking about this, Nicolás Guillén painted a distressing panorama of the situation in Cuba for us. "The only thing I see for the future," he concluded, "is a kid who's getting a lot done over in Mexico." He paused like a clairvoyant, and concluded:

"His name is Fidel Castro."

As for his own arrival in Havana at the height of revolutionary fervor, Gabo recalled it the following way:

Before noon we landed between the Babylonian mansions of the richest of the rich of Havana: in the Campo Columbia airport, then baptized with the name Ciudad Libertad, the former Batista fort where a few days earlier Camilo Cienfuegos had camped with his column of astonished peasants. The first impression was rather comical, for we were greeted by members of the former military air force who at the last minute had gone over to the Revolution and were keeping to their barracks while their beards grew enough to look like old revolutionaries.

WITH THE PUBLICATION and spectacular success of *One Hundred Years of Solitude*, the year 1967 was one of the great milestones in the life of Gabriel García Márquez. From that moment on, Gabo and his family enjoyed economic stability and he was internationally acclaimed, deservedly so, as one of the great novelists of his era. For the next twenty years, Gabo remained at the literary pinnacle, publishing his other great works, such as *The Autumn of the Patriarch* and *Love in the Time of Cholera.* Much less well known to his millions of readers outside of Latin America, Gabo continued to be a journalist as well, albeit with an increasingly political focus.

The 1970s saw rising political tensions in Latin America ushered in by the Cuban Revolution and the violent counterinsurgency policies introduced by the United States to roll back communism. At this time, García Márquez embarked on a phase of militant journalism. When the socialist Chilean president Salvador Allende was brutally overthrown by General Augusto Pinochet in 1972, for instance, Gabo went so far as to declare that he would not publish another book until the regime had fallen. Although he didn't follow through on that promise, he did begin to express his sympathies with leftist causes more openly from then on.

Together with some Colombian journalist friends, he founded *Alternativa,* a leftist magazine; he wrote articles and columns that were critical of U.S. policies and in favor of Cuba and of Fidel Castro, with whom he also began to develop a close friendship. He wrote a long and flattering article about the Cuban military expedition in Angola and another, included in this volume, entitled "The Sandinista Heist: Chronicle of the Assault on the 'Hog House,'" in which he rendered the circumstances of a mass abduction of Nicaraguan parliamentarians by a group of Sandinista guerrillas as a heroic epic.

In the article "The Cubans Face the Blockade," included in this anthology, Gabo used his narrative skills to make his readers understand the implications of the famous trade embargo—"blockade," to the Cubans—which the United States had imposed against Cuba in 1961. He wrote:

> That night, the first of the blockade, in Cuba there were 482,560 automobiles, 343,300 refrigerators, 549,700 radios, 303,500 television sets, 352,900 electric irons, 286,400 fans, 41,800 washing machines, 3,510,000 wristwatches, sixty-three locomotives, and twelve merchant ships. All these things, except for the wristwatches, which were Swiss, had been made in the United States.
>
> It seems that a certain amount of time had to pass before the

Cubans realized what those mortal numbers meant to their lives. From the point of view of production, Cuba soon found that it was not actually a distinct country but rather a commercial peninsula of the United States.

Because of texts like these, Gabo was widely criticized by conservative media in the United States and Latin America, which branded him, not altogether inaccurately, as a propagandist of the Cuban regime. Some went so far, more unfairly, as to call him Fidel Castro's useful idiot. Gabo was undeterred by these critiques, however, and carried on supporting those causes he believed in, which were on the left, by and large, and definitely included advocacy for Cuba and the region's left-wing causes. Behind the scenes, he also used his political access and Nobel clout to play a diplomatic role in efforts to broker dialogue between the United States and Cuba, as well as between Colombian guerrilla leaders and the government.

TOWARD THE END of the 1990s, Gabo was diagnosed with lymphatic cancer—and although he recovered from that illness, he became weaker in the final decade and a half of his life.

In 1996, before his health problems began, he published the book *News of a Kidnapping,* one of his few in-depth journalistic works, and the only one to become widely known internationally. It is the story of the terrifying ordeal of a group of influential Colombians, most of them journalists, who were taken hostage by Pablo Escobar in an effort to convince the Colombian government to abandon the extradition agreement for narcotraffickers it had signed with the United States.

In 1998, Gabo used part of the money he received from his Nobel Prize to buy *Cambio,* a magazine owned by a friend of his, and to relaunch it with a new team of editors and reporters. In *Cambio* he published some of his last pieces of journalism, including a profile of the singer Shakira, who is from Barranquilla, and another of the Venezuelan strongman Hugo Chávez. In the end, the magazine didn't work out, but while it lasted, Gabo greatly enjoyed being immersed, once again, in "the best job in the world."

In 1994, Gabo had launched the Gabriel García Márquez Foundation for New Ibero-American Journalism, with its headquarters in the place he had begun his reporting life all those years before, Cartagena de Indias. Gabo founded it for the purpose of imparting new journalistic techniques and providing encouragement to a new generation of Latin American journalists. In a conversation we had in 1999, he invited me to become one of the teachers at the foundation, enthusiastically describing his vision of a future hemispheric fraternity of reporters and chroniclers as a "mafia of friends" that would not only elevate the standards of Latin America's journalism, but also help to fortify its democracies.

Remarkably, Gabo's vision has come true, with the resulting paradox that one of the most emblematic authors of the Latin American Boom in fiction should also be regarded today as the maximum godfather of a new boom in Latin American journalism. But so it is. In the years that have transpired since its founding, thousands of journalists have attended the foundation's workshops and have competed for the annual awards given out in the Gabriel García Márquez Journalism Prize. Many have attributed their later professional success to their stints with the "Gabo Foundation," as they call it, and some have gone on to write books and found magazines and websites of their own, specializing in long-form journalism and investigative reporting.

After Gabo's death, a law passed by the Colombian congress established that in his beloved Cartagena de Indias, there would be a permanent "Gabo Center," to operate in tandem with his foundation, so that along with his other legacies, his devotion to journalism could be acknowledged and passed on to new generations.

—JON LEE ANDERSON

# Editor's Note

*To the memory of Carmen Balcells
and Claudio López de Lamadrid*

Gabriel García Márquez called journalism "the best job in the world," and he identified more as a journalist than a writer: "I am basically a journalist. All my life I have been a journalist. My books are the books of a journalist, even if it's not so noticeable," he once said.

These fifty journalistic pieces by García Márquez, published between 1950 and 1984, were selected from the hundreds compiled in Jacques Gilard's monumental five-volume collection, *Obra periodística*, in order to provide readers of his fiction a sample of his writings for the newspapers and magazines for whom he worked a great part of his life. He always considered his training as a journalist the foundation of his work in fiction. In many of the writings collected here, readers of his novels and short stories will find a recognizable narrative voice in the making.

Those who want to delve into the subject can find an exciting and erudite explanation of García Márquez's journalism career in the prologues of Gilard's compilation. As Gilard wrote, "García Márquez's journalism was mainly an education for his style, and an apprenticeship toward an original rhetoric." The first works of journalism published as books were the reportage *Relato de un náufrago* (*The Story of a Ship-*

*wrecked Sailor,* 1970) and an anthology of articles written in Venezuela, *Cuando era feliz e indocumentado* (*When I Was Happy and Undocumented,* 1973). *Crónicas y reportajes* (*Chronicles and Reportages*), a selection made by the author, was published in 1976 by the Instituto Colombiano de Cultura. A compendium selected by García Márquez's journalist colleagues, *Gabo periodista,* published in 2012 by the Fundación para el Nuevo Periodismo Iberoamericano and Mexico's Conaculta, also provides a detailed chronology of his career.

Although some of his first fictional stories were written before he worked as a reporter, it was journalism that allowed the young García Márquez to leave his law studies and start writing for *El Universal* in Cartagena and *El Heraldo* in Barranquilla. He later traveled to Europe as a correspondent for *El Espectador* of Bogotá. Upon his return, and thanks to his friend and fellow journalist Plinio Apuleyo Mendoza, he continued to write in Venezuela for the magazines *Élite* and *Momento,* until moving to New York City in 1961 as a correspondent for the Cuban news agency Prensa Latina. Later that year he settled in Mexico City with his wife, Mercedes Barcha, and his son Rodrigo, where he published *No One Writes to the Colonel,* began working in screenwriting, and later devoted all his time to writing *One Hundred Years of Solitude.* Although his work as a writer would occupy most of his time, he always returned to his passion for journalism. During his lifetime he founded six publications, including *Alternativa* and *Cambio:* "I do not want to be remembered for *One Hundred Years of Solitude,* nor for the Nobel Prize, but for the newspapers," he said.

*The Scandal of the Century* takes its title from the masterful reportage sent by García Márquez from Rome and published in fourteen consecutive installments in *El Espectador* in September of 1955. In those five words we find a condensed journalistic headline with a touch of literary hyperbole. The subtitle's fantastical and evocative imagery is signature García Márquez: "In Death Wilma Montesi Walks the Earth."

Among the pieces are press releases, news reports, columns, op-eds, features, and profiles. The reader will also find a few literary pieces published concurrently in the press or in literary magazines.

In selecting these writings, I have tried to avoid any academic, stylistic, or historical categorization. As a reader and editor of García Márquez, I have chosen texts that contain a latent narrative tension between journalism and literature, where the seams of reality are stretched by his unstoppable narrative impulse, offering us the chance to once again enjoy the "storyteller" that he was.

In these works, readers will also see the journalistic skills that García Márquez brought to his works of fiction. "But those books have such an amount of research and fact checking, and historical rigor," he said of his novels, "that in fact they are basically great fictional or fantastic reports, but the method of investigation and the way of handling the information and the facts is that of a journalist."

The reader will find journalistic texts from his youth in which the budding narrator tries to find a reason to cross the line into literature, as in the opening story about the president's barber, early snippets of narrations where characters or places that will populate *One Hundred Years of Solitude* begin to appear; a reportage from Rome about a young woman's mysterious death in which the country's political and artistic elites appear to be implicated, where García Márquez attempts a mixture of police procedural and the society pages that brings to mind *La Dolce Vita;* an investigation into trafficking of women from Paris to Latin America that ends with an interrogation; overseas wire dispatches presented as short stories; reflections on his craft, as he does in many of the articles written for *El País* in later years; and dozens of other stories that bring us back the García Márquez we miss.

For this edition, I have worked with Anne McLean to bring to the English translation the same feeling of immediacy of the original, avoiding any notes, as García Márquez advised in his article "Poor Good Translators," included here. Remembering Gregory Rabassa's masterful work on *One Hundred Years of Solitude,* he writes, "He never explains anything in a footnote, which is the least valid and unfortunately most well worn resource of bad translators." The same goes for the decision not to fix some mistaken Italian names or the incorrect lyrics of some Beatles songs. About that, he writes that a text should "pass into the other language just as it was, not only with its virtues, but also with its defects. It is a duty of loyalty to the reader in the new language." Finally, a paragraph and a half, missing in Gilard's edition from a section titled "A crucial half hour" within "The Scandal of the Century," was restored from the original version found in *Crónicas y reportajes*.

I owe a special debt to Carmen Balcells and Claudio López de Lamadrid, who put this project in my hands. I had already worked with García Márquez on his memoirs, and we had spent a lot of time in his house in El Pedregal working on *I'm Not Here to Give a Speech*. As always, my immense gratitude to Mercedes, Rodrigo, and Gonzalo for their suggestions and advice. The legacy of the journalistic work of Gabriel García Márquez continues its journey through the Fundación para el Nuevo Periodismo Iberoamericano, lead by Jaime Abello, through workshops where hundreds of journalists from around the world have been and still are trained every year. My greatest thanks to Gabo himself, for his confidence and support of my work. And especially for his friendship.

—CRISTÓBAL PERA

# Scandal of the Century

# The Presidential Barber

Aphotograph of His Excellency, President of the Republic, Mariano Ospina Pérez, appeared a few days ago in a government newspaper inaugurating the new direct telephone service between Bogotá and Medellín. The chief executive looks serious and worried in the picture, surrounded by ten or fifteen telephone sets, which seem to be the cause of the president's concentrated, attentive look. I don't think there is any object that gives a clearer impression of a busy man, of a public servant entirely dedicated to finding the solution to complicated dissimilar problems, than this flock of telephones (and I request, parenthetically, applause for the surrealistically corny metaphor) that adorn the presidential image. From the look of the man who's using them, it seems that each receiver might put him in touch with a different one of the many problems of state, and that *el señor presidente* finds himself obliged to spend twelve hours of every day trying to channel them by long distance from his remote head of state's office. However, in spite of this sensation of an incalculably busy man, Señor Ospina Pérez is still, even in the photograph I'm looking at, an appropriately dressed man, the strands of his snowy summit carefully combed, his closely shaved chin soft and smooth, as evidence of the frequency with which the president turns to the intimate and efficient complicity of his barber. And, in fact, this is the question I've posed as I contemplate the latest photo of the best-shaved leader in the Americas: Who is the palace barber?

Señor Ospina is a cautious, astute, and wary man, who seems to profoundly know the nature of those who serve him. His ministers are men who have his complete trust, whom it is not possible to imagine committing sins against presidential friendship, be they sins of word or thought. The palace chef, if the palace has a chef, must be a functionary of irrevocable ideological conviction, who prepares with exquisite care the stews that a few hours later will serve as a highly nutritious factor for the Republic's first digestion, which must be a good, carefree digestion. Furthermore, given that the opposition's malicious slanders must penetrate as far as the palace kitchen, clandestinely, the president's table will not lack an honest taster. If all this happens with the ministers, the chef, the advisor, how must he be with the barber, the only voting mortal who can allow himself the democratic liberty of caressing the president's chin with the sharpened steel of a razor blade? Besides, who is this influential gentleman to whom every morning Señor Ospina communicates his preoccupations of the previous night, to whom he relates, with meticulous detail, the plot of his nightmares, and who is, after all, an efficient advisor, as all worthy barbers must be?

Often a republic's fate depends more on a single barber than on all its leaders, as in most cases—according to the poet—that of a genius depends on the midwife. Señor Ospina knows it and that's why, perhaps, before going to inaugurate the direct telephone service between Bogotá and Medellín, the head of state, with his eyes closed and legs outstretched, submitted to the pleasure of feeling the cold and ironic contact of the blade very close to his jugular, while a crowded parade of all the complicated problems he'll need to solve during the day marched through his head. It's possible the president would have told his barber that later the same morning he was going to inaugurate a perfect telephone service, an honor to his government. "Who should I call in Medellín?" he must have asked, as he felt the sharp edge on his throat. And the barber, who is a discreet family man, who strolls the city in his free time, must have kept a prudent but significant silence. Because in reality—the barber must have thought—if instead of being what he was, he were president, he would have attended the inauguration of the telephonic service, would have picked up a receiver, and, visibly preoccupied, would have said in the voice of an efficient public servant, "Operator, connect me to public opinion."

March 16, 1950, *El Heraldo*, Barranquilla

# Topic for a Topical Piece

There are those who turn the lack of a topic into a topic for a journalistic piece. The choice is absurd in a world like ours, where things of incalculable interest are happening. Someone who thinks of sitting down to write about nothing need only flip casually through the day's newspaper to make the initial problem turn into its exact opposite: how to know which topic to choose out of the many on offer. See, for example, the front page of your average newspaper. "Two children burned while playing with flying saucers." Light a cigarette. Look over, very carefully, the scrambled alphabet of the Underwood and begin with the most attractive letter. Think—once you've read the information—of the painful loss of prestige flying saucers have just suffered. Remember the number of articles that have been written about them, since they appeared for the first time—almost two years ago, somewhere around Arkansas—until now, when they've turned into simple yet dangerous children's toys. Consider the situation of the poor little flying saucers, who, like ghosts, get no respect from humanity despite their elevated category of interplanetary element. Light another cigarette and consider, finally, that it's a useless topic due to its excessive speed.

Then read the international news. "Brazil will not have a surplus of coffee at its disposal this year." Ask yourself, "Who could care about this?" And carry on reading. "The problem of the Mares settlers is not a simple legal case." "El Carare, a great surprise." Read the editorials. In each adjective, find the fingerprint of the implacable censor. All, in reality, of undeniable interest. But none seem like an appropriate topic. What to do? The most logical thing: look at the comic strips. Pancho cannot leave his house. Tío Barbas attends a pistol duel to the death. Clark Kent has to fight against Superman and vice versa. Tarzan becomes a dealer in skulls. Avivato stole, as usual, a string of fish. Penny attends a philosophy class. How awful! And now what: the society page. Two who are getting married when life is so expensive and the climate so hot. Generalísimo Franco's daughter marries a gentleman who will henceforth be known as none other than the dictator's "son-in-lawísimo." One dies and seven are born. Light another cigarette. Think that you're getting to the end of the newspaper and still haven't decided on a topic. Remember your wife, the scene of children waiting, starving to death, and who will continue dying indefinitely as long as there's no appropriate topic. It's terrible! We're starting to get sentimental. No! There are still the movie ads. Ah, but yesterday we wrote about cinema. After this, the flood!

Light another cigarette and discover—with horror—that it was the last one in the pack. And the last match! Night is falling and the hands of the clock turn, turn, turn, performing the dance of the hours (Caliban). And now what? Throw in the towel like a mediocre boxer? Journalism is the profession that most resembles boxing, with the advantage that the typewriter always wins and the disadvantage that you're not allowed to throw in the towel. We'd be left with no *Jirafa* column. Great, so many will applaud the idea. However, you once heard a phrase that is now affected and worn out from use and abuse: "It's never too late to make a good start." That is, starting is the difficult part. We begin, then, now without cigarettes, without matches, to find a topic. We write a first sentence: "There are those who turn the lack of a topic into a topic for a journalistic piece." The choice is absurd . . . but so damn easy! Isn't it?

April 11, 1950, *El Heraldo,* Barranquilla

# An Understandable Mistake

It was Tuesday in Cali. The gentleman, for whom the weekend was a murky timeless period—three days without trace—had been decorously and obstinately raising glass after glass until midnight on Monday. On Tuesday morning, when he opened his eyes and felt his room was completely full of a giant headache, the gentleman believed that he had only been partying the night before and was waking up on Sunday morning. He didn't remember anything. However, he felt a dignified regret over some mortal sin he might have committed, without knowing exactly to which of the seven his regret might correspond. It was just a regret. A lone, unconditional, rabidly independent, and incorruptibly anarchist regret.

The only thing the gentleman knew for sure was that he was in Cali. At least—he must have thought—while that building that stood outside his window was the Hotel Alférez Real and while no one proved to him mathematically that the building had been moved to another city on Saturday night, he could rest assured he was in Cali. When he opened his eyes all the way, the headache that was filling the room sat down beside his bed. Someone called the gentleman by his name, but he did not turn to look. He simply thought that someone, in the next room, was calling a person who was a complete stranger to him. The left side of the gap began on Saturday evening. The other side was this unpleasant daybreak. That was all. He tried asking himself who he really was. Only when he remembered his name did he realize it was he who was being called in the next room. However, he was too busy with his regret to worry about an unimportant call.

All of a sudden, something thin and flat and gleaming came in through the window and hit the floor, a short distance from his bed. The gentleman must have thought it was a leaf blown in by the wind, and kept his eyes fixed on the ceiling that had become mobile, floating, wrapped in the fog of his headache. But something was tapping on the floorboards beside his bed. The gentleman sat up, looked on the other side of the pillow, and saw a tiny fish in the middle of his room. He smiled sardonically; he stopped looking and turned his face to the wall. "How bizarre!" the gentleman thought. "A fish in my room, on the third floor, here in Cali so far away from the sea." And he kept on laughing sardonically.

But all of a sudden, he leapt out of bed. "A fish," he shouted. "A fish, a fish in my room." And he fled panting, exasperated, toward the corner. Regret came out to meet him. He had always laughed at scorpions with umbrellas, pink elephants. But now he could not have the slightest doubt. What was jumping, what was struggling, what was gleaming in the middle of his room, was a fish!

The gentleman closed his eyes, clenched his teeth, and judged the distance. Then came the vertigo, the endless void of the street. He had jumped out the window.

The next day, when the gentleman opened his eyes, he was in a hospital room. He remembered everything, but now he felt well. He wasn't even feeling pain under the bandages. Within his reach was the day's newspaper. The gentleman wanted something to do. Distractedly he picked up the newspaper and began to read:

"Cali. April 18. Today, in the early hours of the morning, a stranger jumped out the window of his apartment located on the third floor of a building in the city. The decision seemed to have been due to the nervous excitement produced by alcohol. The injured man is now in the hospital, where his condition does not appear to be serious."

The gentleman recognized himself in the news item, but he now felt too calm, too serene, to worry about the previous day's nightmare. He turned the page and carried on reading the local news. There was another article. And the gentleman, feeling again the headache that prowled around his bed, read the following information:

"Cali. April 18. Inhabitants of the capital of the Cauca Valley had an extraordinary surprise today, as they observed in a downtown city street the presence of hundreds of small silvery fish, approximately two inches long, that appeared strewn all over the place."

April 20, 1950, *El Heraldo*, Barranquilla

# The Lonely Hearts Killer

When Raymond Fernández and Martha Beck met in New York, a few years ago, one of those startling idylls was born, the most favorable setting of which are little fleabag hotels, between long kisses and deadly pistols; Martha and Raymond—two magnificent names for characters in Don Arturo Suárez's next novel—must have arrived at the state of spiritual purity in which the police surprised them, by way of a scrupulous check of their mutual feelings, proved by common interests and abilities. Life was not good to them. It was a sort of dog tied up in the corridor of the building where they lived, that during the day showed them its ferocious and hungry gleaming teeth and howled all night long, troubling their sleep and threatening, hour after hour, to break its chains. That was life for Martha and Raymond, two lovers who maybe, during their courtship, instead of plucking the petals off nostalgic daisies like the protagonists of romantic novels, fired a machine gun against the walls of their house repeating the classic refrain: "She loves me, she loves me not . . ."

Later, when they went to live in the small apartment with the tied-up dog, they discovered the way to throw a little digestive fuel on that love, which would eventually have cooled off, if not for that providential appeal, for lack of a little hot soup in the heart. Raymond and Martha discovered the vulnerable flank of a widow, a Mrs. Janet

Flay, enrolled in one of those melancholy clubs poetically called lonely hearts. Mrs. Flay seemed to have what Martha and Raymond lacked to triumph over the dog and seemed to lack, instead, what they had in abundance during their nights of shared beds and fright.

Things must have gotten serious when Raymond communicated with the widow and proposed the exchange. She would contribute money and he at least one of the innumerable enamored fibers that were already hardening in his heart, for want of a cup of broth. The plan was perfected—at least in the way Raymond saw things—and began to develop slowly, setting in motion its innumerable little secret plays, until the day when something went wrong, something hampered the perfectly devised mechanism, and Raymond and Martha, without knowing how, ended up in jail with their deadly dueling pistol love, their dog, and all the rest.

This sentimental story would have ended there, if not for the self-sacrificing Martha, who suffers from the contagious ailment of lonely hearts and starts to flirt with a guard in Sing Sing prison. William Ritcher, Fernández's lawyer, got the federal judge, Sylvester Ryan, to expedite an edict of habeas corpus ordering the prisoner's transfer to New York, since the unexpected feelings Martha has displayed toward her jailer have subjected Raymond to "mental torture," which did not figure in his sentence.

But the trip—according to the cable—did not manage to mitigate Raymond's ailment. He has been seen wandering around his cell, talking to himself, tormented by the memories of those fleabag hotel nights, which now seem happy in spite of the dog and in spite of the rats fighting over an editorial page under the bed in their love nest. "The Lonely Hearts Killer," as he's now known, has become one of the members of that club, in the New York prison, and has requested an efficient therapy for his ailment. A therapy of high voltage, which will no doubt transform the current grumbling Raymond into a new euphoric Raymond, when the prison officers bring into operation the efficient mechanism of the electric chair.

September 27, 1950, *El Heraldo*, Barranquilla

# Death Is an Unpunctual Lady

Reading a piece of news from Middlesboro, Kentucky, I remembered the beautiful parable of the slave who fled to Samarra because he met Death in the market and she made a gesture the slave interpreted as threatening. A few hours later the slave's owner, who seemed to be a personal friend of Death, met with her and asked, "Why did you make a threatening gesture this morning when you saw my slave?" And Death answered, "It was not a threatening gesture but rather one of surprise. I was startled to see him there, since he had an appointment with me this evening in Samarra."

That parable is, in a way, the diametrical opposite of something that happened two days ago in Middlesboro, Kentucky, to a man who that morning had an appointment with Death, and, for reasons that have not yet been possible to establish, it was Death, and not the man, who failed to arrive for the appointment. Because James Longworth, a sixty-nine-year-old mountain man, got up earlier than ever that morning, took a bath, and prepared as if for a trip. Then he lay down in his bed, closed his eyes, and said all the prayers he knew, while outside, pressed up against the window, more than two hundred people waited for the invisible boat to arrive that would take him away forever.

The expectation had begun three years ago, one morning when the hillbilly spoke of his dreams at breakfast time and said that in one of them Death had appeared and promised to come for him at 8:20 a.m. on June 28, 1952. The announcement spread through the local population and then around the district and then all over the state of Kentucky. Sooner or later all citizens had to die. But the mortality of James Longworth was from that day on different from that of his neighbors, because he was now a mortal man who could have done anything, even subsist on a diet of mercuric chloride, sure that Death's word of honor, so gravely pledged, would not be taken back after such precise and peremptory notification. Since that day, James Longworth, more than anything else, was known in the streets and the district of Middlesboro and in the state of Kentucky simply as "the man who is going to die."

So when they woke up, two days ago, all the inhabitants of the district remembered that it was June 28 and that in two hours Death would come to keep her appointment with James Longworth. What should have been a morning of mourning was in a way a bit of a holiday, when the curious citizens planned to show up late for work in order to walk a stretch and attend a man's death. In reality, it's not likely that people would have thought that James Longworth's death should be different from any other. But even so, something was at stake in it that we mortals have been interested in checking since the beginning of the world: the fidelity of Death's word of honor. And men, women, and children went to check, while James Longworth waved goodbye to them from his bed as if he were doing so from the boarding step of that invisible vehicle that, three years earlier, had allowed him to know one of the innumerable millions of stops on its endless itinerary.

Suddenly, with their hearts in their throats, the spectators established that it was exactly twenty minutes past eight and Death had not yet arrived. There was a sort of haughty desolation, a dashed hope in the two hundred heads pressing against the window. But the minute elapsed. And the next one elapsed, and nothing happened. Then James Longworth sat up disconcertedly in his bed, and said, "I'll be disappointed if I don't die soon." And it's possible that by now, the two hundred people who got up early and walked a long way and were then gasping in the luminous morning of this sweltering summer are in the town square calling for Death. Not to be dragged away by her, but to lynch her.

July 1, 1952, *El Heraldo*, Barranquilla

# The Strange Idolatry of La Sierpe

The Extravagant Veneration of Jesusito.

A Syndicate of Idols.

Saint Plank and the Holy Kidney.

Pacha Pérez

I dolatry has acquired an extraordinary prestige in La Sierpe since the long-ago date when a woman believed she discovered supernatural powers in a cedar plank. The woman was transporting a case of soap when one of the slats fell off and all efforts to reattach it were futile; nails bent even in the weakest part of the wood. Finally, the woman observed the plank closely, and in its knots and grain, she said, she discovered the image of the Virgin. The consecration was instantaneous and the canonization immediate, with neither metaphor nor circumlocution: *Santa Tabla*, Saint Plank, a strip of cedar that performs miracles and is paraded in supplication when winter threatens the crops.

The find gave rise to an extravagant and profuse calendar of saints' days, incorporating cattle horns and hooves, worshipped by those who aspire to banish disease from their animals; gourds that were specialists in safeguarding travelers against the dangers of wild beasts; pieces of metal or domestic utensils that provided maidens with made-to-measure grooms. And among so many others, Saint Kidney, canonized by a butcher who believed he had discovered in a cow's kidney a startling resemblance to the face of Jesus crowned by thorns, and to which those who suffer afflictions of the internal organs appeal.

### JESUSITO

A small altar set up in a corner of the square is an indispensable element at the celebrations held every year in the one-horse towns around La Sierpe. Men and women converge on this place to leave alms and seek miracles. It is a niche made from the fronds of royal palms, in the center of which, on a little box covered in shiny colored paper, is the most popular idol and the one with the biggest clientele in the region: a tiny little black man, carved out of a piece of wood two inches tall and set in a gold ring. He has a simple and familiar name: Jesusito. And he is invoked by the inhabitants of La Sierpe in the event of any emergency, under the serious commitment to place at his feet an object made of gold, to commemorate the miracle. This is why around Jesusito's altar today there is a pile of golden figures worth a fortune: gold eyes donated by those who were blind and recovered their sight; gold legs, from one who was paralyzed and walked again; gold tigers, deposited by travelers who escaped the dangers of wild beasts; and innumerable gold children, of different sizes and various shapes, because the image of the little black man set in the ring is especially trusted by La Sierpe's women who are about to go into labor.

Jesusito is a venerable saint, his origin unknown. He has been handed down from one generation to the next and over many years has been the means of subsistence of his various proprietors. Jesusito is subject to the law of supply and demand. He is a coveted object, susceptible to appropriation by means of honorable transactions, which correspond in an adequate way to the buyers' sacrifices. By tradition, the proprietor of Jesusito is also the proprietor of the alms and gold votive offerings, but not of the animals presented to the idol to enrich his own patrimony. The last time Jesusito was sold, three years ago, he was acquired by a rancher with excellent commercial vision, who resolved to change businesses, sold off his cattle and his lands, and began to travel from town to town, from one fair to the next, with his prosperous tent of miracles.

### THE NIGHT JESUSITO WAS STOLEN

Eight years ago Jesusito was stolen. It was the first time that happened and will surely be the last, because the author of said act is known and pitied by everyone who has gone beyond the swamps of La Guaripa ever since. It happened on January 20, 1946, in La Ventura, during celebrations of the night of El Dulce Nombre. In the early hours, when enthusiasm was beginning to wane, a runaway rider burst into the village square and knocked over the musicians' table amid an uproar of scattered instruments and roulette wheels and trampled dancers. It was a minute-long storm. But when it ended, Jesusito had disappeared from his altar. They searched for him in vain among the strewn objects, through the spilled food. In vain they took apart the niche and shook out cloths and patted down the perplexed inhabitants of La Ventura. Jesusito had disappeared, and that was not only a cause for general concern, but a symptom of the idol not approving of their Dulce Nombre supplications.

Three days later, a man on horseback, with monstrously swollen hands, rode down the single long street of La Ventura, dismounted in front of the police post, and placed in the inspector's hands the tiny man set in a gold ring. He did not have the strength to get back on his horse nor the courage to defy the fury of the group pounding on the door. All he needed and requested at the top of his lungs was a goldsmith to urgently make a pair of little gold hands.

### THE LOST SAINT

On one previous occasion Jesusito was missing for a year. To find him all the inhabitants of the region were in action, for three hundred and sixty-five days and nights. The circumstances in which he disappeared that time were similar to those surrounding his loss on the night of El Dulce Nombre in La Ventura. A well-known local troublemaker, for no reason whatsoever, grabbed the idol and threw it into a neighbor's garden. Without allowing their confusion or puzzlement to get ahead of them, the devout immediately insisted on cleaning the garden, inch by inch. Twelve hours later there was not a blade of grass, but Jesusito was still lost. Then they began to scratch the earth. And they scratched and scraped fruitlessly for that whole week and the next. Finally, after fifteen days of searching, it was decreed that collaboration in that endeavor would constitute a penance and that the discovery of Jesusito would bring the finder an indulgence. The garden turned into a place of pilgrimage from then on, and later into a public market. People set up stalls around it, and men and women from the most remote parts of La Sierpe came to scratch at the earth, to dig, to turn over the much-turned ground, to locate Jesusito. Those who know firsthand say that the lost Jesusito was still performing miracles, just not that of reappearing. It was a bad year for La Sierpe. The harvests were diminished, the quality of grain went down, and the profits were insufficient to look after local needs, which had never been as numerous as they were that year.

### THE MULTIPLICATION OF JESUSITO

There are many colorful anecdotes about the bad year when Jesusito was missing. In a house somewhere in La Sierpe a falsified Jesusito appeared, carved by a funny man from Antioquia who defied popular indignation in this way and was on the verge of coming off very badly from his little adventure. That episode was the first in a series of falsifications, production on a grand scale of apocryphal Jesusitos, which appeared all over the place and came to confuse souls to such an extent that at a certain moment people began to wonder if that considerable quantity of false idols might not be authentic. At first the instinct that the inhabitants of La Sierpe have to distinguish the artificial from the legitimate was the only resource the proprietor of Jesusito could rely on to identify his image. People examined the little statue and said, simply, "This isn't him." And the proprietor refused it, because even if that had been the legitimate Jesusito, it would have been of no use if his devotees were sure it was one of the false ones. But a moment came when controversies rose up around the identity of the idols. Eight months after he went missing, Jesusito's prestige began to be in doubt. The faith of those devoted to him was shaken, and a mound of idols of arguable reputation was incinerated, because someone maintained that the legitimate Jesusito was invulnerable to fire.

## A SYNDICATE OF IDOLS

Once the problem of the numerous false Jesusitos was resolved, the imagination of fanatics came up with new ideas to locate the idol. Saint Plank, the Holy Kidney, the whole complicated gallery of horns, hooves, rings, and cooking utensils that constituted the prosperous calendar of La Sierpe saints, was brought to the garden on rotation to reinforce, in tight trade union solidarity, the exhaustive search for Jesusito. But that too proved futile.

When exactly a year had passed since the night of the loss, some expert in Jesusito's demands and habits conceived of a providential appeal; he said what Jesusito desired was a huge festival of bullfights.

The region's ranchers contributed money and fierce bulls and five days of paid vacation for their laborers. The festival was the best attended, most intense, and rowdiest anyone remembers in La Sierpe, but its five days passed without Jesusito appearing. One morning, after the last night, when the laborers were going back to their work and the fanatics were inventing new and extravagant penances and ways to make Jesusito appear, a woman who was walking six leagues away from the garden found a carved little black man lying in the middle of the path. In the yard of the nearest house a bonfire was burning, and she threw the figure into it. When the fire went out, the idol was still there, perfect in its entirety of the authentic Jesusito.

## JESUSITO'S PRIVATE HACIENDA

That was the beginning of Jesusito's private wealth. The proprietor of the garden transferred his rights, on the condition that the land was considered as the image's own patrimony and not that of his pro-prietor. Since then Jesusito receives heads of cattle and good grazing pastures with flowing streams from his devoted followers. Of course the administrator of these possessions is the idol's proprietor. But no one can point out any irregularities in the management of the hacienda at present. In this way Jesusito is the owner of a garden, two houses, and a well-cared-for pasture where cows, bulls, horses, and mules graze distinguished by their particular brand. Something similar to what happens with the Villa de San Benito Christ, against whom a charge of rustling was brought a few years ago, because someone else's cattle appeared to have been branded with his iron.

### A WAKE IN LA SIERPE

Housewives in La Sierpe go out shopping whenever a person dies. The wake is the center of a commercial and social activity in a region whose inhabitants have no other opportunity to meet, to get together and enjoy themselves than that eventually provided by the death of some-one they know. That's why the wake is a picturesque and boisterous fairground spectacle, where the least important, most circumstantial and trivial thing is the corpse.

When a person dies in La Sierpe, two others go off in opposite directions: one to La Guaripa, to buy the coffin, and the other into the swamp, to spread the news. Preparations begin at the home with cleaning up the yard and the gathering up of any object that might get in the way of visitors' freedom of movement that night and for the next eight nights. In the furthest corner, where he won't be an obstacle to anyone, where he won't be in the way, the dead person is laid down on the floor, stretched out on two boards. People begin to arrive at dusk. They go directly into the courtyard, and against the fence they set up stalls of pots and pans, of fried food, of cheap lotions, gasoline, and matches. By nightfall the yard is transformed into a public market, in the center of which there is a gigantic trough brimming with the local moonshine, home-distilled *aguardiente,* in which float many little cups made out of green gourds. This last, and the pretext of the death, are the only contributions the family provides.

## THE SCHOOL OF LOVE

On one side of the courtyard, beside the biggest table, the maidens gather to roll tobacco leaves. Not all of them: just the ones who aspire to catch a husband. Those who prefer to carry on with less risky activities for the moment can do whatever they please during the wake, except rolling cigars. Although, in general, maidens who do not aspire to find a husband do not attend the fair.

For men who aspire to find a wife there is also a reserved spot, beside the coffee grinder. Women of La Sierpe feel an irresistible attraction, very conventional, but also very symbolic, for men who are able to grind large quantities of coffee at exceptional speeds. Participants in that tiring contest are admitted by turn to the table, where they try to grind down, both at the same time, the hearts of the maidens rolling cigars and the excessive quantities of roast coffee beans with which an impartial and opportunistic judge keeps filling the grinder. More than the diligent and gallant young men, the ones who come off best are the owners of the coffee, who have waited for many days for the opportunity of a dead man and an optimist to untangle their industry's tightest and most difficult knot.

Distributed in groups, the other men talk about business, argue, improve and close deals, and celebrate agreements or make controversies less gruff by periodic trips to the gigantic trough of *aguardiente*. There is also a spot for the idle, for those who have nothing to buy and nothing to sell; they sit in groups, around an oil lamp, to play dominoes or "9" with a Spanish deck of cards.

## PACHA PÉREZ

Crying for the dead—one of the activities on the Atlantic coast that offers the strangest and most extravagant touches—is for natives of La Sierpe an occupation not for the dead person's family, but for a woman who by vocation and experience becomes a professional mourner. Rivalry among the women of this trade is marked by more alarming characteristics and has darker consequences than the cheerful competition of the coffee grinders.

Pacha Pérez was a genius of mourners among the mourners of La Sierpe, an authoritarian and scrawny woman; it was said that she was turned into a snake by the devil at the age of 185. Like La Marquesita, Pacha Pérez was swallowed by legend. No one has had a voice like hers since, no woman has been born in the tangled swamps of La Sierpe since who has her hallucinatory and satanic faculty of condensing the entire history of a dead man in a shriek. Pacha Pérez always had an edge on the competition. When they speak about her, the mourners of today have a way of justifying her, which is at the same time a way of justifying themselves: "It's that Pacha Pérez had a pact with the devil."

### THE THEATER OF THE MOURNERS

Mourners don't intercede to regret the death, but to pay homage to the notable visitors. When the crowd notices the presence of someone who by his economic position is considered a citizen of exceptional merit in the region, the mourner on duty is notified. What follows is an entirely theatrical episode: commercial proposals are interrupted; the maidens take a break from rolling cigars, and their suitors from grinding coffee; the men playing "9" and the women stoking the fires and the stallholders turn in expectant silence toward the center of the yard, where the mourner, with her arms raised and face dramatically constricted, begins to cry. In a long and piercing shriek, the recent arrival then hears the story: with its good moments and bad moments, with its virtues and its defects, with its joys and its bitterness; the story of the deceased who is rotting in the corner, surrounded by pigs and hens, faceup on top of two planks.

What at dusk was a cheerful and picturesque market in the early-morning hours begins to turn toward tragedy. The trough has been filled several times and several times its devious *aguardiente* consumed. Then knots of conversation, of gambling or love, are formed. Tight knots that cannot be undone, which would forever break relations of that intoxicated humanity if at this instant the dead man's offended importance did not reassert itself with tremendous authority. Before dawn someone remembers there is a corpse in the house. And it is as if the news is spreading for the first time, because then all activities are suspended and a group of drunk men and tired women shoo away the pigs and hens, roll the planks with the dead man into the center of the room, so Pánfilo can pray.

Pánfilo is a gigantic man, built like a tree and slightly effeminate, who is now about fifty and for the last thirty years has attended every wake in La Sierpe and has prayed the rosary over all its dead. Pánfilo's virtue, what has made him preferred over all others who pray in the region, is that the rosary he says, the mysteries and prayers, is invented by himself in an original and twisted utilization of Catholic literature and the superstitions of La Sierpe. His complete rosary, christened by Pánfilo, is called "Prayer to Our Lord of All Powers." Pánfilo has no known home, but lives in the house of whoever died most recently, until news arrives of another; he stands in front of the corpse, keeping a count of the mysteries on his raised right hand. There is an instance of call and response between the prayer leader and the crowd, which counters in a chorus, "Take him this way," each time Pánfilo pronounces the name of a saint, almost always of his own invention. As the culmination of the "Prayer to Our Lord of All Powers," the prayer leader looks up, saying, "Guardian angel, take him this way." And points with his index finger toward the ceiling.

Pánfilo is barely fifty years old and is as stout and healthy as a ceiba tree, but—as happened to La Marquesita and Pacha Pérez in their times—he already carries his legend around his neck.

March 28, 1954, Sunday Supplement, *El Espectador*, Bogotá

# A Man Arrives in the Rain

She had been startled in the same way other times she'd sat down to listen to the rain. She heard the iron gate creak; she heard the man's steps on the brick path and the noise of boots scraping the floor, at the threshold. For many nights she waited for the man to knock on the door. But later, when she learned how to decipher the innumerable noises the rain made, she thought the imaginary visitor would never cross the threshold, and she grew accustomed to not waiting for him. It was a definitive resolution, made on that stormy September night, five years ago, when she began to reflect on her life, and said to herself, "At this rate, I'll end up growing old." Since then the noises of the rain changed and other voices replaced the man's footsteps on the brick path.

It's true that in spite of her decision not to wait for him anymore, on occasion the iron gate did creak again and the man did scrape his boots outside the threshold, like before. But by then she was attending to new revelations from the rain. Then she heard Noel again, when he was fifteen, teaching his parrot the catechism; and she heard the distant and sad song of the gramophone they'd sold to a trinket dealer, when the last man in the family died. She had learned to rescue from the rain the voices lost in the house's past, the purest and dearest voices. So there were many wonderful and surprising novelties that stormy night when the man who had so often opened the iron gate walked up the brick path, coughed at the threshold, and knocked twice on the door.

Her face darkened by an irrepressible nervousness, she made a brief gesture with her hand, turned to look toward the other woman, and said, "Here he is now."

The other was beside the table, her elbows leaning on the thick, unpolished oak panels. When she heard the raps, she turned her eyes to the lamp and seemed shaken by a gloomy anxiety.

"Who can that be at this hour?" she said.

And, serene once more, with the security of someone speaking a sentence that has been maturing for many years, she said:

"That's the least of it. Whoever it is must be drenched."

The other stood up, followed meticulously by her gaze. She saw her pick up the lamp. She saw her disappear down the corridor. She heard, from the semidarkness of the parlor between the sound of the rain that the darkness made more intense, the footsteps of the other, moving away from her, tripping on the loose and worn-out bricks of the entrance hall. Then she heard the noise of the lamp as it banged against the wall and then the latch bar, scraping through the rusty loops.

For a moment she didn't hear anything more than distant voices. Noel's remote and happy talk, sitting on the barrel, giving her news about God and his parrot. She heard the creaking of the wheel in the courtyard, when Papá Laurel opened the gate so the two oxen could pull in the cart. She heard Genoveva disturbing the house as usual, because always, "I always find this blessed bathroom in use." And then again Papá Laurel, shouting his soldier's swearwords, bringing down swallows with the same shotgun he used in the last civil war to defeat, all by himself, an entire government division. She even got to thinking that this time the episode would go no further than the knocks at the door, as before it went no further than the boots scraped at the threshold; and she was thinking that the other woman had opened the door and had seen only the flowerpots beneath the rain, and the sad and deserted street.

But then she began to distinguish voices in the darkness. And she heard again the familiar footsteps and saw the shadows stretched up the wall of the entrance hall. Then she knew that after many years of apprenticeship, after many years of vacillation and regret, the man who opened the iron gate had decided to come in.

The other woman returned with the lamp, followed by the recent arrival; she put it down on the table, and he—without leaving the orbit of light—took off his raincoat, turned his face, punished by the storm, to the wall. Then she saw him for the first time. She looked at him solidly at first. Then she deciphered him from head to toe, taking in each limb, with a persevering, conscientious, and serious gaze, as if instead of a man she were examining a bird. Finally she turned her eyes back to the lamp and began to think, "It's him, in any case. Even if I imagined him a little bit taller."

The other woman rolled a chair over to the table. The man sat down, crossed one leg, and untied his bootlace. The other woman sat beside him, speaking spontaneously to him about something that she, in the rocking chair, did not manage to understand. But at the wordless gestures she felt redeemed of her abandonment and noticed that the dusty and sterile air smelled again as it used to, as if it were again the time when there were men who came into the bedrooms sweating, and Úrsula, scatterbrained and healthy, went running every afternoon at five past four, to wave goodbye to the train from the window. She saw him gesticulate and was pleased that the stranger was behaving like that; that he understood that after a difficult and often-altered trip, he had at last found the house lost in the storm.

The man began to unbutton his shirt. He had taken off his boots and was leaning over the table, trying to dry out by the heat of the lamp. Then the other woman stood up, walked over to the cupboard, and returned to the table with a half-full bottle and a glass. The man grasped the bottle by the neck, pulled the cork out with his teeth, and poured himself half a glass of the thick green liqueur. Then he drank without a breath, with an exalted haste. And she, from the rocking chair, watching him, remembered that night when the gate creaked for the first time—so long ago . . . !—and she thought that there was nothing in the house to give the visitor, except that bottle of crème de menthe. She had said to her companion, "We must leave that bottle in the cupboard. Someone might need it sometime."

The other had said, "Who?" And she had answered, "Anyone. It's always good to be prepared in case anyone comes when it rains." Many years had passed since then. And now the predicted man was there, pouring more liqueur into the glass.

But this time the man didn't drink. When he was about to, his eyes got lost in the shadows, over the top of the lamp, and she felt for the first time the warm contact of his gaze. She understood that up until that instant the man had not realized there was another woman in the house; and then she began to rock.

For a moment the man examined her with indiscreet attention. A possibly deliberate indiscretion. She was disconcerted at first, but then she noticed that this gaze was also familiar, and despite its penetrating and somewhat impertinent obstinacy there was much in it of Noel's mischievous goodness and also a bit of the patient and honorable awkwardness of his parrot. That's why she began to rock, thinking, "Even if it's not the same one who opened the iron gate, it's as if he were, anyway." And still rocking, while he watched her, she thought, "Papá Laurel would have invited him to hunt rabbits in the garden."

Before midnight the storm grew stronger. The other woman had moved her chair over to the rocking chair and the two women sat still in silence, contemplating the man drying off by the lamp. A branch from the almond tree next door banged against the window several times without clinging, and the air in the room grew humid invaded by a gust of the elements. She felt on her face the sharp edge of the hailstorm, but she didn't move, until she saw the man drain the last drop of the crème de menthe. She thought there was something symbolic in that spectacle. And then she remembered Papá Laurel, fighting on his own, entrenched in the corral, picking off government soldiers with a pellet gun meant for swallows. And she remembered a letter Colonel Aureliano Buendía had written him and the title of captain Papá Laurel turned down, saying, "Tell Aureliano I didn't do that for the war, but to keep those savages from eating my rabbits." It was as if with that memory she too had drained the last drop of the past that was left in the house.

"Is there anything in the cupboard?" she asked somberly.

And the other, in the same accent, in the same tone, which she supposed he wouldn't be able to hear, said:

"Nothing else. Remember on Monday we ate the last handful of kidney beans."

And then, fearing that the man had heard them, they looked toward the table again, but saw only darkness, not the table or the man. Nevertheless, they knew the man was there, invisible beside the extinguished lamp. They knew he wouldn't leave the house while it was still raining, and the darkness had shrunken the room so much that it would not be at all strange if he'd heard them.

May 9, 1954, *El Espectador*, Bogotá

# The House of the Buendías

(Notes for a Novel)

The house is cool; damp at night, even in the summer. It is in the north, at the end of the village's only street, built on a high and solid concrete sidewalk. The tall doorframe, without steps; the long living room sensitively and sparsely furnished, with two full-sized windows onto the street, is perhaps the only thing that sets it apart from other houses in the village. No one remembers having seen the doors closed during the day. No one remembers having seen the four wicker rocking chairs in any other place or in different positions: placed in a square, in the middle of the room, with the appearance of having lost their ability to provide rest and now having only a simple and useless ornamental function. Now there is a gramophone in the corner, beside the disabled girl. But before, during the early years of the century, the house was silent, desolate; perhaps the most silent and desolate in the village, with that immense living room barely occupied by the four [. . .] (now the water jar has a stone filter, with moss) in the opposite corner from the girl.

On either side of the door that leads to the only bedroom, there are two old portraits, marked with funerary ribbons. The air itself, inside the living room, has a cold but elemental and healthy severity, like the small bundle of wedding clothes that swings on the lintel of the bedroom or like the dry sprig of aloe vera that decorates the inside of the threshold of the door to the street.

When Aureliano Buendía returned to the village, the civil war had ended. Maybe the new colonel had nothing left from his harsh pilgrimage. He was left with only the military title and a vague unawareness of his disaster. But he was also left with half the death of the last Buendía and a full portion of hunger. He was left with nostalgia for domesticity and the desire to have a calm, peaceful house, without any war, that would have a tall doorframe to let the sun in and a hammock in the courtyard, between two posts.

In the village, where the house of his elders had been, the colonel and his wife found nothing but the incinerated stumps of the posts and the high terrace, now swept every day by the wind. No one would have recognized the place where a house had once been. "So clear, everything so clean," the colonel had said, remembering. But among the ashes where the backyard had been the almond tree still grew green, like a crucifix among the rubble, beside the little wooden outhouse. The tree, on one side, was the same that had shaded the old Buendías' yard. But on the other, the side that fell over the house, funereal, charred branches stretched out, as if half the almond tree was in autumn and the other half in springtime. The colonel remembered the destroyed house. He remembered it for its light, for its disorganized music, made by the scraps of all the noises that inhabited it to overflowing. But he also remembered the sour and penetrating smell of the latrine beside the almond tree and the inside of the little room weighed down by profound silences, divided up into vegetal spaces. Among the rubble, stirring up the dirt as she swept, Doña Soledad found a plaster Saint Raphael with a broken wing, and the glass of a lamp. There they built the house, facing the sunset; in the opposite direction from the Buendías killed in the war.

Construction began when it stopped raining, without preparations, without any preconceived order. In the hole where the first post would stand, they fit in the plaster Saint Rafael, without any ceremony. Maybe the colonel didn't think about it like that when he drew the plan in the dirt, but beside the almond tree, where the outhouse was, the air kept the same density of coolness it had when this place was the backyard. So when they dug the four holes and he said, "This is how the house will be, with a big room where the children can play," the best of it was already made. It was as if the men who took the measurements outdoors had marked out the limits of the house exactly where the silence of the courtyard ended. Because when the four support posts were erected, the enclosed space was already clean and humid, as the house is now. Within it were enclosed the freshness of the tree and the profound and mysterious silence of the latrine. Outside was the village, with the heat and the noise. And three months later, when the roof was built, when the walls were plastered and the doors hung, the inside of the house—still—had something of the courtyard about it.

June 3, 1954, *Crónica*, Barranquilla

# Literaturism

There are still those who protest at the gruesomeness of those high-flying melodramas, in which there is more blood than there are protagonists per square mile, and whose readers or spectators should take precautions in order not to become victims themselves of the tragedy. However, real life is on occasion even more gruesome.

There is the case that happened in the municipality of San Rafael, Antioquia, which any literary critic would condemn for its exaggeration and for not being true to life. In the foreground it seems to be a case of rivalry between two families, which might seem to disqualify it literarily, because very few people are disposed to attribute the validity to such a situation that it had two centuries ago. However, the bloody drama of San Rafael originated in a rivalry between families, and those to whom this situation seems false will have no choice but to condemn life for its lack of imagination and excessive fondness for conventionalism.

As is to be expected, there was a crime. Not a simple crime, but a spectacular homicide, in which the killer, to begin with, fired a shotgun at the victim. And then all hell broke loose for literature: after firing the weapon at the victim, the killer attacked the corpse with a machete, and finally, in an excess of impiety that could lead to thinking in a certain way of the Tartar ancestry of some Colombians, he severed the tongue without stopping to think what he would do with it, as in fact he did nothing.

The news has not earned—at the current exchange rate of the journalistic peso—more than two columns on the regional news page. It is a bloody crime, like any other. With the difference that these days there is nothing extraordinary about it, since as a news item it is too common and as a novel too gruesome.

It would be best to recommend that real-life exercise a bit more discretion.

June 23, 1954, *El Espectador,* Bogotá

# The Precursors

Without doubt the first sensational news produced—after creation—was the expulsion of Adam and Eve from Paradise. It would have been an unforgettable front page: Adam and Eve Expelled from Paradise (across eight columns). "You'll earn your bread by the sweat of your brow," said God. "An angel with a flaming sword carried out the sentence yesterday and stood guard at the gates of Eden. An apple was the cause of the tragedy."

How many years since that news happened? It is as difficult to answer that question as to predict when the moment will arrive to write the last great sensational feature story: the Last Judgment, which will be a sort of definitive evaluation of humanity. But before that hour arrives, who knows how many modifications journalism will undergo, that exhausting activity that began when a neighbor told another what a third did the previous night, and which has a curious variety in our towns, where a man who reads the newspapers every day comments in writing on the news, in an article with an unmistakable editorial tone or in the light and insignificant style of a press release, according to its importance, and reads it that afternoon in the drugstore, where public opinion considers itself to have a duty to get its bearings.

That commentator of the daily event, who can be found in at least forty percent of our towns, is the journalist without a newspaper, a man who exercises his profession against the hard and unalterable circumstance of not even having a hand press to express his ideas and expresses them out in public, with such obvious results that might be an incontrovertible demonstration that journalism is a biological necessity of humanity, which at the same time has the capacity to survive even newspapers themselves. There will always be a man reading an article in the corner of a drugstore, and there will always—because this is the funny thing—be a group of citizens ready to listen to him, even if just to feel the democratic pleasure of not agreeing with him.

August 10, 1954, *El Espectador,* Bogotá

# The Postman Rings a Thousand Times

## A Visit to the Cemetery of Lost Letters

*Which Is the Destination of Correspondence
That Can Never Be Delivered. Letters for the Invisible Man.
An Office Where Nonsense Is Entirely Natural.
The Only Persons with Legal Authorization
to Open the Correspondence*

Someone posted a letter that never reached its destination and was never returned to its sender. In the instant of writing it, the address was correct, the postage was stamped irreproachably, and the name of the addressee was perfectly legible. The postal workers processed it with scrupulous reliability. It did not miss a single connection. The complex administrative mechanism functioned with absolute precision, the same with that letter, which never arrived, as with thousands of letters that were posted that same day and arrived in good time at their destinations.

The postman rang several times, checked the address, asked around in the neighborhood, and received a reply: the addressee had moved house. He was provided with the new address, with precise particulars, and the letter was finally passed to the poste restante, where it was available to its addressee for thirty days. The thousands of persons who go to post offices daily in search of a letter that has never been written saw the letter there that had been written and never reached its destination.

The letter was returned to its sender. But the sender had also changed address. Thirty more days the returned letter waited for him in the post restante, while he wondered why he had not received a reply. Finally that simple message, those four lines that might not have said anything in particular or might have been decisive in a man's life, were put into a sack, with another thousand anonymous letters, and sent to the poor and dusty house at number 567, on Carrera Octava. That is the cemetery of lost letters.

### EPISTOLARY SLEUTHING

Thousands of unclaimed letters have passed through that single-story house, with its low roof and peeling walls where nobody seems to live. Some of them have gone all around the world and returned to their destination, in hopes of a claimant who may have died while waiting for it.

The letter cemetery resembles a human cemetery. Tranquil, silent, with long and deep corridors and dark galleries full of letters crowded together. Nevertheless, unlike what happens at the human cemetery, in the letter cemetery a lot of time passes before all hope is lost. Six methodical, scrupulous civil servants, covered by the rust of routine, keep doing everything possible to find clues that might allow them to locate an unknown addressee.

Three of these six persons are the only ones in the country who can open a letter without being charged with violating correspondence. But even this legal recourse is futile in the majority of cases: the text of the letter gives no clue. And something stranger: of every hundred envelopes stamped and processed with a mistaken address, at least two have nothing inside. They are letters without letters.

### WHERE DOES THE INVISIBLE MAN LIVE?

The change of address of both sender and receiver, although it seems far-fetched, is the simplest and most frequent. Those in charge of the office of unclaimed letters—the official name of the cemetery of lost letters—have lost count of the situations that can come up in the confusing labyrinth of messages gone astray. Of an average one hundred unclaimed letters received every day, at least ten have been properly franked and processed but the envelopes are perfectly blank. "Letters for the invisible man," they call them, and they've been dropped into the mailbox by someone who had the idea of writing a letter to someone who does not exist and therefore lives nowhere.

### LETTERS TO UFEMIA

"José. Bogotá," says the envelope of one of the lost letters. The envelope has been opened, and inside it they found a two-page, handwritten letter signed by "Diógenes." The only clue to finding its intended recipient is in its opening: "My dear Enrique."

Envelopes with only a name or only a surname that have arrived at the office of unclaimed letters number in the thousands. Thousands of letters for Alberto, for Isabel, for Gutiérrez and Medina and Francisco José. That's one of the most common cases.

In that office where absurdity is entirely natural, there is a letter in a mourning envelope, on which neither the name nor the address of the recipient has been written, instead a phrase in violet ink: "I'm sending it in a black envelope so it will arrive more lightly."

### WHO'S WHO!

These pieces of absurdity, multiplied ad infinitum, which would be enough to drive a normal person crazy, have not altered the nervous systems of the six civil servants who for eight hours a day do everything possible to find the intended recipients of thousands of lost letters.

Hundreds of letters with no names arrive from the Agua de Dios leper colony, especially around Christmas time. They all ask for help: "To the gentleman who has a little shop on Calle 28-South, two houses past the butcher's," it says on the envelope. The postman discovers that not only is it impossible to find the precise store on a fifty-block-long street, but that in the entire neighborhood there is not a single butcher shop. Nevertheless, one letter from Agua de Dios does reach its destination, with the following information: "For the lady who goes to the five-thirty mass every morning at the Iglesia de Egipto." By insisting and investigating, the employees and messengers of the unclaimed letters office managed to identify the anonymous addressee.

### IN SPITE OF EVERYTHING . . .

Letters that get declared definitively dead do not constitute the majority of those arriving daily at the unclaimed letters office. Don Enrique Posada Ucrós, a phlegmatic, white-haired man, who after five years of running this office is no longer surprised by anything, has his senses sharpened by the fabulous task of finding clues where none appear to exist. He is a fanatic for order in an office that exists only by virtue of the country's correspondents' abysmal disorder. "Nobody goes to read the poste restante," the head of the unclaimed letters office says. And those who go to read them constitute a very small percentage of people who really do have a letter without an address. The poste restante of the Bogotá mail department is constantly full of people expecting to receive a letter. However, on a list of 170 letters with mistaken addresses, only six were collected by their intended recipients.

### HOMONYMS

Ignorance, carelessness, negligence, and the lack of a sense of cooperation on the part of the public are the main causes of a letter not reaching its destination. The number of Colombians who change addresses and make the corresponding announcement at the post office is very small. As long as this situation continues, the efforts of the employees of the unclaimed letters office—where to this day there is an unclaimed letter that has been there for many years, addressed in the following way: "For you, sir, sent by your fiancée"—will be in vain. And right there, packages from all over the world, with newspapers, magazines, reproductions of famous paintings, academic diplomas, and strange objects with no apparent application. Two rooms are stuffed with those unclaimed items from all over the world whose recipients it has not been possible to locate. Parcels have been seen there for Alfonso López, Eduardo Santos, Gustavo Rojas, Laureano Gómez, who are not the same citizens that anyone might imagine. And among them, a package of philosophical journals and bulletins for the lawyer and sociologist from the Caribbean coast, Luis Eduardo Nieto Artesa, currently residing in Barranquilla.

### THE POSTMAN RINGS A THOUSAND TIMES

Not all the packages found at the lost letters office have the wrong address. Many of them have simply been refused by their intended recipients. Men and women who buy things by mail order and then change their minds obstinately refuse to receive the shipment. They won't open the door to the messenger. They are indifferent to the telephone calls from Señor Posada Ucrós, who looks up the addressee's number in the phone book, and implores them to receive a parcel from Germany. The messenger, accustomed to these sorts of incidents, resorts to all kinds of cunning ruses to get the addressee to sign the corresponding receipt and keep the shipment. In most cases all efforts are futile. And the package, which also in many cases has no return address, goes definitively to the archive of unclaimed objects.

This is the same case with prohibited imports that arrive at customs, and allowable imports that are not claimed because the duties are higher than the price of the merchandise. In the last room of the cemetery of lost letters, there are nine bundles sent by the customs house at the Cúcuta border. Nine bundles containing all kinds of valuable objects, but which arrived without consignment documents and which therefore do not legally exist. Merchandise that no one knows where it came from or where it's going.

## BROAD AND ALIEN IS THE WORLD

Sometimes the complex mechanism of worldwide mail delivery fails and a letter or parcel that shouldn't have traveled 100 miles, and has traveled 100,000, arrives at the Bogotá unclaimed letters office. Very often letters arrive from Japan, especially since the first group of Colombian soldiers came back from Korea. Many of them are love letters, written in an indecipherable Spanish, where Japanese characters are confusingly mixed with roman printing. "Cabo 1.º La Habana" was the only address one of those letters bore.

Just a month ago, a letter intended for someone in a tiny, remote village in the Italian Alps, with a perfectly legible name and address, was returned to Paris.

November 1, 1954, *El Espectador,* Bogotá

# The Aracataca Tiger

Aracataca, in the banana-growing region of Santa Marta, does not get many opportunities to appear in print, and not because they ran out of As for the linotype machines, but because it has been a peaceful and predictable town, since the green tempest of the banana plantations passed. These days its name has once again appeared in the newspapers relating its five repeated and frenetic vowels with the two syllables of a tiger, which might be one of the *tres tristes tigres* of the Spanish tongue twister, now stuck in the tongue twister of Aracataca itself.

Even if it were true, as it undoubtedly is, the news of the Aracataca tiger does not seem to be. There are no tigers in Aracataca, and he who's telling you has more than enough reasons to know that. The region's tigers were killed off many years ago, and sold to make rugs in different parts of the world, when Aracataca was a cosmopolitan town where no one got down off his horse to pick up a five-peso bill. Later, when the banana fever ended and the Chinese, Russian, English, and emigrants from all over the rest of the world went somewhere else, they didn't leave any traces of its former splendor, but they didn't leave any tigers, either. In Aracataca they left nothing.

Nevertheless, it would be worthwhile for the story of the tiger to be true so the linotype machines could again insist five times on the same letter and someone might remember Aracataca again—the land of Radragaz, as a professional author of jokes has said—and someone might think of it as sooner or later they think of all the municipalities of Colombia, even those with names not so difficult to forget.

We must remember Aracataca before it gets eaten by the tiger.

February 1, 1955, *El Espectador,* Bogotá

# H.H. Goes on Vacation

## (Fragment)

The pope went on vacation. This afternoon, at five o'clock
sharp, he settled into his own Mercedes, license plate
SCV-7, and drove out through the Holy Office gate, to the
Castel Gandolfo Palace, twenty miles from Rome. Two gigantic Swiss
Guards saluted him at the gate. One of them, the taller and heftier
one, is a blond teenager with a flattened nose, like a boxer's nose, the
result of a traffic accident.

Very few tourists were expecting to see the papal sedan pass through
Saint Peter's Square. Discreetly, the Catholic newspapers announced
His Holiness's trip this morning. But they said the automobile would
be leaving the Vatican courtyards at 6:30 in the evening, and he left at
five. As always, Pius XII was early: his collective audiences, his trips,
and blessings of tourists always happen a little bit before the scheduled
time.

### NINETY-FIVE DEGREES IN THE SHADE

The traveler was alone in his sedan, in the back seat, naturally. In the
front seat a uniformed driver seemed indifferent to the manifestations
of devotion and sympathy from Romans and tourists, who waved to

the sedan as it passed over Janiculum Hill, where there are statues of Garibaldi—who looks like a pirate out of a Salgari book—and one of his wife, who also looks like a Salgari pirate, on horseback like a man.

For the first time all year, this afternoon the pope was within reach of children, perfectly visible through the sedan's rolled-up window. Inside the vehicle it must have been terribly hot, because the pontifical car does not have air conditioning. However, the pope did not appear uncomfortable in the temperature, in spite of not wearing what might be called "vacation clothes." While through the streets of Rome stout workers drive like lunatics on their Vespas, in shorts and shirtless, His Holiness goes off on vacation in his hermetically sealed car imparting blessings left and right, not concerned about the heat.

### THE HOUSEKEEPER

Another two sedans, identical to that of His Holiness, were following the pontifical car. In one of them was Sister Pascualina, the ancient and dynamic administrator of His Holiness's private life. She is a German nun, strong in body and spirit, who takes personal charge of the pope's clothing, supervises his diet, and exercises an inflexible sovereignty over him. She, more than anyone, and even more than His Holiness's top doctors, can say how the pope was when he woke up. And she is the one who helped him recover from his ailments a few months ago, to such an extent that the Supreme Pontiff has now put on weight, and has recovered the spontaneity of movement in his arms. And he has gone back to working normally. The front page of today's *L'Osservatore Romano* announces:

"The office of His Holiness's master of chambers lets it be known that, during his stay in Castel Gandolfo, the Holy Father will be so kind as to grant an audience to the faithful and to pilgrims, twice a week. These audiences will take place on Wednesdays and Saturdays, at six in the evening. Those who wish to participate in these audiences will have to obtain the usual ticket, from the office of His Holiness's master of chambers."

That announcement has been taken as an indication of the pope's good health. It is also known that in the third sedan were Vatican City officials, with a briefcase full of paperwork that His Holiness would have to study during his vacation.

### ACCIDENTS ALONG THE WAY

The last time the pope drove along the beautiful road to Castel Gandolfo, he believed that it really would be the last time. It was at the end of last summer, and his health was alarmingly weakened. Nevertheless, today he has driven it again, and he has moved his lean, olive-skinned face close to the sedan's windows several times to bless the many Italians who raced over on their Vespas to wait for his car to come along the highway.

But not all of them waited on the road. Most were concentrated in Castel Gandolfo's narrow little square, a little square surrounded by trees and with stores displaying their eye-catching merchandise on the doorframes, like in Girardot. The pope arrived at the palace shortly before six. His trip had a ten-minute interruption: an enormous truck loaded with bricks was blocking traffic on the Vía Apia Nuova. When the pope's sedan reached that spot, a colossal driver in his underwear was swearing in the middle of the road.

### SATURDAY IN TOLIMA

No one in Castel Gandolfo noticed which entrance the pope took into his holiday palace. He entered from the west side, into a garden with an avenue bordered by hundred-year-old trees. The little town square was full of banners, like the Espinal square on Saint Peter's Day. And exactly like in Espinal before the bullfights start, the authorities are in a wooden box for distinguished persons and the musicians in another. When they found out His Holiness was in the palace, the band—a typical *papayera* rural—burst out playing at full volume. Except they didn't play a *bunde* from Tolima, but a moving hymn: "Blanco Padre." Schoolchildren, sweating buckets in their woolen uniforms, were waving yellow-and-white pennants—Vatican colors—on a Saturday afternoon that was no vacation for them because they had to attend the pope's vacation.

## A WOMAN'S HEAD

Traditionally His Holiness begins his rest period in the early days of July. This time he's almost a month late, and people's interpretations of that delay are numerous and very wide-ranging. One of those interpretations has a lot to do with a gory article from the local crime pages. Twenty days ago the decapitated body of a woman appeared on the shore of Lake Albano in Castel Gandolfo. The police put the body in deep-freeze. It was examined inch by inch, and the details of three hundred missing women were studied in recent days. One by one, the three hundred women have been appearing. Unintentionally, many things have been discovered, as an additional benefit of the investigative activity: adultery, rapes, runaways. But the head of the decapitated woman of Castel Gandolfo has not appeared anywhere in spite of the government divers, working around the clock every day, sounding out the lake inch by inch.

Tomorrow, on his first day of vacation, the pope will lean out the window of his summer palace to contemplate the blue surface of Castel Gandolfo's beautiful lake. And even if we have no news that His Holiness takes an interest in the bountiful and scandalous crime pages of the Rome newspapers, he might not be able to avoid the sight of the police boats and divers. And he might just be the only person who can observe—from a window that overlooks the whole surface of the lake—what all Romans are desperate to see: the head that, sooner or later, the divers will recover from the waters of Castel Gandolfo.

August 8, 1955, *El Espectador*, Bogotá

# The Scandal of the Century

In Death Wilma Montesi Walks the Earth

T he night of Thursday, April 9, 1953, the carpenter Rodolfo Montesi was waiting for his daughter Wilma to come home. The carpenter lived with his wife, Petti María, with his seventeen-year-old son, Sergio, and with another unmarried daughter, Wanda, who was twenty-five, at number 76 Vía Tagliamento, in Rome. It is an enormous three-story residence, built at the beginning of the twentieth century, with four hundred apartments constructed around a beautiful circular courtyard, full of flowers and with a small fountain in the center. There is only one entrance to the building: a gigantic gate with an archway of broken and dusty little windows. To the left of the entrance is the concierge's room, and above her door, an image of the Heart of Jesus, illuminated by an electric lightbulb. From six in the morning until eleven at night the concierge keeps a rigorous eye on access to the building.

### THE FIRST STEP

Rodolfo Montesi waited for his twenty-one-year-old daughter Wilma until 8:30. Her prolonged absence was alarming, because the girl had been out since the afternoon. Tired of waiting, the carpenter headed first to the nearby general hospital, where there was no news of any accidents that day. Later, on foot, he headed to the Lungotevere, where he looked for his daughter for two hours along the banks of the Tiber. At 10:30, tired of his fruitless search and fearing a calamity, Rodolfo Montesi went to the police station on Vía Salaria, a few blocks from his house, to ask for help in locating Wilma.

### "I DON'T LIKE THAT MOVIE"

The carpenter told the officer on duty, Andrea Lomanto, that after lunch that day, at approximately one o'clock, he had returned as usual to his carpentry workshop, located at number 16 Vía de Sebino. He said his whole family had been home when he left, and when he came back, his wife and his daughter Wanda had told him that Wilma had not yet returned. According to the carpenter, the two women told him they had gone to the Excelsior Theater, on nearby Viale Liegi, to see a movie called *The Golden Coach*. They left the house at 4:30, but Wilma did not want to go with them because, as she said, she didn't like that kind of picture.

At 5:30—according to what Rodolfo Montesi said at the police station—the concierge saw Wilma leave, alone, with a black leather purse. Unusually, Wilma was not wearing the pearl earrings and necklace her fiancé had given her a few months earlier. Wilma's fiancé was Angelo Giuliani, a police officer in Potenza.

### A STRANGER'S CALL

Since his daughter had gone out without fixing herself up, contrary to her habits, and also without any money or her identification documents, Rodolfo Montesi came up with the hypothesis at the police station that Wilma had committed suicide. The girl had, according to her father, a motive for suicide: she was in despair at the prospect of having to abandon her family and move to Potenza, after her imminent marriage to the police officer.

However, Wanda, Wilma's sister, had a different opinion: she thought the girl had gone out without fixing herself up simply because she hadn't had time. Maybe, she thought, she'd had to leave the house in a rush, after an urgent telephone call.

However, there was a third hypothesis: Wilma had run away with her fiancé and had traveled to Potenza that very night. To establish that, Rodolfo Montesi phoned Giuliani, Friday, April 10, at seven in the morning. But the disconcerted carpenter got nothing but the astonished reply of his future son-in-law. Giuliani had no news of Wilma, except for a letter that had arrived the previous afternoon. That letter offered no clues. It was just a conventional love letter.

Worried about his fiancée's disappearance, Giuliani prepared to travel to Rome immediately. But he needed an urgent excuse to give to his superiors. So he told Rodolfo Montesi to send him a telegram. And at noon Rodolfo Montesi sent him a dramatic telegram. In four words, he said that Wilma had committed suicide.

### A BODY ON THE BEACH

During the night of the 10th, the Montesi family and the Rome police force continued their search. It was a futile search, which Wilma's fiancé joined after midnight, as soon as he arrived from Potenza. Nothing had been discovered by seven o'clock in the morning of the following day, Saturday, when a bricklayer, Fortunato Bettini, arrived by bicycle at a police station, to say there was a dead woman on Torvaianica beach, twenty-five miles from Rome.

Bettini told the police that when he was on his way to work he had seen the body on the beach, almost parallel to the water's edge, with her head resting on her right shoulder, and that same arm raised and her hand beside her chin. The left arm was stretched down along her side. The body was missing her skirt, shoes, and stockings. She was wearing only an ivory-colored slip, a tight-fitting pair of white piqué underpants with embroidered edges, and a light sweater. Around her neck, held by a single button, she had a coat with green hexagons on a dark yellow background. The jacket was almost completely covered in sand, and open like a wing in the direction of the waves.

### THE DEAD CHANGE POSITION

Bettini's revelation was given to the agent on duty, Andreozzi Gino. At 9:30 in the morning, Carabinieri Amadeo Tondi, Sergeant Alessandro Carducci, and the local doctor, Agostino di Giorgio, met at the place of the macabre discovery. They discovered that the corpse was not in the same position in which the bricklayer said he'd found it: it was almost perpendicular to the shore, head toward the sea and feet toward the beach. But they did not think the bricklayer had lied, but rather that the waves had moved it from its earlier position.

After a brief examination of the cadaver, Dr. Di Giorgio verified:

a)  That it was in the early stages of rigor mortis.
b)  That external appearances suggested death had been caused by drowning, and had occurred approximately eighteen hours before discovery.
c)  That the condition of the clothing and external appearance of the corpse ruled out a long period of time in the water.

### "IT'S HER!"

At 11:30 Sergeant Carducci sent a telegram to the attorney general of the Republic, announcing the find. But at seven that night, having received no response, he decided to make a telephone call. Half an hour later the order was given to remove the cadaver and transport it to the Rome mortuary. It arrived there at midnight.

The next day, Sunday, at ten in the morning, Rodolfo Montesi and Angelo Giuliani went to the mortuary to see the corpse. Recognition was instantaneous: it was the body of Wilma Montesi.

*The Reader Should Remember*

a)  That the concierge saw Wilma leave at 5:30, as she revealed to Rodolfo Montesi, who in turn reported it the police.
b)  That on the night of April 9 nobody in the Montesi family

home mentioned a probable visit to Ostia on the part of the girl.

c) That Wanda Montesi spoke of a mysterious telephone call.

In his report on April 12, Sergeant Carducci expressed the opinion, based on Dr. Di Giorgio's conclusions, that Wilma Montesi's death had been caused by asphyxiation due to drowning and there were no lesions caused by acts of violence. He also declared that, based on the same report, three hypotheses could be established: accident, suicide, or homicide. He also expressed the belief that the cadaver, from the area of Ostia, had been swept away by the sea and returned to the beach in the early hours of April 10. The same informant declared that on the night of April 10 a violent storm had raged in the area, and that the sea had afterward remained in a state of agitation, due to the effects of the wind that continued to blow in a northeasterly direction.

### A CRUCIAL HALF HOUR

On April 14, the Salaria police station produced its own report on the Montesi family. According to that report, the carpenter's family enjoyed a good reputation. Wilma was known to be a serious, reserved young woman without friends, who was officially engaged, since September 1952, to Officer Giuliani, who had been transferred, a few months before the death of his fiancée, from Marino to Potenza.

According to that report, Wilma's behavior toward her family had always been excellent. She wrote to her fiancé often, and the last of those letters, dated April 8, which she had copied out in a notebook seized by the police, revealed a serene and calm affection.

The building's concierge, according to the same report, agreed with Rodolfo Montesi on every point except one: she said she'd seen Wilma leave at five o'clock. Rodolfo Montesi said it had been 5:30.

That half-hour difference was crucial, because in Italy trains are very punctual. And Doctoresa Passarelli, a serious and reliable employee at the War Ministry, said she'd seen Wilma Montesi the afternoon of April 9 on the train to Ostia. And on April 9 the train to Ostia left at exactly 5:30.

## THE HOUSE KEYS

After seeing photos of Wilma Montesi and reading about her death in the newspapers, Doctoresa Passarelli turned up on Monday the 13th, very early, at the family's apartment, to tell them what she had seen on the Thursday. She said that Wilma had been in the same compartment of the train to Ostia as she, and that the girl had been traveling alone. Nobody had approached her or talked to her during the trip. According to Passarelli, Wilma got off the train at Ostia Lido, without haste, as soon as the train stopped.

The police established with the family what other garments Wilma was wearing when she left home, apart from those found on the body. She had been wearing stockings and high-heeled, deerskin shoes. She was also wearing a short, wool skirt, of the same material as the coat found on the body, and elastic garters. The family confirmed that when she went out she had left behind not only all the gold jewelry her fiancé had given her, but also his photograph. They also confirmed what the concierge had said: Wilma was carrying a square black leather purse, with a gold-colored metal handle. Inside the purse she had a little white comb, a small mirror, and a white handkerchief. She also had a key to their apartment.

## NO ONE KNOWS ANYTHING

This first police report declared that they hadn't been able to establish any reason for suicide. Moreover, in the letter she had written to her fiancé the previous day, there was no indication that she would have made such a decision. It was also established that no member of the family, neither on the mother's side nor on the father's, had suffered mental disturbances. Wilma was in very good health. But it supplied a piece of information that could be of extraordinary importance in the investigation: on April 9 Wilma had just finished her menstrual cycle.

Despite numerous investigations, it could not be established that Wilma's family had any knowledge of a possible trip to Ostia she might have planned. Her father had looked for her insistently along the Lungotevere, believing she had thrown herself in the river, but he could give no explanation other than a premonition. It was clearly established that the family had no idea if the girl knew anyone in Ostia. They assured the police that they didn't even know the way or the bus or streetcar connections they'd need to take to get to San Pablo station, where the trains leave for Ostia.

### AN ENIGMA FOR THE EXPERTS

On the afternoon of April 14, at the Institute of Forensic Medicine in Rome, Professors Frache and Carella performed an autopsy on Wilma Montesi. The police presented the experts with a questionnaire, with the aim of establishing the precise time and cause of death. And they specifically wanted them to determine whether it had been the result of drowning or if the girl was already dead when she was thrown into the water. They should also establish the nature of any anatomical irregularities discovered in the cadaver, and the eventual presence in the intestines of any poisonous or narcotic substances.

The experts were also requested to specify if death had really been caused by drowning, and the distance from the beach that Wilma fell into the water. They were asked to establish at the same time if the death could have been a consequence of special physiological conditions, or from the state of her digestion. This investigation was important, for it could be related to the fact that Wilma had wanted to dip her feet in the sea during the process of digestion.

### SIX THINGS TO REMEMBER

On October 2, 1953, the experts returned the questionnaire with the following answers:

1. The death of Wilma Montesi had occurred on the "ninth of April," between four and six hours after her final meal. According to the examination, her last meal (which must have been lunch at home) had been verified at between 2 and 3:30 in the afternoon. So the death must have occurred between 6 and 8 that night, for the digestive process was completely concluded. The team of specialists established that shortly before she died, Wilma Montesi had eaten ice cream.

2. Death had been occasioned by the asphyxia of total immersion and not by syncope in the water. No traces of any poisonous or sedative substances were found in the viscera.

3. At the moment of death, Montesi was in an immediate postmenstrual phase, that is to say, in circumstances of greater sensitivity to an unexpected immersion of her lower extremities in cold water.

4. The presence of sand in the lungs, in the gastrointestinal tract, should be interpreted as proof that the asphyxia had occurred in proximity of the beach, where the seawater has a notable quantity of sand in suspension. But at the same time, the ferruginous content of that sand was not consistent with the sand at Torvaianica beach, but rather with the sand from another nearby beach.

5. They observed, among other things, the presence of small ecchymosis, almost round in shape, on the lateral surface of the right thigh and on the upper third of the upper face of the left leg. They considered that those small bruises had been caused before death, but they were not deemed to have any forensic significance.

6. They did not find any elements that would allow them to determine if death resulted from "an accidental misfortune," suicide, or homicide. The hypothesis of an accident was founded exclusively on the possibility that Wilma Montesi had suffered from a fainting spell while wading in the sea in the special physiological conditions she was in that day.

*The Press Sounds the Alarm*

Four days after the cadaver of Wilma Montesi was identified—on April 16—the investigation was considered definitively concluded, described as "an unfortunate accident." The victim's family, which on the day of the disappearance presented the police with sufficient arguments to sustain the hypothesis of suicide, contributed to the destruction of that hypothesis in the days following the identification of the corpse.

Contradicting everything she had said on the first day, Wanda Montesi declared before the investigating magistrates that her dead sister had invited her to go to Ostia on the morning of the 9th, "just" for a footbath in the sea. She wanted, according to what Wanda said, to submit an irritation on her heels caused by her shoes to the action of the seawater. To confirm that statement, Wanda remembered at the last minute that on that morning she'd gone to her father's workshop, at Wilma's request, to get a more comfortable pair of shoes. She said previously that both of them suffered from the same irritation and had tried to cure it with tincture of iodine. Later, methylated spirits having proved useless, they had resolved to travel "one of these days" to the beach at Ostia, in the hope that the natural iodine of seawater would bring them the longed-for improvement. But they had not spoken again about that trip. Only on the morning of the 9th, according to Wanda, her sister had remembered the trip again. But Wanda declined, because she was interested in seeing *The Golden Coach*.

### IF SHE'D SAID SO EARLIER

After her refusal, Wanda said that Wilma did not mention the trip to Ostia again but said that she'd rather stay home while her mother and sister went to the cinema. And unlike what she'd said the first time, Wanda explained to the police that her sister had left her gold jewelry at home because her mother had repeatedly begged her to do so, to prevent them from getting lost or deteriorating. She also declared that she had not taken her fiancé's portrait with her because she was not in the habit of taking it outside. Finally, she offered two important pieces of information to rule out the suicide hypothesis: In the first place, Wilma had seemed very serene on the morning of the 9th. And in the second place, before leaving she had washed her undergarments, after changing the ones she'd been wearing, for a clean set.

### THE MYSTERY OF THE GARTER

In the inquiry carried out among Wilma's relatives, neighbors, and acquaintances, another important truth was established: Wilma did not know how to swim. That's why the previous year, when she was in Ostia with her family during the summer vacations, she had only sunbathed on the beach in her bathing suit or waded up to her ankles in the sea.

Wilma's father also took back his original version that the girl had committed suicide. Rodolfo Montesi justified his first impression that Wilma had taken her own life with a very comfortable explanation: he said when he went out to look for her, on the night of the 9th, he did not know she'd invited her sister to travel to Ostia to take a footbath. And he explained that the dramatic telegram he had sent to Giuliani had been suggested by him during the telephone call: only with this shocking news could he get quick permission to travel to Rome that very night.

One thing still needed to be established: Rodolfo Montesi's opinion on the fact that his daughter's body had been found without her garter, which is intimate apparel, and which does not need to be removed for a footbath. Rodolfo Montesi explained: Wilma was an exuberantly shapely girl and did not enjoy sufficient freedom of movement when submitted to the pressure of garter belts.

### A PAIR OF GLOVES

Signora Montesi also ruled out the hypothesis that her daughter had committed suicide. And she set out a strong argument: Wilma had taken her house keys with her, which demonstrated that she intended to return. However, she did not agree with the accident hypothesis, but instead tried to reinforce that of homicide. According to Signora Montesi, her daughter had been the victim of a seducer, who had found it necessary to remove her garters to carry out his brutal intentions. And to demonstrate how difficult it is to take a woman's garter off, she showed the investigator one of Wanda's garters, similar to the one Wilma was wearing and which was not found on the corpse. It was a black satin garter, eight inches high on the front side, decreasing toward the back, with a metal fastening of hooks and eyes. And she made the police realize that not only her skirt and shoes had disappeared but her black leather purse had disappeared as well.

### The Reader Should Remember

a)  That the notebook in which Wilma copied the letter she'd sent to her fiancé had been impounded as evidence.

b)  That the Salaria police station's report affirmed that the concierge saw Wilma leave at 5:00 p.m., and not at 5:30, as Rodolfo Montesi had said.

c)  That the experts observed small bruises, but did not suggest the hypothesis that Wilma had been forcibly grabbed.

d)  That the analysis to establish the presence of poisonous or sedative substances had only been done on the viscera.

e)  Doctoresa Passarelli's declaration.

On that occasion, Signora Montesi enriched the inventory of her daughter's clothing with other objects. According to her, Wilma was wearing a pair of black musketeer's gloves and a gold-plated wristwatch.

#### THE SILENT ADMIRER

However, Signora Montesi's arguments were not given sufficient weight, and more importance was attributed to the reasons stated by Wanda to rule out the homicide hypothesis. Wanda explained that, when she told the police that her sister had left after an urgent telephone call, she'd forgotten two things: the conversation about the trip to Ostia, and the fact that there was nothing in Wilma's life she didn't know about. And incidentally, she remembered a recent case, five days before the death. Wilma told her that a young man had followed her in his automobile from Plaza Quadrata to her building, but without saying a word to her. According to Wanda, her sister had not seen her silent admirer again, for she surely would have told her.

### NOBODY SENT HER FLOWERS

After that investigation, rushed through in four days, the police reached the conclusion that Wilma was an exceptionally serious and reserved girl, who had not had any love in her life for anyone but Giuliani. It was accepted that she only went out in the company of her mother and her sister, in spite of these two admitting that in recent months—after her fiancé was transferred to Potenza—Wilma had acquired the habit of going out alone almost every day, and always at the same time: from 5:30 to 6:30 in the evening.

The building's concierge, Adalgisa Roscini, remembered in turn never having received a bouquet of flowers for Wilma. And she assured the investigators that the girl had never received a letter from anyone except her fiancé.

### NOTHING'S HAPPENED HERE

On the basis of these declarations it was concluded—in a report dated April 16—that, since there were no reasons to doubt the Montesi family's declarations, it should be taken as certain that, in fact, Wilma had gone to Ostia to take a footbath. It was supposed that the girl had chosen a part of the beach that she knew from having been there the year before and had begun to take her clothes off, sure that she couldn't be seen by anyone. The girl had lost her balance due to a hollow in the sandy bottom, and had drowned accidentally. The report finished by saying that death must have occurred between 6:15 and 6:30, since

Wilma—who never arrived home later than 8 at night—should have taken the 7:30 train.

## "THE SCANDAL OF THE CENTURY"

That would have been the melancholy ending to the Montesi case, if there had not been newspapers in the streets telling people there was much more to it than met the eye. It started on the very day the body was identified, when Angelo Giuliani, Wilma's fiancé, observed the small bruises that the newspapers would later talk about, without conferring any importance to them. When he left the morgue, Giuliani told a journalist of his observation and declared his certainty that Wilma had been murdered.

While the police considered that Wilma Montesi had died by accident, the press kept demanding justice. On May 4 *Il Roma*, a newspaper based in Naples, dropped the dynamite bomb that would set off "the scandal of the century." According to an article published by that paper, Wilma Montesi's missing garments had been left at Rome's central police station, where they had been destroyed. They had been taken there by a young man in whose company Wilma Montesi had been seen in the first half of March, in an automobile that got stuck in the sand, near the Ostia beach. The name of the young man was published: Gian Piero Piccioni. He was none other than the son of Italy's minister of foreign relations.

### Public Opinion Comes into Play

The spectacular news published in *Il Roma*, a rabidly monarchic newspaper, was picked up, prettied up, and augmented by every paper in the country. But the police were going in another direction. On May 15, the Ostia Lido police produced a report on the only indications they'd found to establish Wilma Montesi's presence in Ostia, on the afternoon of April 9. These were the declarations of a nursemaid, Giovanna Capra, and of a manager of a newspaper kiosk in Ostia station, Pierina Schiano.

According to the nursemaid, at six o'clock on the evening of April 9, she had seen a girl who looked like Wilma Montesi, according to the pictures in the papers, heading toward the Marechiaro establishment. But she hadn't noticed the color of her coat.

The manager of the newspaper kiosk told the police, without hesitating, that Wilma Montesi had bought a postcard in Ostia station, had written it there and then, and mailed it. Later, according to this declaration, Wilma had gone, alone the entire time, toward the marshland canal. The card Wilma had written had been addressed to "a soldier in Potenza."

### THE CARD NEVER ARRIVED

The investigators questioned the two witnesses and dismissed both statements. But while the first did not remember any of the personal characteristics of the girl she saw on the beach at Ostia, the second declared with no hesitation that she was wearing a white sweater. The manager of the newspaper kiosk confirmed that the postcard was addressed to "a soldier in Potenza," but could not supply any detail of the address.

In a later interrogation of Giuliani, the police confirmed that he had not received any postcards. And Wilma's mother and sister verified that the girl did not have a pen in her purse. Finally it was established that the place where the nursemaid said she saw Wilma at 6:00 is more than two miles away from the Ostia station newspaper kiosk.

### THE GIRL IN THE AUTOMOBILE

But while the police went on destroying testimonies, the newspapers continued stirring up the scandal. And it was discovered that on April 14, two days after the discovery of Wilma's corpse, a mechanic from Ostia had gone to the police post to tell the story of the automobile stuck in the sand that *Il Roma* had mentioned in its sensational article. The mechanic's name was Mario Piccini. And he told the police that in early March, when he was working for the Ostia railway station, he had been summoned by a young man, shortly before dawn, to help him tow his automobile. Piccini says he went with pleasure, and that during the maneuver he noticed the presence of a girl aboard a bogged-down automobile. That girl looked very much like the pictures of Wilma Montesi published by the newspapers.

### IT HAS TO DO WITH PRINCES

The Rome police did not show the slightest interest in the mechanic's spontaneous declaration. But the judicial police did a quick investigation and discovered something different. They discovered that at six o'clock on the evening of the 9th or 10th of April an automobile had passed by that same place driven by a well-known young Italian aristocrat, Prince Maurizio D'Assia. According to that investigation, the distinguished gentleman was accompanied by a girl, who was not Wilma Montesi. The aforementioned automobile was seen by the guard Anastasia Lilli, Carabinieri Lituri, and a worker called Ziliante Triffelli.

### THE BOMB!

The Ostia police officially abandoned their search for the items of clothing the corpse was missing. A lawyer called Scapucci and one of his sons, who were walking near Castelporziano on April 30, found a pair of women's shoes. Believing they were Wilma Montesi's, they took them to the police. But the victim's relatives declared that they were not the shoes the girl had been wearing the last time she left her house.

In light of the fact that there was nothing to be done, the attorney general of the Republic prepared to close the case, confirming the hypothesis of accidental death. That was when the modest and scandalous monthly magazine *Attualità*, in its October issue, put another stick of dynamite under the investigation. Under the byline of its editor in chief, the magazine published a sensational chronicle: "The Truth About the Death of Wilma Montesi."

The editor of *Attualità* was Silvano Muto, an audacious thirty-year-old journalist, with the face of a movie star, who dressed like a movie star, with a silk scarf and dark sunglasses. His magazine, it is said, was the least read in all of Italy—therefore, the poorest. Muto wrote it from the first page to the last. He himself sold advertising space and kept it afloat by the skin of his teeth, simply out of the desire to have a magazine.

But after the October 1953 issue, *Attualità* turned into an enormous monster. Readers punched each other every month at the doors of its offices to get a copy.

That unexpected popularity was due to the scandalous article on the Montesi case, which was the first firm step public opinion took toward finding out the truth.

### The Reader Should Remember

a) That Wanda Montesi did not remember that Wilma had invited her to Ostia until several days after her disappearance.
b) That the police did not interrogate the mechanic Mario Piccini.
c) The testimony of Carabinieri Lituri relative to the sighting of Prince D'Assia's automobile.
d) The name Andrea Bisaccia.

#### NAMELESS PERPETRATOR

In his article, Muto affirmed:

a) The person responsible for Wilma Montesi's death was a young musician from Italian radio, son of a prominent political personality.
b) Due to political influences, the investigation had gone forward in such a way that little by little silence would fall over it.
c) He highlighted the reserve maintained around the results of the autopsy.

d) He accused the authorities of not wanting to identify the culprit.

e) He related Wilma Montesi's death with the trafficking of narcotics, to which he found it linked; he also talked about orgies in the area, in Castelporziano and Capacotta, with drug abuse, during one of which Montesi had died, not being a habitual user of narcotics.

f) The people present at the party moved the body to the neighboring beach of Torvaianica, to avoid a scandal.

### CASE CLOSED

On October 24, 1953, Silvano Muto was summoned by the Roman district attorney's office to be held to account for his article. Muto calmly declared that it was all lies, that he'd written the article only to increase circulation of his magazine, and he admitted to having proceeded flippantly. In view of that overwhelming retraction, Muto was charged with "spreading false and tendentious news and for disrupting public order." And the brief of the Montesi case was shelved in January 1954, by order of the attorney general's office.

### AGAIN?

However, when Silvano Muto showed up in court to answer for his scandalous article, he again said what he'd written and added new details. And for the first time he gave proper names; he said the material for his article had been supplied by Orlando Triffelli, according to whom his brother had recognized Montesi in an automobile stuck in the sand on the 9th or 10th of April 1953, in front of the Capacotta security guard's hut. Furthermore, he said he had received confidential revelations from two of those present at the epic orgies of liquor and drugs: Andrea Bisaccia and the television actress Anna María Caglio.

### THE DANCE BEGINS

Andrea Bisaccia was summoned to testify. In an alarming state of nervousness, she denied having said anything to Silvano Muto. She said that it was a fantastical story, invented with the aim of destroying her intimate friendship with Gian Piero Piccioni, son of the minister of foreign relations and well-known composer of popular music. She finished off by saying that Silvano Muto's idiotic scheme had made such an impression on her that on the 9th of January she had attempted suicide.

The only place left for Muto was jail, and for the Montesi dossier a definitive stay in the dusty judicial archives of Rome. But on February 6, Anna María Caglio turned up at a police station and very serenely, in her professional announcer's voice, told the dramatic story of her life.

### Secret Rendezvous in the Ministry of the Interior

Anna María Caglio was the lover of Ugo Montagna, an affluent gentleman, friend of notable personalities, and famous for his romantic adventures. He called himself "the Marchese of Montagna," and he was known and treated as a marchese in all circles. Anna María Caglio told the police that she didn't know Wilma Montesi. But she had seen her picture in the papers and identified her as the dark-haired, well-built, and elegant young woman who, on the evening of January 7, 1953, had come out of one of Montagna's apartments in Rome, accompanied by him. Both got into an automobile driven by the marchese.

That night, Anna María Caglio—according to what she told the police—had been involved in a violent jealous scene when her lover returned home.

### "THERE'S MORE TO THIS THAN MEETS THE EYE"

When Anna María Caglio read the article in *Attualità*, she believed that the Signor X mentioned in that article was her own lover, the Marchese of Montagna. That's why she approached the journalist, and told him that everything in his article was true. The night of October 26 she was with her lover, in an automobile. She asked him for an explanation, as she told the police. And the marchese, who was irritated, and a little nervous, threatened to throw her out of the car.

To calm her lover, Anna María Caglio suggested they go home, to read Muto's article in peace; Montagna read Muto's article and didn't say anything. But when Anna María Caglio went to put the magazine in the drawer of the nightstand, she saw a packet with two golden cigarettes and an ashtray made of precious gems. That discovery reinforced her suspicion that her lover was connected to some band of narcotics traffickers.

### A MYSTERIOUS MEETING

Caglio insisted to the police that she had gone to Milan, her hometown, on April 7, and returned on the 10th. When she arrived in Rome, her lover was visibly nervous and upset by her unexpected return. Nevertheless, he took her home, where that night Montagna received a call from the son of the minister of foreign relations, Gian Piero Piccioni, who was preparing for a trip.

Later, Anna María Caglio found out that in November of the previous year, a certain "Gioben Jo" had lost thirteen million lire playing cards in Capacotta with Montagna, Piccioni, and a high-ranking police official.

### THE NIGHT OF APRIL 29

Anna María Caglio was dining with her lover in his luxurious apartment and getting ready to go to see a movie at Supercinema. A few days earlier, Caglio says that Montagna had told her that Piccioni was "a poor boy he had to help, because he'd got himself into a mess." That night, when she was putting her coat on to leave, Anna María Caglio realized that Piccioni called Montagna on the telephone and told him he should go immediately to speak to the chief of police. Montagna rushed out and met Piccioni at the Ministry of the Interior.

*The Reader Should Remember*

   a) Anna María Caglio's declaration that Montagna and Piccioni
      had visited the Ministry of the Interior on April 29, 1953.
   b) The slip of paper that says, "I'm going to the Capacotta and
      I'll spend the night there. How will I end up?"
   c) "The certain Gioben Jo," who lost thirteen million lire at
      cards.


## "*A VOLAR*"

An hour and a half later, when Montagna returned to the automobile
where Ana María Caglio was waiting for him, he said he had been trying to stop the investigation into the death of Wilma Montesi. Anna
María Caglio told him that was despicable, since whoever committed
the crime should pay for it, even if he were a minister's son. Montagna
told her that Piccioni was innocent, since the day of the crime he had
been in Amalfi. Then the girl asked Montagna:

   "And when did Piccioni return to Rome?"

Montagna was indignant, and did not answer her question. He
looked her in the eye and said:

   "Girlie, you know too much. You better get a change of scene."


## "*TI BUTTO A MARE*"

In effect, Anna María Caglio demonstrated that the next day she'd
been sent back to Milan, with a special letter for the director of the
television station. She returned to Rome on the 22nd of the same
month, to celebrate her first anniversary of meeting Montagna. On
July 27 they moved into separate homes, but continued to see each
other in the apartment on Vía Gennargentu. At the end of November they broke up definitively, after the incidents caused by Muto's
article.

Anna María Caglio told the police she had felt terror during those
days. Her lover was becoming more and more mysterious. He received

strange telephone calls and seemed to be involved in shady business deals. One night, exhausted by the nervous tension, Anna María Caglio says she asked her lover a question related to his businesses and Montagna answered her in a threatening tone:

"If you don't behave yourself, I'll throw you in the sea."

### THE WILL

Anna María Caglio, in her dramatic tale to the police, said that since that night she'd been harboring the certainty that she would be murdered. On November 22, after having dinner with Montagna at the Matriciana restaurant, on Vía Gracchi, she had the sensation she'd been poisoned. Alone in her apartment, she remembered that her lover had gone to the kitchen personally, to collaborate in the preparation of the meal.

Terrorized, Anna María Caglio left the next day for Milan. Her nerves were shattered. She didn't know what to do, but she was sure she had to do something. That's why she went to visit the Jesuit Father Dall'Olio and told him the whole story of her life with Montagna. The priest, tremendously shocked by the girl's tale, repeated the story to the minister of the interior. Anna María Caglio, tormented by a feeling of persecution, took refuge in the convent on Vía Lucchesi. But there was something she had not told the police: before she left for Milan, she gave her landlady in Rome a sealed letter with the following instructions: "In the case of my death, deliver this letter to the Attorney General of the Republic."

### "HOW WILL I END UP?"

The landlady, Adelmira Biaggioni, in whose hands Anna María Caglio had left the letter, was called to make a statement. She went to see the police with three letters, written in Caglio's handwriting, and a little piece of paper the girl had slipped under her door before going out on October 29, 1953. The paper said, "I'm going to the Capacotta Estate and I'll spend the night there. How will I end up?"

Adelmira Biaggioni revealed that the night Anna María Caglio thought Montagna had poisoned her, she wrote a will that she presented to her the next day, before leaving for Milan, with the task of taking it to the attorney general if she turned up dead. The landlady held on to the letter for several days. Then, not wanting to bear that responsibility, she put it in another envelope and addressed it to Anna María Caglio, at the convent where she'd taken refuge.

The police ordered the seizure of that letter and called Anna María Caglio again, to identify it as hers. Among many other things, the letter said, "I want everyone to know that I have never been aware of the business dealings of Ugo Montagna [. . .] But I am otherwise convinced that the one responsible is Ugo Montagna (with the collaboration of many women [. . .]) He is the brains behind the organization, while Piero Piccioni is the murderer."

### Loud Kinky Parties with Alida Valli

Anna María Caglio's dramatic will started an earthquake in public opinion. The press, and especially the opposition newspapers, began a barrage of heavy artillery fire against the judicial establishment, against the police, against everything that had anything to do with the government. Between the blasts, Ugo Montagna and Gian Piero Piccioni were summoned to testify.

Well dressed, in a dark pinstriped suit and with a smiling seriousness, Ugo Montagna responded to the inquiry. He said he had never met Wilma Montesi. He denied that she was the lady Anna María Caglio said she'd seen him with on January 7, 1953, in his car and at the door of his apartment building. He emphatically denied that "pleasure parties" had taken place at his Capacotta estate. He said it was not true that Piccioni would have telephoned him on the night of April 10. He ended by saying, without losing his cool, in a sure and convincing voice, that he did not remember having attended an interview with Rome's chief of police at the Ministry of the Interior, as Anna María Caglio had said, and that it was absolutely false that he had ever been in contact with any narcotics traffickers. He also made the observation that Piccioni and the chief of police were old friends and it was neither necessary nor reasonable, therefore, that he should have had to serve as an intermediary between them.

### THE FATAL DATE

Less serene than Montagna, dressed a little sportily, and in a sonorous Italian with a Roman accent, Gian Piero Piccioni declared himself to be an absolute stranger to the Montesi case. On the day of her death, he said, he was taking a short break in Amalfi, returning from there to Rome, by automobile, at 3:30 on the afternoon of April 10. He later declared that same afternoon he had to take to his bed with a bad case of tonsillitis. To prove it, he promised to show them the prescription from Professor Di Filippo, the doctor who had visited him that afternoon.

As far as his supposed visit to Rome's chief of police in Montagna's company, Piccioni declared that it had not been carried out in the malicious way Anna María Caglio told it. Several times, he said, he had visited him alone or with Montagna, but only in order to request his intervention in the way the press was compromising his name in the Montesi case. "Those attacks from the press," he said, "have no other aim than a political one: to harm my father's prestige."

### CASE SHELVED!

In light of the charges not offering any new perspective or seeming sufficiently valid to rule out the hypothesis of accidental death while taking a footbath, the Wilma Montesi case was shelved for the second time on March 2, 1954. But the press did not shelve their campaign. The trial of the journalist Muto proceeded, and each time someone showed up to testify, the Montesi case was stirred up again.

*The Reader Should Remember*

a) The date on which Piero Piccioni said he returned from Amalfi.

b) The prescription from Professor Di Filippo, which Piero Piccioni promised to show the police.

Among many others summoned to declare, Franccimei, a painter, said he had lived for a week with Andrea Bisaccia, one of the two women who Muto named as his sources of information. Franccimei told the police an intense story. Andrea Bisaccia—he said—suffered from nightmares. She talked in distressed tones while she slept. In one of those nightmares, she began to shout in terror: "Water . . . ! No . . . I don't want to drown . . . No, I don't want to die the same way . . . Let me go!"

While the painter was making his dramatic declaration, a woman driven mad by the abuse of narcotics threw herself off a third-story balcony of a hotel in Alessandría. In her purse, the police found, written down on a little piece of paper, two telephone numbers that were not listed in Rome's telephone directory. Both were private numbers. One belonged to Ugo Montagna. The other to Piero Piccioni.

### A WHOLE LIFE

The woman who jumped from the third floor was Corinna Versolatto, an adventurer who in less than a year had practiced all sorts of trades. She was a nurse in a respectable clinic; a coat-check girl at the Piccolo Slam nightclub, later closed by the police; and in her leisure time, a clandestine prostitute.

At the moment of her suicide attempt, Corinna Versolatto was the private secretary of Mario Amelotti, a Venezuelan who was fond of traveling and suspected of involvement in narcotics trafficking and the white slave trade. In a moment of lucidity, Corinna told journalists, in the presence of the doctor at the clinic she'd been driven to and an Alessandrian police officer, that in recent months she had fallen out of favor with Amelotti, her boss, because she had refused to collaborate in his illicit undertakings. She said, "That's all I can say. Mario is an unscrupulous man. He has bought off the police and he is a friend to many influential people."

Finally, Corinna revealed that her boss was a friend of someone who smoked marijuana cigarettes. And that together with a photographer friend of his, he ran a studio that made and sold pornographic postcards.

### THIS SEEMS LIKE A MOVIE

While this was going on, the press continued shouting. And the police carried on receiving anonymous tips. When Wilma Montesi's case was shelved for the second time, they received more than six hundred anonymous tips. One of them, signed Gianna la Rossa, said, "I am in the know about the events that occurred in April 1953, concerning the death of Wilma Montesi. I am terrified at the cruelty of Montagna and Piccioni, who tried to put her in contact with narcotics traffickers in the province of Parma, specifically in Traversetolo. I made a corresponding denunciation to the Parma police, in good time. But they buried it. A few months ago, I deposited a second letter for safekeeping at the office of the parish priest, in a little village in the region of Traversetolo. I sent that letter because I was convinced that I would suffer the same fate as Wilma Montesi. The priest will hand that letter over to whoever presents the attached half ticket. The other half is in his hands."

Gianna la Rossa went on in her letter explaining the reasons she preferred to shelter behind a pseudonym. The letter ended: "My hide is worth nothing, but it happens to be all I have."

### HOW HIGH DOES THE WATER GO?

The police conducted a swift investigation of the two previous cases. In relation to the background of the woman who attempted suicide, they established that in Rome she frequented the Victor club and in the hotel where she lived she organized loud kinky parties, attended by notable personalities and two movie actresses. One of them was Alida Valli.

The hotel where Corinna lived in Alessandria, and where she'd jumped out the window, was searched by the police. In the suicidal woman's room they found two press cuttings. One was the news of the closure of Piccolo Slam. The other was about the Montesi case.

### "LET'S SEE, FATHER"

In relation to the letter from Gianna la Rossa, the police discovered that the parish priest was Tonnino Onnis, curate of Bannone di Traversetolo and an engineering student. And along they went to his parish, with the half ticket included in the letter, a fifty-lire entry ticket to the Ministry of Education's general headquarters of antiquities and fine arts. The parish priest showed them the letter, on the envelope of which he had written: "Deposited into my safekeeping on May 16, 1953, to be handed over only to whomever presents the other half of the attached ticket, which must have the number A.N.629190." On the back of the envelope he had made a second explanation: "Sealed by me. I do not know the name or address of the person who wrote it."

The letter was opened and its sensational text read.

### The Dark Histories of the Witnesses

The letter handed over by the parish priest to the police was dated May 16 and said, among other things, "If you are reading this letter, I am dead. But I want it to be known that I did not die a natural death. I have been finished off by the Marchese Montagna and Piero Piccioni . . . I have lived my last months under the nightmare of suffering the same death as Wilma Montesi . . . I am putting into practice a plan to unmask the band of narcotics traffickers . . . If this plan fails, I will meet the same fate as Wilma . . .

"This letter will only be handed over to whomever is in possession of a special password . . ."

## THE TRICK

Father Onnis was not satisfied with merely showing this letter to the police, but took the opportunity to tell a story that sounded like a bandit movie. He said that in August or September 1953, on a Friday, when he was getting ready to leave Parma on his motorcycle, two individuals approached him who had just gotten out of a car with French license plates. With simulated foreign accents, through which the parish priest believed he detected the accent of southern Italy, the two individuals begged him to take a package. He refused, started up his motorcycle, and took off at full speed. But when he reached the village he was arrested by the police and taken to the precinct. The officers on duty searched the package that the priest had on his back seat. It was a radio to repair.

Then the police showed him an anonymous note they'd received a few hours earlier with the license plate number of his motorcycle, the time he would pass through the village, and the accusation that Father Onnis was in contact with a gang of drug traffickers.

## ALIDA VALLI ON THE PHONE

The investigators made something very important immediately clear: the letter presented by Father Onnis was dated May 16, when the name Piero Piccioni had not yet been associated with that of Montagna. Ana María Caglio's declarations were made in October.

Around the same time, the newspapers were insisting on another important event in the Montesi case: the telephone call the actress Alida Valli made from Venice to Piero Piccioni, with whom she had an intimate friendship. Alida Valli had been with Piccioni in Amalfi during the trip he told the police about to defend himself. Later the actress traveled to Venice to work filming the movie *The Stranger's Hand*. Two days after Alida Valli arrived in Venice, the Montesi scandal broke at. A journalist, an actor, a film director, and a parliamentary deputy all declared that the actress had phoned Piccioni from a

Venetian tobacconist shop. The actress denied the conversation had taken place.

## NO ROOM FOR DOUBTS

According to the witnesses, Alida Valli, obviously quite worked up, said to Piccioni:

"What the hell have you done? What happened to that girl?"

The actress carried on the conversation in a loud voice, because it was a long-distance call. It was a public place. When she hung up, she was in such a state of agitation that she said out loud, as if she were still calling long distance, "You'll see what a mess that imbecile's got himself into."

### The Reader Should Remember

a) The telephone call Alida Valli made to Piero Piccioni from Venice.
b) The results of the first autopsy performed on Wilma Montesi, published in the second installment of this series.
c) Wilma Montesi's family's declarations, after her body was found on Torvaianica beach.
d) The items of clothing found on the body.

The organ of the Italian Communist Party, *L'Unità,* reported on the scandal of the telephone call. According to that newspaper, the call had been placed on April 29, 1953. The actress wrote a letter to the editors protesting the ease with which they spread "fantastical and tendentious news." And she stated that on April 29 she had been in Rome. But the police had seized her telephone book and established that, in effect, the call had been made.

## DARK STORIES

Another declaration was heard at the trial of the journalist Muto: that of Gioben Jo, who according to Ana María Caglio had lost thirteen million lire playing cards at Capacotta, with Montagna, Piccioni, and a high-ranking police official. Gioben Jo declared that an acquaintance of hers, Gianni Cortesse, who had emigrated to Brazil, and written from there to say that he was "very well settled in," had been "ship's purser" in Genoa several years ago, and a notorious narcotics dealer. She said that the aforementioned Cortesse supplied a dentist friend with large quantities of cocaine. That friend, according to Gioben Jo, had introduced her to Montagna, who was a close friend.

Another witness finally declared that several years before he had been a guest of Montagna. There had been a lawyer, a friend of both, known for his fondness for drugs, who even suffered attacks of delirium tremens due to his abuse of narcotics. In April or June of 1947, according to the witness, Montagna, the lawyer friend, and a woman came into his room, completely naked, and had woken him up with vulgar phrases and dark words.

## WHOM TO BELIEVE?

The journalist Muto's trial really turned into a many-legged creature. Each time someone was summoned to testify, more witnesses had to be called, to establish the truth of the testimonies. It was like a game of *da que te vienen dando* (give as good as you get). New names kept coming up. And the press, for its part, conducted spontaneous investigations, and every day dawned on new revelations. Among the people testifying at Muto's trial was Vittorio Feroldi de Rosa, who said he had driven, in July or August of 1953, from Rome to Ostia, along with several people, one of whom was Andrea Bisaccia. According to Feroldi, Bisaccia had told her travel companion that narcotics were trafficked along the Ostia-Torva coast; that she had met Wilma Montesi; that she had participated in some of the "pleasure meetings" at Castelporziano, and that she had seen Montesi's garter "in someone's hands."

The other occupants of the automobile were summoned to testify, and one of them, Silvana Isola, declared that she hadn't heard anything, because she was fast asleep for the whole trip. But another of the travelers, Gastone Prettenati, admitted that, in fact, Andrea

Bisaccia had revealed some confidences during that trip. She had told them, among other things, that Montesi, on "a pleasure outing" she'd attended and during which she'd smoked "certain cigarettes," had suffered a collapse. Then she'd been left on the beach, because the others there thought she was dead.

Another witness, Franco Marramei, declared finally that one night he'd found himself in a small bar on Vía del Balbuino and had heard Andrea Bisaccia say in a loud voice, "The Montesi girl couldn't have died by accident, because I knew her very well."

### BACK TO THE BEGINNING

Faced with the tremendous uproar in the press and public opinion's evident disapproval, Rome's Court of Appeals demanded that the attorney general reopen the twice-closed case. On March 29, 1954—almost a year after Montesi's death—the examining office took charge of the confusing and hefty dossier and began the formal proceedings of the Montesi case.

For a year, the voluminous and smiley presiding magistrate, Rafaelle Sepe, working day and night, put that chilling mountain of contradictions, errors, and false testimonies in order. He had to start over again from the beginning. Wilma Montesi's cadaver was exhumed for a new autopsy. What Magistrate Sepe did was put the deck in order, with the cards facedown.

### Twenty-Four Lost Hours in Wilma's Life

Since he was starting from scratch, Magistrate Sepe began by trying to establish the precise hour that Wilma Montesi left her house on the afternoon of April 9. Up until that moment there were two different testimonies: that of the victim's father, who on the night of the 9th told the police that the concierge Adalgisa Roscini had said that Wilma left at 5:30; and that of the Salaria police department, which in their first report on Tuesday, April 14, declared that the concierge herself had said another time: five o'clock on the dot.

The investigating magistrate called Adalgisa Roscini directly and she declared without hesitation that Wilma had not left the house before 5:15. The concierge had a reason for that categorical statement. During the days when the events occurred, a group of laborers were working on the building and stopped at exactly five o'clock. Then they went to wash up at the fountain in the courtyard and took no less than ten minutes. When the laborers finished their work on April 9, Wilma had not yet gone out. When they finished washing up and left the building, she still hadn't gone out. Adalgisa Roscini saw her leave a few minutes after the laborers. Shortly after 5:15.

### "A HARD BONE"

In this investigation, the concierge of number 76 Tagliamento made another revelation that cast shadows of doubt onto the Montesi family's behavior. In reality, the attitude of the victim's relatives had changed fundamentally since the day her body was identified. Adalgisa Roscini declared that a few days after Wilma's death, her mother had pressed her to modify her earlier declaration that the girl had left at 5:30. The concierge refused. And then Wilma's mother said to her:

"Then how did Doctoresa Passarelli manage to travel on the train with her at that very time?"

The concierge says she replied:

"She must have seen the clock wrong."

And then, feeling indignant at the pressure they were trying to put on her, she exclaimed:

"You've come upon a tough nut to crack, because I'm not changing the time."

### DOCTORESA PASSARELLI

To start right at the beginning, Doctoresa Passarelli was summoned again. She showed up in a state of worrying agitation. This time she didn't seem so sure of having seen Wilma Montesi on the train. "I thought I saw her," was all she said. And she described the girl again. She was a young woman between twenty-eight and thirty years of age. Her hair was styled "high above her forehead, tight on the sides, and with a large bun in the back." She wasn't wearing gloves. She was wearing loafers and a coat the predominant color of which was green.

However, Wilma had just turned twenty-one a few months before, and according to the testimony of many people who knew her she looked younger than she was. Furthermore, on the afternoon she left her house for the last time she wasn't wearing loafers, but very eye-catching shoes, of gold fabric. Her hairstyle was not as Passarelli described it, because Wilma had had short hair for the last several months.

### SAVED BY A THREAD

The investigator showed Doctoresa Passarelli the coat found on the body. When she saw it, the doctoresa seemed disconcerted. It was a yellow coat, eye-catching and unmistakable. She turned it over, as if to see if it was green on the other side. Then she roundly denied that this was the coat the girl on the train had been wearing.

Magistrate Sepe demonstrated that the doctoresa had not been shown the body of Wilma Montesi. The identification had been limited to the examination of a few pieces of clothing. However, he considered it necessary to investigate the woman's conduct. He established that she was a humanities graduate, employed by the Ministry of Defense, daughter of a high-ranking army official, and belonging to a distinguished Roman family. But at the same time he established that she suffered from mild nearsightedness but did not wear glasses, and had an impulsive, not very reflexive, temperament with a tendency toward fantasy. She was saved by a thread: she managed to prove where she got the money to buy, a few days after her first spontaneous declaration, an apartment that cost 5,600,000 lire.

### "FROM HERE TO ETERNITY"

Once Passarelli's testimony was demolished, the investigating magistrate proposed to establish how long it takes a person to get from number 76 Vía Tagliamento to the Ostia train station. The police, the urban transport management, and the Ministry of Defense collaborated in this investigation.

## The Reader Should Know

Starting with this installment, the reader will find in the text the answers to the points that "the readers should remember," which were published in the previous installments.

From this moment on, it will be established in strict order:

a) Wilma Montesi's alleged trip to Ostia.
b) The time and place of her death.
c) Cause of death and judicial definition of the deed.
d) The real habits, morality, and family atmosphere of Wilma Montesi's life.
e) Narcotics trafficking.
f) Gatherings at Capacotta.
g) Accusations against Prince D'Assia.
h) Facts against Ugo Montagna and Piero Piccioni and against the ex-chief of police of Rome, Severo Polito.

There are 3.9 miles from number 76 Vía Tagliamento to the door of the station, by the shortest route. To cover that distance, in ideal transit conditions and not considering possible red lights, a taxi would take exactly thirteen minutes. On foot, at a normal pace, it would take between an hour and a quarter and an hour and twenty-one minutes. At a fast pace, fifty minutes. The journey is covered by a streetcar route (the rápido B), which normally takes twenty-four minutes. Supposing that Wilma Montesi had used that means of transport, we would have to add at least three minutes, which was the time the girl would have needed to walk from her door to the bus stop, 220 yards away.

And that's still without counting the time to buy a ticket at the station and get to the train, on a platform more than 300 yards from the ticket office. It was an important conclusion: Wilma Montesi did not travel to Ostia on the 5:30 train. She very probably could not have done so even if she had actually left the house at 5:00.

### THE TIME OF DEATH

Those who produced the first reports did not realize something essential: Dr. Di Giorgio, the first doctor to examine the corpse on the Torvaianica beach, declared that it was in the early stages of rigor mortis. After a certain time, a cadaver begins to stiffen: this is the period of the cadaveric rigidity. Subsequently, the contrary phenomenon comes into operation. Dr. Di Giorgio established that Wilma Montesi's body was "partially rigid." But he had a reason for stating that it was in the process "of progressive stiffening": the rigidity presented in the jaw, the neck, and the upper extremities. Nysten's law, duly proven, explains: "Rigor mortis begins in the muscles of mastication; continues to those of the neck and upper extremities." Based on this law, Dr. Di Giorgio prepared his report: death must have occurred approximately eighteen hours before the examination. And the examination was verified on Saturday, April 11, at 9:30 in the morning.

### HERE THE ERROR BEGAN

The corpse was exposed to the sun for the whole day, while waiting for instructions from Rome. Those instructions arrived after dark. A few hours later, the cadaver was transported to the autopsy room. When Rodolfo Montesi and Angelo Giuliani entered to identify it, more than twenty-four hours had gone by since the find. When the postmortem was done and the report prepared, it said death had occurred on the night of April 9, because the cadaver presented a first point of putrefaction and due to the phenomenon of "anserine skin." A year after her death, a group of professors from the Faculty of Medicine prepared a new expert opinion, after a careful examination of the cadaver, and established that the incursion of putrefaction could have been precipitated by the corpse's long exposure to the sun and humidity on the Torvaianica beach, during the whole day of April 11.

In relation to the phenomenon of the "anserine skin," they demonstrated that this phenomenon is common in the bodies of drowning victims, but it can even present before death, due to terror or prolonged agony. But in the case of Wilma Montesi, it could also have been caused by the long time the corpse was kept in cold storage before the autopsy was carried out. All in all, the first report, that of Dr. Di Giorgio, was fundamental: the rigidity was partial. And the conclusion was indisputable: Wilma Montesi had died on the night of April 10, twenty-four hours after the concierge Adalgisa Roscini saw her leave her home.

What did she do in those twenty-four hours?

### Twenty-Four Lost Hours in Wilma's Life

Another important truth needed to be established: the place Wilma Montesi died. For it had been accepted as true that the girl had gone to the beach at Ostia to bathe her feet when she suffered a collapse and then, once she'd drowned, was carried by the waves to Torvaianica beach, twelve miles away.

To reinforce this hypothesis the Ostia police reported that on the night of April 10 a violent storm had raged in that region, with strong northwesterly winds. The investigator in charge of the proceedings, Magistrate Sepe, turned to the meteorology professors at the meteorological institute to verify that fact. The report, with weather bulletins from the entire month of April 1953, said that the Ostia-Torvaianica sector did not register any such storm. The most notable phenomenon had occurred on April 11 at the exact time Wilma Montesi's body was found: a northeasterly wind of eight miles per hour.

### THE REVEALING CARMINE

The autopsy by the new experts made it clear that the cadaver had no bite marks from marine animals or insects, which are abundant on Torvaianica beach. The magistrate drew the conclusion, from this information, that the corpse had not spent much time in the water, and not much time on the beach, either, before being found. The first deduction was already a principle of certainty to rule out the hypothesis that the body had been carried twelve miles by the waves.

But they found more important evidence. Wilma Montesi's crimson nail polish was intact. The experts confirmed that the substance was resistant to seawater. But they investigated the density of sand in suspension in the water between Ostia and Torvaianica. And they concluded that it would have been difficult for her nail polish to stand up to the friction of the sand on a long and fast twelve-mile journey.

### BY WAY OF EXAMPLE: A BUTTON

Magistrate Sepe was the only one to take any interest in the coat that was buttoned around the corpse's neck. When Wilma Montesi's body was found on the beach, Carabinieri Augusto Tondi understood that this coat would be an obstacle to transporting the body, so he pulled the button and removed it without much difficulty.

Magistrate Sepe counted the threads used to sew the button on: there were seventeen. The experts demonstrated that those seventeen threads would not have withstood the marine journey, the coat battered by the waves, if a carabinieri had needed only a tug to pull it off.

These conclusions and others of an indigestible scientific nature allowed him to rule out the hypothesis of the corpse's long sea journey from the beach at Ostia to that of Torvaianica. New experts demonstrated that the ferruginous density of the sand found in the lungs of the cadaver was not conclusive proof to establish the place where the victim lost her life. Wilma Montesi drowned a few feet from the place where her body was found.

### FURTHERMORE

However, fifteen feet out from the beach at Torvaianica the water is not even a foot and a half deep. It's true that Wilma did not know how to swim. But it is not likely that a person who doesn't know how to swim will drown, just because she doesn't know how to swim, in a foot and a half of water. There must be other causes. And Magistrate Sepe resolved to discover them.

Super expert advice was called for. A doctor of irreproachable conduct and five university professors of forensic medicine duly investigated studying the presence of sand and plankton in the lungs and intestines of the corpse. Due to the quantity and profundity, they concluded that death had not occurred in normal circumstances. From the first swallow of water until the moment of death, four minutes elapsed, at most.

The new expert advice demonstrated that Wilma Montesi died in a slow and prolonged drowning, between ten and twenty minutes after her first contact with the water. That's how they explained how she had drowned in a foot and a half of water: Wilma Montesi was exhausted when she began to drown.

### SUICIDE TAKES NOTHING

Once this important conclusion was obtained, Magistrate Sepe resolved to analyze the three hypotheses:

a) Suicide.
b) Accident.
c) Homicide.

The only time Wilma's possible suicide was mentioned was on the night of April 9, when her father went to look for her in the Tiber and later, when he went to the police and when he sent the telegram to Giuliani. Rodolfo Montesi said that his daughter wanted to commit suicide due to the imminence of her wedding and resulting separation from her family, by moving to Potenza, where her fiancé was working. But Wilma's marriage had not been imposed by her family. She enjoyed enough independence, had reached the age of majority, and could have canceled her engagement to Giuliani whenever she wanted. It was a weak explanation.

Her mother's argument had carried a lot of weight in destroying the suicide hypothesis: Wilma had taken her house keys with her, which she didn't always do. And her sister's argument: before going out, Wilma left her underwear that she'd just changed out of soaking in soapy water in the bathroom sink. Finally, someone who examined the true circumstances in which Wilma Montesi died stated, "It would have necessitated violating her instinct of self-preservation to superhuman extremes to keep drowning herself for a quarter of an hour, in such shallow water." Suicide doesn't take such hard work.

### BIG GAME STEPS

Magistrate Sepe discarded suicide and began to study accidental death. He accepted as valid the first autopsy's explanation: Wilma did not die from having gone into the water while in the process of digestion, because that process was finished. And even if that had not been the case, it was not very likely that she would have suffered a collapse from dipping her feet in the water after lunch.

The circumstance that Wilma was in the immediate postmenstrual phase was not considered valid to explain a collapse either. Any upset she might have suffered, owing to that particular circumstance, would not have prevented her from dragging herself back onto the beach, according to the experts. They also ruled out, after the new autopsy, any other kind of disorder: Wilma had been in good health. But her heart was small in relation to her height, as was the capacity of her aorta.

On the other hand, Magistrate Sepe considered it advisable to establish the precise origin of the foot-bathing hypothesis. It arose many days after the death, when Wanda Montesi "remembered" that her sister had spoken to her of a trip to Ostia. That was after the funeral, when the whole family began to look for an explanation for the death. The attitude was considered suspicious: Wilma Montesi's family always demonstrated an excessive interest in giving credit to Wanda's version. Based on her declaration, the case was shelved for the first time, with the definition of "accidental death." However, all the elements contributed to an admission of the truth: Wilma's family had no news of any trip to Ostia, or any supposed footbath.

## "LET'S GO THIS WAY"

The experts did establish, though, that Wilma Montesi had no lesions, irritation, or eczema on her heels. She had no signs of hardened or peeling skin caused by her shoes. That suspicious attitude on the part of her family was meticulously analyzed by the magistrate. Wilma's father, who inexplicably took charge of the accidental death hypothesis, explained that the girl had taken her garter belt off for more freedom of movement while wading in the sea. And yet she did not take off her coat. And it has to be imagined that a person who wants freedom of movement while bathing her feet would be more likely to take off her coat before her garters. She might even take off her coat in order to have more freedom of movement to take off her garter.

Finally, it is inconceivable that in order to bathe her feet Wilma Montesi would have walked twelve miles from the Ostia train station to Torvaianica beach, when the sea was a few yards away from the station. Magistrate Sepe was not taken in by the accidental death while foot-bathing idea and carried on investigating. Now he had a more important piece of information in hand: the size of Wilma Montesi's heart. That could have something to do with narcotics.

### They Threw Her, Unconscious, into the Sea

When Angelo Giuliani saw the corpse of his fiancée, he observed certain marks on her arms and legs, which made him think of homicide. He was the one who told a journalist, on his way out of the mortuary. The first autopsy confirmed the existence of those five small bruises, but did not attribute any medical or legal importance to them.

The consultation ordered by Magistrate Sepe, to reexamine the cadaver, meticulously, and even to carry out a detailed radiographic exploration, demonstrated that there were no broken bones. Some superficial scratches were observed on the face, especially on the nose and brows: results of the body's friction against the sand. However, the examination confirmed that the five small bruises had occurred before death. The experts considered that they could have happened any time between the beginning of her death throes and five or six hours before death.

### THERE WAS NO CARNAL VIOLENCE

In consideration of her particular situation and the absence of other characteristic signs, the hypothesis that the five bruises were the product of an act of sexual violence was ruled out. There were two on her left arm and two on her left thigh and one on her right leg. Those bruises, according to the specialists, due to their location, quantity, and superficiality, had the characteristics of a "grasping" of an inert body.

They were not signs of struggle or force, for it could be clearly established that when they were produced the body offered no resistance. In an act of carnal violence, the characteristics would have been different. The quantity would have been different and the location very different.

### THE VISCERA ARE NOT ENOUGH

As will be recalled, after the first autopsy a chemical examination of the viscera was executed, to check for the presence of narcotics. The result of that examination was negative. One year later, the forensic specialists affirmed that the "state of unconsciousness preexistent to death was not incompatible with the absence of traces of narcotics in the viscera." The original investigation had been incomplete, as it did not check for the presence of narcotics in the blood, the brain, or the spinal cord. Consequently, the negative of the chemical examination of the intestines could not be considered absolute. Wilma Montesi could have been the victim of narcotics, even though the chemical exam of her viscera did not reveal their presence.

### MAKING HEADWAY

Furthermore, it could have been an alkaloid that left no trace in the stomach. That could have occurred through elimination, while the body was still alive or after death, or due to transformations occurred after dying. That assertion is much more valid in cases of volatile substances or those that break down rapidly.

Faced with these circumstances, the superior magistrates considered that it had not been established forensically whether or not Wilma Montesi had utilized some dose of narcotics. Therefore, the exam was not negative, but rather useless, since it had only checked to make sure there were no traces of narcotics in the stomach at the time of investigation. Those traces could have been found in other organs, and even in the stomach itself, at a previous moment.

### "YOUR SMALL HEART"

Magistrate Sepe was struck by the small size of Wilma Montesi's heart. He asked the specialists if that circumstance could have provoked a fainting spell when the girl was bathing her feet. The experts said no: the hypothesis was absolutely indemonstrable that Wilma's particular physiological condition could have caused a collapse due to the small size of her heart.

However, they said something else: "The small size of her heart could have produced a collapse, given the provision of narcotics."

The detailed examination of the body allowed it to be established that Wilma had a lower than normal sexual sensitivity. Magistrate Sepe considered that this could be an explanation for the provision of narcotics, for anyone might have put that resource in practice to provoke an arousal that would not have occurred in normal circumstances. Or to break down the victim's resistance.

### INSIDE AND OUT

They had to definitively discard the hypothesis that the sea had removed Wilma's garments. In order for that to have occured the body would have had to be submitted to violent wave action, which the seventeen threads of the coat's single button would not have withstood. However, the corpse was not wearing a garter, an item so tightly attached to her body that a former servant of the Montesi family declared that on several occasions, to remove it or put it on, Wilma had requested her help.

It was necessary to accept that someone other than Wilma had removed her clothes, probably by force, or probably when she was under the effect of narcotics. However, the coat continued to be an enigma: it is strange that they would have taken off her garter but not the easiest garment to remove—her coat.

Why not think of something more logical? For example: Wilma was completely undressed when she suffered the collapse. In his nervousness, her unknown companion, trying to destroy the traces of his action, had tried to hurriedly dress her. That's why the coat was there. Because it was the easiest item to take off, but also the easiest to put back on. And that's why the garter belt was gone.

### THE DEFINITION

Magistrate Sepe, having examined these and other details, not all of which are indispensable, arrived at the conclusion that the state of unconsciousness Wilma Montesi was in before her death was the result of a culpable act, or a malicious act. Those were the alternatives. Culpable homicide would have to prove that the person responsible did not know Wilma was still alive when he abandoned her body on the beach. Curiously, one of the first to give a statement had said that Wilma had participated in a pleasure party, had suffered a collapse because of the drugs, and had been abandoned on the beach.

## TWO LINKED QUESTIONS

Faced with such an alternative, there is a principle in Italian law called *favor rei,* the king's favor. This means that, in the case of doubt between a serious crime and a less serious one, the suspect must be tried for the less serious crime. The first part of article 83 of the Italian penal code says: "If through an error in the use of the means of execution of the crime, or for another cause, an event different from that desired is occasioned [concealment of an alleged corpse, in this case], the guilty party responds, by way of guilt, for the undesired event, when the event has been provided for by the law as a culpable crime." On the basis of that article, Magistrate Sepe defined the death of Wilma Montesi as a culpable homicide. Who committed that homicide?

## THE CENTRAL CHARACTER

For the time being, Magistrate Sepe could not mention any names. But there were some important things: from the five bruises, it could be deduced that the positioning of the body in the water, on Torvaianica beach, could have happened when Wilma was unconscious. That is, the accident had occurred somewhere else and the victim had been transported to the deserted spot. In that place, the seashore is more than forty feet away from the paved road, where the car that was carrying Wilma Montesi must have stopped. Between the road and the sea there is a sandy area, difficult to cross. In consideration of the victim's weight and the location of the five bruises, Sepe concluded that Wilma Montesi was carried from the car to the beach by at least two individuals.

"Who are those two individuals?" Sepe must have asked himself, scratching his bald and shiny head. Until now, he only had one clue: the possibility that Wilma Montesi had been in contact with drug traffickers. That was when the investigator, perhaps jumping up out of his chair as detectives do in the movies, asked himself the surprising question that nobody had asked up till then: "Who was Wilma Montesi?"

*The Myth of the Ingenuous Girl Collapses*

From the very first police reports the public was given the impression that the Montesi family was an example of modesty, tact, and innocence. The newspapers themselves contributed to creating that impression, devising the ideal image of Wilma Montesi: an ingenuous girl, free of malice or guilt, victim of the monstrous drug traffickers. There was, however, a bulging contradiction: it was inconceivable that a girl adorned with such exalted attributes would have had any connection to that class of people or would have participated, as was said, in a "pleasure party" that cost her her life.

Sepe realized the character was badly constructed and arranged to verify it with an in-depth investigation into the true family atmosphere and into Wilma Montesi's secret life.

### THE FALLEN IDOL

"Wilma's mother," wrote the magistrate once his investigation was completed, "did not enjoy a good reputation in the neighborhood and had imparted to her daughter, from the early years of her childhood, a not very strict upbringing, accustoming her to not washing and to dressing with a luxury disproportionate to her economic and social condition." Wilma Montesi's image as a poor, ingenuous girl, victim of drug traffickers, began to crumble before the onslaught of a cold and impartial investigation. Wilma Montesi's own mother set a bad example at home of pompous elegance and bad taste. "She was," says the summary, "authoritarian with her husband, despotic toward the whole family, and even violent to her own mother, uttering vulgar words and coarse expressions during the frequent scenes of domestic strife."

### THE MYSTERY OF THE PURSE

That behavior influenced Wilma's upbringing to such an extent that in an altercation she recently had with a neighbor, she used a string of unpublishable swearwords, literally transcribed in the summary. Shortly after her death, the proprietor of the Di Crema department store, on Vía Nazionale, heard that two girls who knew Wilma, but not later identified, said, referring to the victim, "It was to be expected, the life she lived couldn't have ended any other way."

Rodolfo Montesi's daily earnings were no more than fifteen hundred lire. However, in the final days of Wilma Montesi's life she owned a genuine crocodile-skin purse, estimated by experts to be worth eighty thousand lire. It was not possible to establish the origin of that purse.

### STRONG WORDS

One of the first things the police had proven seemed to have been forgotten: after her fiancé was transferred to Potenza the girl acquired the habit of going out every day, in the afternoon. She never returned home later than half past seven, it was claimed. But an unidentified doctor, who lived in the last building of number 76 Tagliamento, told a pharmacist on Vía Sebazio, who in turn revealed to the police, that he had, on occasion, opened the main door for Wilma after midnight.

For five months, Annunciata Gionni worked as a servant for the Montesi family household. The maid revealed to the police the exact opposite of what the family had told them: loud arguments were frequent in Rodolfo Montesi's absence, and sometimes Wilma's mother had shouted at her using very strong expressive words, which slightly toned down might be translated as "whore" and "wretch."

### TWO LITTLE SISTERS

It was also said that every morning, around eight, once their father had left the house, the two sisters would go out, until two in the afternoon. The former maid confirmed that fact, but said she hadn't thought it important because she imagined the two girls must have jobs.

In the afternoons, even after her engagement to Giuliani, Wilma Montesi received numerous telephone calls. Before answering, she closed the door of the room and spoke in a low and cautious voice. But nobody was in a position to say whether it was always the same caller, or whether they were long-distance calls. If this were the case, they couldn't have been from Giuliani, in the last months, because at the time Wilma Montesi died there was not yet direct telephone communication between Rome and Potenza.

### SUSPICIOUS ATTITUDE

As for the behavior of the family after Wilma's death, the magistrate verifies, by tapping their telephone, that Wilma's mother took advantage of the publicity the newspapers gave to her daughter's death. She herself charged several hundred lire for information and "on a certain occasion," says the brief, "deplored the scanty fee and urged the journalists to write a spicier article." From this and other inquiries, the investigating magistrate reached the conclusion that Wilma Montesi had led "a double life." Used to luxury beyond the means of her social position from an early age, raised in a family environment not exactly characterized by excessive severity in its habits and customs, Wilma dreamed of a better future and enjoyed total freedom to go out when she wanted, morning or afternoon.

It was therefore not implausible that this real Wilma Montesi—so different from the one constructed by the newspapers—should have been in contact with drug traffickers and might have participated in a "pleasure party."

### THE TELEPHONE

The magistrate then looked back and remembered Wanda Montesi's first declaration, later amended: "Wilma had gone out without fixing herself up, simply because she hadn't had time. Maybe she'd had to run out after an urgent telephone call." That declaration leads us to think that Wanda was sure that her sister could receive urgent telephone calls and rush out without previous plans and that she even had secret relationships, never revealed by the family to the police.

Rodolfo Montesi, the only person who could have imposed an atmosphere of severity in his home, did not have time to attend to such obligations. His work absorbed almost all his hours and he barely had time to go home for lunch.

## WHAT DID THE PRINCE DO?

But before going any further, one testimony must be analyzed: someone declared that they'd seen Prince D'Assia in a light-colored automobile in the company of a girl, on the afternoon of April 9, near the area where the crime was committed. A lawyer heard about this and told the lawyer representing Ugo Montagna, who stirred up a huge scandal: he spoke to the witness, who confirmed the testimony. When the witness's wife learned that he had spoken, she exclaimed, "Idiot. I told you to keep your mouth shut. That girl was Wilma Montesi."

Prince Mauricio D'Assia, a young Italian aristocrat, over six feet tall and as thin as a rake, was called to make a statement. He denied that his companion had been Wilma Montesi. But he also refused to reveal the girl's name, because Prince D'Assia is a total gentleman.

## LET'S SEE

However, chivalry must be set to one side, for Magistrate Sepe does not accept such alibis as valid. He revealed the name of a distinguished young lady of Roman high society, who was called to make a statement, and confirmed the prince's version of his trip to the Capacotta estate on April 9. Furthermore, the gasoline receipt demonstrated that the prince had bought five gallons of fuel that afternoon for the trip.

The allegations against Prince D'Assia turned out to be inconsistent. But there were other concrete allegations that it was necessary to examine: those against Ugo Montagna and Piero Piccioni. But before going any further it is time to inform the reader of something he has undoubtedly been wanting to know for several days, but only now is it appropriate to reveal: Wilma Montesi was a virgin.

*Revelations About Piccioni and Montagna*

The magistrate for the Montesi case established the following facts about the life of Piero Piccioni: He had a bachelor's apartment on Vía Acherusio, at number 20, for his exclusive use, at which he organized parties in the company of friends and women. That apartment was not registered with the building's concierge. The actress Alida Valli admitted having been to that place several times "to listen to records."

According to various testimonies, Piero Piccioni is a man "of refined taste in love." They revealed that he resorted to the use of narcotics as stimulants.

It was demonstrated that, in Montagna's company, he frequented a small bar on Vía del Babuino, where, as will be recalled, someone heard Andrea Bisaccia say, "Wilma Montesi could not have died by accident, because I knew her very well." That establishment was closed by the police, owing to the fact that "young existentialists, and people who used narcotics or were at least of dubious morality, congregated there."

## "THE MARCHESE"

Regarding the life of Ugo Montagna, known as the Marchese of San Bartolomeo, an elegant and well-connected man, it was established, according to the terms of the pretrial brief:

"Born in Grotte, in the province of Palermo, on November 16, 1910, into a family of very modest social and economic position, some of whom had prison or police records. His father, Diego, was arrested on the first of April 1931, 'on the orders of a higher court,' in Pistoia, and banished on the 27th of the same month. One of his brothers was condemned to several years in prison for fraud and concealment.

"In 1930, Ugo Montagna left his hometown and moved to Pistoia, and later returned to Palermo, where he was arrested for the first time for falsifying bills of exchange. Released from prison, with provisional liberty, on May 23, 1936, he was banished to Rome on the 28th of the same month."

### MARRIED WITH CHILDREN

"Ugo Montagna"—the brief went on—"married Elsa Anibaldi in Rome, in 1935. Imprisoned again, he was freed, by an amnesty, in 1937, when he was serving a sentence for the usurpation of the title of a chartered accountant.

"After a brief period of cohabitation with his wife, with whom he had a son, he separated from her for reasons of jealousy and interests and, especially, because, dissipating all his earning on women of easy virtue and pleasure trips, he did not even provide her with the basic means of subsistence.

"In May of 1941, due to a neighbor's complaints, he was advised by police to abstain from holding the nocturnal parties that, with dancing, singing, and commotion, took place in his residence, in the Flaminio area, and went on past midnight, to entertain his numerous string of guests of both sexes." Currently he is a multimillionaire.

### WITNESSES

The mechanic Piccini, who a year before had rushed to declare to the police his certainty that Wilma Montesi had been with a man, in an automobile stuck in the sand near the Capacotta estate, in the first half of March, was now summoned to make a formal statement. Piccini stated what he had seen: the man was approximately the same height as himself, five foot nine, balding, elegant, hatless, who spoke proper Italian, with a slight Roman accent.

However, this time it was revealed that Piccini had not gone alone to help the stranger. He'd gone with a workmate whose surname was De Francesco, who agreed with everything, except that the man spoke Italian properly. According to De Francesco, the man in the car had a slight foreign accent. The two witnesses confronted each other. Piccini remained firm and in a formal identification picked out Piero Piccioni from among another three individuals with similar physical characteristics. Nevertheless, the fact should be taken into account that

Piero Piccioni's photograph had appeared, by that time, on innumerable occasions in all the newspapers.

## THE MAN ON THE TELEPHONE

Among the things that Piccini said in his declaration, he remembered that the man in the automobile had been in a suspicious hurry to make a telephone call. At that hour it is not frequent for someone to speak on the telephone. The investigator called the administrator of the tobacco kiosk at the Ostia station, Remo Bigliozzi, so he could describe the man who made the telephone call. As far as he could remember, Bigliozzi described a swarthy man, with an oval face, dark hair, receding hairline, and in an incredible hurry to make a call. The witness said that as soon as he saw the photographs of Piero Piccioni, he had recognized him as the man who made the telephone call from his tobacco kiosk, in early March.

To accept that Wilma Montesi was the girl in the car—and the witnesses concurred in their descriptions—would put the Montesi family's assertions in doubt, according to which Wilma was never away from home very late. But the real behavior of that family, perfectly verified by the investigator, and the not forgotten circumstance that the mother of the Montesi family tried to induce the concierge to modify her statement, allows us to think that they knew something, a secret link their daughter had that they wanted to keep hidden at any cost. That's why their statements were not taken into account, to rule out the possibility that the girl in the automobile was Wilma Montesi.

## WERE THERE NO BYSTANDERS?

Moreover, the investigator resolved to call some people to give statements who hadn't been taken into account by the two previous investigations before they were shelved, and who surely had something to say: the eyewitnesses who went to Torvaianica beach to see the corpse. Nobody had remembered them, specifically Anna Salvi and Jale Balleli. Called to make statements, they concurred in having recognized the corpse of Wilma Montesi as a girl who at 5:30 on April 10, 1953, had gone past their houses, in Torvaianica, in a dark-colored automobile in the company of a man. They also concurred in their descriptions of the man. And they stated that they had been on the beach looking at the body, but then they read in the press that the girl had died on the 9th, drowned off the beach at Ostia, and took no more interest in the case.

LOOSE ENDS

There were still a confusing number of loose ends. There was the declaration of another man who had seen the corpse on the beach. The previous afternoon, that man and his wife had walked past a black automobile, near Capacotta, and he had taken a long look at the girl who was in the car. His wife said, "You cheeky devil, you're eyeing up that girl." The next day, after having been on the beach looking at the corpse, the man went to find his wife and told her, "Guess what? The girl we saw yesterday afternoon turned up dead on the beach this morning." But his wife did not want to confirm his statements to the investigator. However, Magistrate Sepe did not get demoralized for a single moment. Determined to move his work forward, he prepared to take the next step. A decisive step: a face-to-face meeting between Ana María Caglio and Ugo Montagna.

### The Police Destroyed Wilma's Clothes

Ana María Caglio arrived for the confrontation in complete command of herself. She confirmed all the charges laid out in her will. And she added a few new pieces of information, to extend them. She said that due to some publications giving publicity to the black car stuck in the sand in the first half of March (Piccini's testimony), she had seen an Alfa 1900 outside the door to Piero Piccioni's room. She said that when she saw that automobile she had remembered the publications she had seen in the press and tried to remember the license plate number, but that Montagna had discovered her aim and prevented her very ably. She remained firm in her charge that Piccioni and Montagna had visited the chief of police while she waited in the car. The charge was denied by Piccioni. But later it was proven that, in fact, that visit had taken place.

### IN SPITE OF ACRIMONY

After all of Ana María Caglio's charges had been examined and many of her statements verified, the magistrate reached the following conclusion: "It is necessary to consider Ana María Caglio's various statements worthy of consideration in the course of the formal investigation, just as those previous to the second closure of the case and those of Muto's trial, in virtue of the substantial uniformity of her statements, held firm with extreme exuberance, revealing her radical conviction, even in the dramatic face-to-face encounters with Montagna and Piccioni.

"It is true that Miss Caglio," the magistrate continued, "was inspired by acrimonious feelings toward Montagna, having been abandoned by him after a not inconsiderable period of intimacy, which had provoked and established a profound affection in the girl's spirits, constantly demonstrated in her correspondence"; but he concluded that this feeling could be the explanation of her behavior, that it should not be considered unfounded fruit of jealousy, or as rash revenge.

### A BAD MOVIE

The actress Alida Valli summoned to make a statement about her telephone call from Venice, which she'd denied in the press, admitted that, in fact, the call had taken place, but that it had been completely different from the way the witnesses had described it. She said her account of that conversation had come from some newspaper cuttings, which mentioned Piccioni. Those cuttings—the actress said—had been sent to her house by the Milan agency, *L'Eco della Stampa*. To prove it, she showed the cuttings: one from *La Notte*, from May 6; another from *Milano Sera*, with the same date; another from *Il Momento Sera*, from the 5th, and another from *L'Unità*, from Milan, with the same date. Nevertheless, Alida Valli had forgotten something fundamental: her telephone call had been made on April 29. A week before the cuttings she presented as an alibi appeared in the press.

## "THE AMALFI TONSILLITIS"

Something else still needed to be examined: Piccioni's Amalfi tonsillitis. As has been said, the young composer of popular music said he'd been in Amalfi, with the actress Alida Valli, and that he'd returned to Rome on April 10. That night, both of them should have attended a get-together. However, it was found that Piccioni had not attended. But he had an explanation: he had been confined to his bed with tonsillitis, that very afternoon, and to prove it he presented Dr. Di Filippo's prescription, carefully retained for a year. And he also presented a certificate of a urine analysis.

So much time had passed that Dr. Di Filippo did not remember the exact date on which he'd issued the prescription. But the investigator meticulously examined the medical books and found that the consultation did not accord with the date of Piccioni's prescription.

In light of this suspicious difference, the prescription presented by Piccioni was submitted to a technical exam, and the graphologists agreed that the date on the prescription had been altered.

## ANOTHER FALL

They then proceeded to investigate the authenticity of the certificate of the urine analysis. A Professor Salvattorelli, in charge of the bacteriological institute that had presumably done the analysis, declared that he did not know who had signed the certificate. Also, he looked in the appointment book and found that Piero Piccioni's name did not appear in it or in any others related to the analyses the institute conducted. Trying to identify the signature, the handwriting experts attributed it to Dr. Carducci, who worked at the same institute. Dr. Carducci, in effect, recognized the signature as his own, but did not find in his books, or in his memory, any record of a urine analysis for anyone by the name of Piero Piccioni. Voluntarily, Dr. Carducci himself suggested the hypothesis that a false certificate had been written above his signature, on a blank piece of paper, or after erasing an authentic certificate.

## "PLEASURE PARTIES"

Finally, the magistrate paid a visit to the house at Capacotta, where Gioben Jo must have lost, as declared, thirteen million lire. According to numerous testimonies, the famous "pleasure parties" were held in that house. It is a house situated a short distance from the place where Montesi's body was found.

The investigating magistrate managed to establish that in that house Montagna and some of his friends would get together and occasionally swim in the sea, completely naked, on the neighboring beach. And he established, and wrote in the pretrial brief, that various people had been in that house, for instance, "definitely, more than once, Montagna and Ana María Caglio; at least once, Montagna and Gioben Jo, and on another occasion Montagna himself, a friend of his, and two girls."

## NO ONE IS SPARED

In the arduous task of putting the cards in order, the magistrate then examined one of the most serious charges that had been made in the Montesi case: the destruction of Wilma's clothing by the police. When the Muto trial was held, the editorial offices of *Attualità* were searched and a notebook belonging to the journalist Giuseppe Parlato was found. In one of his notes he said that in the course of a conversation with Signor de Duca, the latter revealed that a policeman had told him in May of 1953 that the day Wilma Montesi's body was found, Piero Piccioni had gone to see the chief of police and handed over the clothing the corpse had been missing. After a painstaking investigation, the magistrate managed to identify a "Signor de Duca." He was called Natal del Duca.

And Natal del Duca not only confirmed the above, but added something more: Wilma Montesi's clothing had remained hidden for a while, but was then destroyed with the consent of the Montesi family. Del Duca then revealed the name of the police officer who had made the revelation. The officer was called to make a statement. And in the end, by virtue of the new testimonies, another charge was left floating in the air: not only had the clothes been destroyed, but also the garments found on the corpse were later substituted, with the consent of the family, to suggest that Wilma had not gone out dressed for a date.

### "YOU TOO?"

At that tremendous charge, the magistrate ordered an analysis of the clothing that he was certain were the clothes found on the corpse. The analysis demonstrated that the content of sodium chloride found in the coat was considerably higher than that found in other garments. And he concluded: with the exception of the coat, none of the other garments had been immersed in seawater, unless they'd been washed or subjected to some other process that had eliminated the sodium chloride. Moreover, they were garments worn from usage, visibly deteriorated and stained in places. The magistrate thought it odd that Wilma Montesi would have changed to go outside, to put on deteriorated undergarments. So he called back the persons who saw the body on the beach and asked them, "What was the clothing like on Wilma Montesi's corpse?" And they all responded the same way. The descriptions of the clothing seen on the corpse did not coincide with the characteristics of the clothing then in the magistrate's power and analyzed by the experts.

Magistrate Sepe advanced the hypothesis that the corpse had really been undressed and the clothing substituted, with the agreement of some members of the Montesi family. The police commissioner of Rome, Severo Polito, was summoned to respond to that charge. And later for others.

*Thirty-Two to Stand Trial!*

The ex-commissioner of Rome, Severo Polito, began his defense saying that, actually, he had never paid much attention to the Montesi case. The investigating magistrate reviewed the files of the commissioner's office and found some things that belied this assertion: among them, a copy of a press bulletin signed by Severo Polito, dated May 5, 1953. In that bulletin, never published by the newspapers, the commissioner said, "The news about the son of an unnamed, but clearly insinuated, high-ranking political personality is devoid of justification."

On May 5 another communiqué had been given to the press, in which it was stated, "No investigation carried out since the discovery of the cadaver has enough validity to modify the result of the early investigations and verifications done by law." That was the time when the hypothesis that Wilma Montesi had died accidentally while taking a footbath arose and was defended tooth and nail.

### MORE PROOF

Besides, there was another piece of evidence proving that Severo Polito had taken a personal interest in the case. On April 15 he sent the chief of police a memorandum in which he confirmed once more the footbath hypothesis. In this memo it was taken as given that the girl had left her house at five o'clock sharp and had been seen on the train, where "she behaved like a perfectly calm, normal person." The disappearance of some of her clothing was explained there: "The girl must have undressed to wade in the water up to her knees, as she had done in the past." The magistrate demonstrated that the memo had three false statements: "In the past," Wilma did not remove intimate apparel to bathe her feet; she did so in a swimsuit. She did not walk in water up to her knees; she only got her feet wet at the edge of the beach. And finally, she did not leave her house at five o'clock sharp.

## IN MILAN?

At this stage of the investigation, the journalist Valerio Valeriani, of *Il Giornale d'Italia*, was summoned to give a statement to demonstrate the authenticity of an interview with Severo Polito, which was published in said newspaper. In that interview, the former police commissioner affirmed:

a) After the discovery of the body he had personally assumed leadership of the investigation.

b) The result of that investigation had confirmed the hypothesis of misfortune, based on solid elements.

c) Montesi suffered from eczema on her heels, which is why she had decided to submerge her feet in seawater.

d) As for the charges against Piero Piccioni, they were unacceptable, for he had demonstrated that the day the events occurred he had been in Milan.

## "I DO NOT KNOW THAT MAN"

Interrogated on his relationship to Ugo Montagna, former police commissioner Polito declared that he had met the gentleman after the death of Wilma Montesi. However, various testimonies demonstrated that they had a long-standing friendship. Furthermore, the former police commissioner did not know one thing: at a certain point in time when Montagna's telephone calls were monitored, he held a conversation with the then police commissioner that was certainly not an indication of a recent friendship. That call was made on July 3, 1953, right after Montagna was summoned to answer questions for the first time. In the course of the conversation, Severo Polito told Montagna, as the brief reports:

"You are a free citizen and can do what you want. You saw that Pompei himself already excluded two things: the question of narcotics and the apartment. You'll see . . ."

And then Montagna, maybe more astute than the commissioner, told him:

"Alright, alright. Can we meet tonight at 11? Or no, let's do it this way: let's meet at 9 and we'll have dinner together."

And Severo Polito responded:

"Splendid."

### THE LAST STRAW

Moreover, the magistrate demonstrated that some pages were missing from the notebook impounded by the police in which Wilma Montesi had transcribed the letter she sent to her fiancé on April 8, evidently torn out after the notebook had been confiscated. It was not possible to establish, however, who tore out those pages, or when or with what objective.

Severo Polito could not give any explanation for his statements related to Piccioni's stay in Milan. Piccioni had not been in Milan, and what's worse, he had never tried to defend himself by saying he'd been in that city.

"Such original acts," says the brief, "were followed by many others: serious omissions, false proofs of nonexistent circumstances, distortions of nonexistent circumstances, distortion of serious circumstances, voluntarily invented mistakes, all of them aimed at frustrating the verification of the cause and the true mode of Montesi's death and removing any suspicion and avoiding any investigation related to the person who from the first moment was indicated and then as the principal author of the crime . . ."

### THIS IS NOT THE END

On June 11, 1955, two years after Wilma Montesi left her house never to return, Piero Piccioni and Ugo Montagna have been summoned to stand trial. The first must answer a charge of culpable homicide. The second, as an accessory. The commissioner, Severo Polito, must answer to the charges previously cited.

But over two years of investigations, obstacles, closures, and reopenings of the case, nine men were added to the list; another twenty persons have been put on trial, most of them for false testimonies.

The arduous task of inquiry by Magistrate Sepe clearly established that Wilma Montesi was away from her home for twenty-four hours. What did she do during those twenty-four hours? That is the great gap in the pretrial brief. In spite of twenty people being tried for giving false witness statements, none of them intended to clear up the mystery; no one spoke of having been or having known of someone who had been with Wilma Montesi during the night of April 9, while her father was looking for her desperately in the Tiber. The next day, when Angelo Giuliani received the telegram saying that his fiancée had committed suicide, Wilma Montesi was still alive. She must have eaten at least twice more before she died. But nobody knows where she ate those meals. Nobody has even dared to insinuate that they saw her on the evening of April 10, eating an ice cream cone. It is possible that next month, during the hearings, we'll find out the other side of this mystery. But it is also very possible that we will never know.

Series of articles from Rome published on
September 17 and 19–30, 1955, *El Espectador*, Bogotá

# The Disappearing Women of Paris— Are They in Caracas?

Madame Jeanne Cazals, the young and elegant wife of a rich French industrialist, left her couturier's shop at seven in the evening, wearing a brand-new mink coat and with fifteen million francs' worth of jewelry all over her body. She blended into the crowd concentrated on Rue Faubourg Saint-Honoré—maybe the most elegant and one of the busiest streets of Paris—on her way to meet her husband. She never arrived at that date. Madame Cazals disappeared without leaving a single trace, a single piece of evidence that would allow any conjecture about her whereabouts. Desperate, the police are clinging to a confidence Madame Cazals seems to have made, some time ago, to a close friend: "I've fallen into a mechanism it seems impossible to get out of." It is an unusual clue. Madame Cazals's habits were absolutely regular. Her reputation irreproachable. But in a city like Paris, where one hundred thousand people disappear mysteriously every year, no possibility should be ruled out.

### MARKET *NÚMERO UNO*: CARACAS

The Cazals case has brought a related problem to the front pages of the newspapers: the white slave trade. It is now a much-discussed question. The police believe in it. All the newspapers that have investigated the matter agree that the main South American market in the white slave trade is the city of Caracas.

But it has been difficult to alarm society, despite the substantial amount of coverage: in recent years, thirty thousand girls have been kidnapped in Paris and sold to numerous cabarets and public places all over the world. The principal markets, according to these investigations, are in North Africa and South America.

For the first time since the existence of this murky trade in human flesh began to be periodically raked up, French public opinion is showing militant concern. This afternoon I attended a public meeting, mostly made up of mothers, who were requesting a more energetic intervention from the French government to deal with the problem. The French justice system knows of many cases. But unfortunately, whenever the newspapers have taken up the issue, public opinion seems to think it is simply journalistic speculation. Now things are different. In the National Assembly, Deputy Francine Lefevre has put all the international and internal political problems to one side in order to raise this question desperately. No doubt remains: the white slave trade exists, and it is run by powerful organizations with agents and clients all over the world, operating in all the great capital cities. Especially in Paris.

### TWO THOUSAND DOLLARS FOR A FRENCHWOMAN

For a start, the police have begun to take rigorous control over certain apparently innocent and tempting classified advertisements: "Simple job, 40,000 francs, for young ladies, eighteen years of age." An eighteen-year-old girl does not easily resist temptation. In many cases it might be an honest job. But the exceptions are tremendous: the applicants are roped into a contract, flown to North Africa, and sold there like any piece of merchandise. It is a business that produces a one hundred percent profit.

The way the agents of the organization operate resembles a fictional film. At the beginning of this year, on the Champs-Élysées, a car stopped at seven in the evening in front of the big illuminated shop windows. A man got out of the car, grabbed a student by the arm, and shoved her into the vehicle. She was never heard from again.

But in reality, the first contacts are usually more ingenious than brutal. A magazine recounts the case of Yvonne Vincent, who one lazy Sunday afternoon was at home in the company of one housemaid. Her mother had gone to the pictures. At dusk, a kind nun had knocked on the door with bad news: her mother had been in a car accident. The nun showed up with false news and false intentions. Parked outside the door, there was a car driven by an accomplice. It was the last time Yvonne Vincent was ever seen.

Another case, told without proper names, is that of a girl who was on her way to catch the Metro after having spent the whole afternoon with her friends in the Bois de Vincennes. While she was waiting for a red light to change, an elderly blind woman asked her to help guide her across the street. Nobody knows what happened on the opposite sidewalk, for that happened on September 18, at quarter after six, and the girl still hasn't arrived home. The police have reason to believe that these two girls—like the majority of the thirty thousand missing girls in recent years—are in some part of the world, working as prostitutes by reason or by force.

The mechanism seems to be very simple: once persuaded, the girls are taken to North Africa or South America. A beautiful, young, compliant Frenchwoman can cost up to half a million francs, almost two thousand dollars. But the person who pays that sum feels he has the right to exploit the merchandise to multiply his investment. Once a girl has been imprisoned by the mechanism, she has very few possibilities of ever returning home. The organization can pursue her to the ends of the earth. However, some have had the courage and luck to escape. One of them was Suzanne Celmonte, who at twenty-one years of age told her incredible adventure on television a few months ago. She was a singer in a modest nightclub in Paris. One night, fate introduced himself to her elegantly disguised as an impresario. He hired her for a cabaret in Damascus for two thousand francs a night. The girl needed to be on the ground before she realized that she was expected to do much more than sing. Without losing her sangfroid she got in contact with the French consul through the authorities and was repatriated. The international police used this case as a springboard in order to dismantle a ring, which is now leading some pretend impresarios to prison.

### ONLY ONE EXPORTER WAS ARRESTED . . .

Pretenses are so well kept up and the agents of the operation so skillful that the police cannot break their solid appearance of legality. They need a stroke of luck, almost a coincidence, like the one that jailed Francis Raban, a comfortable Frenchman who appeared to be as honorable as can be. One night, when he was at Orly preparing to board a flight to South America with a woman who was not his wife, a detective had an impulse to examine their papers closely. The woman's were fake.

That detail disclosed Francis Raban's true personality. He was set up in Paris as a large-scale exporter. He periodically received succulent checks in U.S. dollars from Venezuela. Now he is accused of having exported girls for several years.

The newspapers that point to Caracas as the principal market in South America do not quote many concrete cases. But a popular magazine recently linked Raban's case to that of a servant kidnapped in Paris and sold in Venezuela. According to that source, the girl was hired as a waitress in a bar. But she roundly refused "to be more than nice to the clientele." As punishment, she was driven out to the deserted San Félix ranch, five hundred miles away from Caracas. She managed to escape with the help of two French explorers who arrived by chance. How many cases like that might be found right now in Venezuela?

January 12, 1957, *Elite*, Caracas

# "I Visited Hungary"

## (Fragment)

János Kádár—prime minister of Hungary—made a public appearance on August 20, in front of the six thousand farmworkers who gathered on a soccer field in Újpest, eighty-two miles away from Budapest, to commemorate the anniversary of the socialist constitution. I was there, on the same stage as Kádár, with the first delegation of Western observers that arrived in Hungary after the events of October.

For ten months Budapest had been a forbidden city. The last Western plane that took off from its airport—on November 6, 1956—was an Austrian twin-engine plane chartered by the magazine *Match* to evacuate special correspondent Jean Carles Pedrazzini, mortally wounded in the Battle of Budapest. Hungary has been closed since then and only opened its borders to us again ten months later due to the influences of the committee in charge of preparations for the Moscow festival, which managed to get the Hungarian government to issue an invitation to Budapest for a delegation of eighteen observers. There were two architects, a German lawyer, a Norwegian chess champion, and just one other journalist: Maurice Mayer, a diabolically likable Belgian, with a red mustache, a beer drinker and teller of stupid jokes, who began his career in the Spanish Civil War and was wounded in

Liège during the German occupation. I didn't know any of them. At the border, after the customs authorities examined our papers for three hours, an interpreter gathered us together in the restaurant car, made the introductions, and gave a brief welcome speech. Then he read the program for the next two weeks: museums, lunches with youth organizations, sporting events, and a week of relaxation at Lake Balaton.

Maurice Mayer thanked them for the invitation on behalf of us all, but let it be understood that we were not very interested in tourism. We wanted something else: to know what happened in Hungary, for certain and without political mythifications, and to comprehend the country's actual situation. The interpreter responded that Kádár's government would do everything possible to oblige us. It was three in the afternoon on August 4. At 10:30 that night we arrived at the deserted Budapest station, where a group of perplexed, energetic men waited, who escorted us for the whole two weeks and did everything possible to prevent us from forming a concrete idea of the situation.

We had not finished unloading our luggage when one of those men—who introduced himself as an interpreter—read the official list of our names and nationalities and made us answer as if we were in school. Then he invited us to board the bus. Two details caught my attention: the number of our escorts—eleven, for such a small delegation—and the fact that all of them had introduced themselves as interpreters despite the fact that the majority of them spoke no language other than Hungarian. We crossed the city through somber, deserted streets, saddened by the drizzle. A moment later we were at the Hotel Liberty—one of the best in Budapest—sitting at a banquet table that took up the whole dining room. Some of them had difficulties managing the cutlery. The dining room, with a mirror, large chandeliers, and plush red furniture, seemed made out of new materials but with antiquated taste.

During the course of the meal a disheveled man with a certain romantic disdain in his gaze gave a speech in Hungarian that was translated simultaneously into three languages. It was a brief, absolutely conventional welcome followed by a series of concrete instructions. He recommended that we not go out on the streets, always carry our passports, not speak to strangers, leave our key at reception each time we left the hotel, and remember "Budapest is under martial law and it is therefore forbidden to take photographs." By then there were seven more interpreters. They moved with no objective around the table, talking to each other in Hungarian, in very low voices, and I had the impression that they were frightened. I was not alone in that appraisal. A moment later, Maurice Mayer leaned over toward me and said, "These people are scared to death."

Before we went to bed they collected our passports. Tired from the trip, but not sleepy and a little depressed, I tried to see a piece of the city's nightlife from the window of my room. The gray and crumbling buildings of Rakoczi Avenue looked uninhabited. The limited public lighting, the drizzle falling on the lonely street, the streetcar that grated past amid blue sparks, all contributed to creating a sad atmosphere. When I got into bed I noticed that the walls of my room still showed signs of the impact of projectiles. I couldn't sleep, shuddering at the idea that this room lined with yellowish wallpaper, with old furniture and a strong smell of disinfectant, had been a barricade in October. That was how my first night in Budapest ended.

### LONGER LINES FOR LOTTERY TICKETS THAN FOR BREAD

In the morning the view was less somber. Prepared to outwit the vigilance of the interpreters—who wouldn't arrive until ten—I put the keys in my pocket and walked down the stairs to the lobby. I didn't take the elevator, because it was located right in front of the reception desk and I wouldn't have been able to leave without being seen by the manager. The revolving glass door opened right onto Rakoczi Avenue. Not just the hotel, but all the buildings on the avenue—from the floral pediment of the station to the banks of the Danube—were covered in scaffolding. It's difficult to avoid the sensation created by a commercial avenue whose crowds move among wooden skeletons. A fleeting sensation, for I barely took two steps outside the hotel before someone put a hand on my shoulder. It was one of the interpreters.

In a cordial manner, but without letting go of my arm, he guided me back inside the hotel.

The rest of the delegation came down at ten, as planned. The last one was Maurice Mayer. He entered the dining room in a splendid sports jacket, with his arms wide open, singing "The Internationale." With an exaggerated effusiveness, still singing, he embraced each and every one of the interpreters, who hugged him back with a disconcerting joy. Then he sat down beside me, tucked his napkin into his collar, and nudged me with his knee under the table.

"I've been thinking since last night," he said under his breath. "All these ruffians are armed."

From that moment on we knew what to expect. Our guardian angels accompanied us to museums, historical monuments, official receptions, jealously preventing us from any contact with people in the street. One afternoon—our fourth in Budapest—we went to see the beautiful panorama of the city from atop the Fishermen's Bastion. Near there is a church that had been converted into a mosque by the Turkish invaders that is still decorated with arabesques. A group of delegates detached ourselves from the interpreters and went inside the church. It was enormous and tumbledown, with high, small windows through which shone streams of yellow summer light. On one of the front pews, sitting in an absorbed posture, an old woman in black was eating bread and sausage. Two interpreters came into the church a moment later. They followed us in silence through the naves, without saying anything to us, but they made the woman leave.

By the fifth day the situation had become untenable. We were utterly fed up with visiting old things, historical monstrosities, and with feeling that the city, the people who lined up to buy bread, to board the streetcars, seemed like unreachable objects on the other side of the glass windows of the bus. I made the decision after lunch. I asked for my key at reception, where I told them I was very tired and planned to sleep all afternoon, then I went up the elevator and immediately down the stairs.

At the first stop I hopped on a streetcar, not caring where it was going. The jammed crowd inside the vehicle looked at me like an emigrant from another planet, but there was no curiosity or surprise in their gazes, rather a distrustful reserve. Beside me, an elderly lady in an old hat with artificial fruits was reading a Jack London novel, in Hungarian. I spoke to her in English, then in French, but she didn't even look at me. She got off at the next stop, elbowing her way through the crowd, and I was left with the impression that was not where she should have gotten off. She was frightened too.

The driver spoke to me in Hungarian. I let him understand that I didn't speak the language, and he in turn asked me if I spoke German. He was a fat old man with a beer drinker's nose and glasses mended with wire. When I told him I spoke English, he repeated a phrase I couldn't understand several times. He seemed desperate. At the end of the line, as I was getting off, he handed me a little slip of paper with a phrase written in English: "God save Hungary."

Almost a year after the events that stirred the world, Budapest is still a provisional city. I saw extensive sectors where the streetcar tracks have not been replaced and which are still closed to traffic. The crowds, badly dressed, sad, and concentrated, stand in endless lines to buy basic necessities. The stores that were destroyed and looted are still being rebuilt.

In spite of the boisterous publicity the Western newspapers gave the events in Budapest, I hadn't believed the havoc wreaked was so terrible. Very few central buildings have their façades intact. I later learned that the people of Budapest took refuge in them and fought for four days and four nights against the Russian tanks. The Soviet troops—eighty thousand men ordered to crush the revolt—employed the simple and effective tactic of parking the tanks in front of the buildings and firing straight at them. But the resistance was heroic. The children went out into the streets, climbed onto the tanks, and dropped flaming bottles of gasoline inside. Official information indicates that in those four days five thousand people were killed and twenty thousand injured, but the substantial damage leads one to think that the number of victims was much higher. The Soviet Union has not supplied any figures of their losses.

Dawn broke on November 5 over a destroyed city. The country

was literally paralyzed for five months. The population survived during that time thanks to trainloads of provisions sent by the Soviet Union and the people's democracies. Now the lines are not so long, the grocery stores are beginning to open their doors, but the people of Budapest are still suffering the consequences of the catastrophe. At the lottery ticket kiosks—which are a source of revenue for the Kádár regime—and at pawnshops—which are owned by the state—the lines are longer than the ones at the bakeries. A government official told me that, in effect, the lottery is an inadmissible institution in a socialist regime. "But we can't do anything else," he explained. "It solves one problem for us every Saturday." The same thing happens with the pawnshops. I saw a woman lined up in front of one of them with a baby carriage full of kitchen equipment.

Fear and distrust appear everywhere, in the government as much as in the general population. There are quite a few Hungarians who lived abroad until 1948, and they and their children speak all the languages of the world. But it's difficult for them to speak to foreigners. They think that these days there cannot be a foreigner in Budapest who is not an official invited guest, and that's why they don't dare risk a conversation with any of us. Everybody, in the street, in the cafés, in the tranquil gardens of Margaret Island, distrusts the government and its guests.

The government, for its part, feels that dissent continues. On the walls of Budapest there are notices written with a broad brush: "Hidden counterrevolutionary, fear the power of the people." Others blame Imre Nagy for the October catastrophe. That is an official obsession. While Imre Nagy suffers enforced exile in Romania, Kádár's government daubs the walls, publishes pamphlets, and organizes demonstrations against him. But all the people with whom we've managed to speak—workers, employees, students, and even some communists—are waiting for Nagy's return. At dusk—after having traveled all over the city—I found myself at the Danube, in front of the Elisabeth Bridge, dynamited by the Germans. There was the statue of the poet Petofi, separated from the university by a little square filled with flowers. Ten months earlier—on October 28—a group of students crossed the square shouting for the expulsion of the Soviet troops. One of them climbed the statue with the Hungarian flag and gave a two-hour speech. When he came down, the avenue was teeming with men and women of Budapest singing the poet Petofi's anthem under the bare autumn trees. That's how the uprising began.

Half a mile or so beyond Margaret Island, in the lower Danube, there is a dense proletarian sector where Budapest's workers live and die all on top of each other. There are some closed taverns, warm and full of smoke, where customers drink huge glasses of beer amid that sustained machine gun rattling that is conversation in the Hungarian language. The afternoon of October 28, those people were there when word came that the students had started the uprising. Then they left their glasses of beer, walked up the bank of the Danube to the little square of the poet Petofi, and joined the movement. I went to those taverns at nightfall and discovered that despite the military regime, the Soviet intervention, and the apparent tranquility that reigns in the country, the seed of the uprising is still alive. When I entered the bars, the rattling turned into a dense buzz. Nobody wanted to talk. But when the people are quiet—out of fear or prejudice—you have to enter the washrooms to find out what they're thinking. There I found what I was looking for: in among the pornographic drawings, classics now by all urinals of the world, there was Kádár's name, in an anonymous but extraordinarily significant protest. Those notices represent a valid testimony on the Hungarian situation: "Kádár, murderer of the people," "Kádár, traitor," "Kádár, the Russians' attack dog."

November 15, 1957, *Momento,* Caracas

# The World's Most Famous Year

The international year of 1957 did not begin on the 1st of January. It began on Wednesday the 9th, at six in the evening, in London. At that hour, the British prime minister, the child prodigy of international politics, Sir Anthony Eden, the best-dressed man in the world, opened the door of 10 Downing Street, his official residence, and that was the last time he opened it as prime minister. Wearing a black overcoat with a fur collar, carrying a top hat for solemn occasions, Sir Anthony Eden had just attended a tempestuous cabinet meeting, the last of his mandate and the last of his political career. That afternoon, in less than two hours, Sir Anthony Eden did the most number of definitive things a man of his importance, of his stature, of his upbringing, can allow himself in two hours: he fell out with his ministers, visited Queen Elizabeth for the last time, offered his resignation, packed his bags, moved out of the house, and retired to private life.

More than any other man, Sir Anthony Eden had been born with 10 Downing Street etched on his heart, inscribed in a line on his palm. For thirty years he had bewitched the salons of Europe, as well as foreign offices all over the world, and he had played a prominent role in the biggest political negotiations on earth. He had forged a reputation for physical and moral elegance, rigorous principles, and political audacity, which hid from the wider public certain weaknesses of his character, his whims, his disorder, and his tendency to indecision that in certain circumstances could lead him to decide too quickly, too intensely, alone, and against everyone. Three months earlier—November 2, 1956—Sir Anthony Eden, faced with a secret invitation from France to seize control of the Suez Canal by force, he had shown such indecision that he decided too quickly, too intensely, against the opinion of the majority of his ministers, the archbishop of Canterbury, the press, and even the people of London, who expressed their disagreement with the largest popular demonstration Trafalgar Square has seen this century. As a consequence of the solitary and hasty decision, he had to decide in those two melancholy hours on January 9—and this time with the approval of his ministers, with the approval of the great majority of the subjects of the British Empire—to perform the most significant act of his life: resign.

That very night, while Sir Anthony Eden, accompanied by his wife, Lady Clarissa, Winston Churchill's niece, was driven away in his long black motorcar to their private residence in the London suburbs, a man as tall as he is, just as well dressed, moved from number 11 to number 10 Downing Street. Mr. Harold MacMillan, the new prime minister, only had to walk fifteen yards to take charge of the sensitive business of the British Empire.

That news, however, which exploded like a torpedo on the front page of all the newspapers of the world, must have seemed like a meaningless rumor to the cramped crowd of four thousand people on the other side of the Atlantic who gathered a few hours later outside the small protestant church in Los Angeles, California, to attend the funeral of Humphrey Bogart, who died of throat cancer, on Sunday, January 6. "Believe me," Humphrey Bogart had once said, "I've got more female admirers over the age of eight and under sixty than anyone else in this country, and that's why I earn $200,000 per picture." A few hours before he died, the most beloved gangster in cinema history, Hollywood's tender thug had said to his lifelong friend Frank Sinatra, "The only thing that's doing well is my bank account."

The great movie actor was the third notable death that January: in the same month, the Chilean poet Gabriela Mistral and the Italian orchestra conductor—one of the most famous in the history of music and also one of the richest—Arturo Toscanini also died, while the Polish people ratified their confidence in Wladislaw Gomulka at the ballot box and French drivers lined up at the gas pumps. The Suez adventure only left France with nothing but immense disappointment and a grave fuel crisis. During the transit upheavals caused by the restriction, one of the few things that arrived on time—on January 23—were the seven pounds, two ounces, of Carolina Luisa Margarita, Princess of Monaco, daughter of Rainier III and Grace Kelly.

### IN FEBRUARY THE NEWS OF THE YEAR WAS LOST

*Rock Around the Clock* sold out in London, a million copies in thirty days—the biggest record since *The Third Man*—the morning that Queen Elizabeth II boarded the plane that would take her to Lisbon. That visit to the discreet and paternalistic president of Portugal, Oliveira Salazar, seemed to have such an indecipherable political intention that it was interpreted as a simple pretext of the English sovereign to go to see her husband, Prince Philip of Edinburgh, who for the last four months had been sailing the last high seas of the British Empire on a yacht filled with men. That was a week of indecipherable news, of frustrated predictions, of hopes dashed in the hearts of journalists, who were undoubtedly anticipating the sentimental event of the year: the breakup of Queen Elizabeth and Prince Philip. In the clean and labyrinthine Lisbon airfield, where the Duke of Edinburgh arrived five minutes late—in the first place because he's not English, but Greek, and in the second because he had to shave off his beard to kiss his wife—the anticipated event did not happen, and that was, in 1957, the big news that might have been but was not.

On the other hand, in that same February when Brigitte Bardot wore a neckline that plunged to implausible depths at the Munich carnival and the French prime minister, M. Guy Mollet, crossed the Atlantic to reconcile his country with the United States after the Suez disaster, Moscow released the first surprise of what would be the busiest, most disconcerting and efficient year for the Soviet Union. That surprise, presented by *Pravda* as a secondary event, was the replacement of the sixth Soviet minister of foreign affairs, Dmitri Shepilov, by the new boy wonder of world diplomacy, Andrei Gromyko.

Shepilov, former editor of *Pravda,* had been appointed in June 1956. His time spent in the Ministry of Foreign Affairs constituted a speed record: all his predecessors had remained in the post for an average of eight years. Shepilov lasted eight months. The West, which hasn't been able to understand the complex political chess of the Kremlin, had reasons to think Gromyko would only last eight days.

At 8:33 in the morning, in the fog and cold of the indecisive Washington spring, the vice president of the United States, Mr. Richard Nixon, embarked on a seventeen-day trip to Africa. Thus began the third month, March, the month of travel. With the 10,000 miles in three stages that Mr. Foster Dulles traveled a few days later from Australia to New York, the U.S. secretary of state covered the equivalent of sixteen times around the world, since he took office: 236,000 in total. The president of the United States, General Eisenhower, traveled that same week, on board the battleship *Canberra,* to the idyllic British possession of Bermuda, where he was to hold talks with the British prime minister, Mr. Harold MacMillan, who hopped over the Atlantic in an overnight flight to try to put in order some of the things his predecessor Mr. Eden had left pending.

Golda Meir, one of Israel's ministers, participated in that race against time in a record-breaking trip, from Tel Aviv to Washington, where she intended to remind Mr. Foster Dulles to fulfill American promises to "guarantee that the Gaza Strip would not be occupied again by Egyptian troops and the security of the United States would not allow the strait of Alaska to be closed again." In this confusion of journeys, of comings and goings around the world, the president of the Philippines, Señor Magsaysay, embarked in a new and well-maintained C-47, which a few hours after takeoff plunged to the ground, in a ball of flames. This accident, and we don't know for certain whether it really was an accident, was the only one in a month when a simple engine failure could have reversed—or righted—the history of the world. One

Philippine personality, Señor Néstor Mato, who was traveling in the same plane as the president and miraculously survived the catastrophe, revealed that the disaster had been provoked by a violent explosion on board the plane. While the rescue expeditions searched in vain for the body of President Magsaysay and political circles in the Western world attributed the accident to a communist attack, President Eisenhower, packing his bags to travel to Nassau, took off his jacket in front of an open window and caught a cold. In the torpor of the African spring, Mr. Nixon was at that hour grinding seeds of wild plants, between his tough schoolboy jaws, as proof of his country's sympathy for the healthy-looking, befeathered citizens of Uganda.

### PEDRO INFANTE GOES. BATISTA STAYS

That untimely travel fever among politicians was aimed to patch up the last loose wires after the Suez adventure, which four months later was still causing headaches for the Westerners, despite the UN troops that were stationed between Egypt and Israel and the fact that the engineers had started to remove the ships General Nasser had scuttled in the canal in November. In reality, if Vice President Nixon traveled to Africa, if he took the trouble to eat and drink as many strange things as the primitive monarchs of the dark continent offered him, he did not miss the opportunity to take mint tea in Morocco with Moulay Hassan, the Technicolor movie prince who constituted one of the three pillars of the Arab world. Mr. Harold MacMillan, for his part, tried to convince the president not to entrust the problems of the East entirely to the UN. The president listened to him very attentively, in spite of his cold and in spite of the fact that—for reasons protocol could never explain—during the meeting he had his ears stuffed with cotton.

Very near where this conversation was taking place, in Cuba, where President Batista was beginning to lose sleep due to problems of public order in Oriente Province, the dance of the year, the music that infected the youth of the whole world in less than three months, from Paris to Tokyo, from London to Buenos Aires, suffered its first setback: rock 'n' roll was banned on Cuban television. "It was," said the proscription, "an immoral and degrading dance, the music of which was contributing to the adoption of strange movements, which offend morals and decency." In a curious coincidence, that very same week, at a party in Palm Beach, the Swedish actress Anita Ekberg and her husband Anthony Steel had a fistfight with the Cuban sculptor Joseph Dobronyi, because he had shown a sculpture of a completely nude woman for which, he said, he'd taken the Swedish actress as a model. In the name of morals and decency, she attacked the sculptor with her high heels. Another Swedish actress, Ingrid Bergman, figured that same week in world news, when she won an Oscar for her role in *Anastasia*. That event was interpreted as a reconciliation between Ingrid Bergman and the public of the United States, who for eight years considered her questionable because of her marriage to the Italian director Roberto Rossellini.

The explorer Richard Byrd, who had traveled to the South Pole, died a few days before the French politician Edouard Herriot. France barely had time to observe twenty-four hours of mourning, busy as it was with the Algerian War and with the preparations for the reception of Queen Elizabeth.

A young Cuban lawyer, who on one occasion in Mexico spent his last twenty dollars on the publication of a speech, landed in Cuba with a group of opponents to President Batista. The lawyer's name is Fidel Castro, and he knows strategy better than he does legal codes. President Batista, who is having difficulty explaining why his armed forces have not been able to expel Fidel Castro from the island, gave some exalted speeches to say "all quiet on the eastern front," but the fact is that the disquiet still continued in April. The government's enemies were appearing everywhere: on the Calzada de Puentes Grandes—in Havana—where detectives discovered an arms deposit of modern weapons at the beginning of the month; in the east of the country, where serious signs exist that the civilian population is protecting and helping Fidel Castro's men, as in Miami, in Mexico City, in the key points around the rebellious Caribbean. But public opinion in that minuscule and conflictive corner of the earth, which has not for a single moment been indifferent to political entanglements, forgot about

Cuba's problems to shudder at the death of Pedro Infante, the Mexican singer, victim of an aircraft accident.

### THE SCANDAL OF THE CENTURY ENDS. RESULT: 0

Seven thousand miles from the place where the plane carrying the popular idol crashed, a long and complex drama took on comedic overtones: the Montesi case, tried in Venice, with a complete team of defendants and witnesses, judges and lawyers, journalists and simply curious onlookers who rode to court in gondolas, dissolved into meaningless suppositions. The murder of Wilma Montesi, the modest girl from Vía Tagliamento, considered as the scandal of the century, has gone unpunished, and seems likely to stay that way.

Meanwhile, the inhabitants of Paris, defying the last icy breezes of spring, went out onto the streets to greet, in an outburst of monarchical fervor, Queen Elizabeth II, who crossed the English Channel in her private "Viscount" to tell President Coty, in French, that the two countries were more united and closer than ever after their joint failure at Suez. The French, who love the Queen of England almost as much as President Coty, in spite of maintaining the opposite, have not been bothered for a long time to stand for four hours behind a police cordon to greet a visitor. This time they did, and their shouts of welcome concealed for three days France's tremendous economic crisis, which the prime minister, M. Guy Mollet, tried desperately to repair at the moment when the Queen of England, in Orly, descended from an airplane in which she'd forgotten her parasol.

Secretly, without anyone daring to insinuate it, a fear circulated through the streets of Paris when the British sovereign's topless automobile drove down the Champs-Élysées: it was the fear that the rebels of Algeria, who are infiltrated everywhere, who in their country confront groups of paratroopers and in Paris play hide-and-seek with the police, would throw a bomb at the royal automobile. That would have been the most spectacular episode of an anonymous war, almost a clandestine war, which has been going on for three years, and which in 1957 was again not resolved as the world waits impatiently.

## BOGOTANOS IN PAJAMAS BRING DOWN ROJAS

The inhabitants of Bogotá, many of them in pajamas, went outside, on May 10, at four in the morning, to celebrate the fall of General Gustavo Rojas Pinilla, who had been in power since June 13, 1953. Since May 7—three days earlier—the country was practically paralyzed in protest at the presidential maneuver of convening the National Constituent Assembly to get himself reelected for another term. Banks, businesses, and factories all closed their doors for seventy-two hours, in a show of passive resistance supported by all the forces of the country. When on May 10, at four in the morning, the capital of Colombia spilled into the streets to celebrate the fall of Rojas Pinilla, he was in the San Carlos Palace, meeting with his most faithful collaborators, and he must surely have had to ask one of them what was happening in the city. In reality, Rojas Pinilla, who flew to Spain with 216 suitcases, did not actually resign until four hours later: at eight in the morning. That same morning, another government collapsed: that of Guy Mollet, in France, which had lasted fifteen months, and was the longest lasting of French governments, after that of Poincaré. Although M. Mollet managed to fall "due to the economy," observers of French politics knew the true cause was something else: the war in Algeria, which had bled the country's finances dry and was the real cause of the two crises of 1957.

In Rome, the James Dean club, made up of teenagers who drive seventy-five miles per hour in cars without brakes, in homage to the actor who died last year in a car accident, kept on meeting in secret, after the police interceded in May to put a stop to their activities, at the request of their fathers. None of them had suffered the slightest accident, when the French novelist Françoise Sagan—who profoundly hates being called "the James Dean of French literature"—crashed her car, on the outskirts of Paris. For a week the twenty-two-year-old writer, who four months earlier had scandalized the good bourgeois readers of France with her first novel, *Bonjour Tristesse,* was in a coma on the brink of death. When she left the hospital, a month later, her new book went to press: *Those Without Shadows.* Its sales were record-breaking: the first edition had sold out before the fall of the new French government, presided over by M. Bourges Maunouri. Things happened so fast in those two weeks that many of James Dean's admirers decided to go to the barbershop and have their heads shaved in one fell swoop to follow the fashion set by Yul Brynner.

### A PROPOSAL, MAO'S BEST JOKE

An insignificant-looking woman, Mrs. Liu Chi-Jean, showed up one June morning at the doors of the United States embassy in Taiwan, with a sign in English and Chinese, calling American Sergeant Robert Reynolds a murderer and calling on the population of the island to demonstrate against the decision of the court-martial that had declared him innocent. A few weeks earlier, the wife of that same Sergeant Robert Reynolds, whom Mrs. Liu Chi-Jean called a murderer, was taking a shower in her house in Taipei. All of a sudden she started shouting in protest because, according to her, a man was looking through a crack in the window. Mrs. Reynolds's husband, who was reading the newspaper in the living room, went out in the yard with his revolver, with the intention, according to what he told the court, "to keep the individual at bay until the police arrived." The next morning a corpse was found in the garden, riddled with bullets from Sergeant Reynolds's revolver. The corpse was that of Mrs. Liu Chi-Jean's husband. A court-martial made up of three sergeants and three colonels judged the American sergeant and gave its verdict: "Legitimate defense."

The demonstrations provoked by this event, which the population of Taiwan considered a simple judicial comedy, were the first serious incidents between the Republic of China and the United States, since Mr. Chiang Kai Shek, president of the Republic of China, was expelled from the continent by the communists and took power in Taiwan, with the favor and financial and political support of Washington. Liu Chi-Jean's protests unleashed a storm of anti-American protests in Taiwan that the prime minister of Red China, Chu En-Lai, knew exactly how to evaluate. Convinced that things were not going well between Taiwan and the United States, the rulers of communist

China made a proposal to Chiang Kai Shek: that he could stay in Taiwan, with his armies, his people, and his ninety-two private cars, but as administrator of the island on behalf of the government of Mao Tse-Tung. Chiang Kai Shek, who must have considered the proposal as a joke in bad taste, did not even make the effort of replying. Mao Tse-Tung shrugged his shoulders. "In any case," he said, "time will take care of the problem of Taiwan: Chiang Kai Shek's armies are getting old. Within ten years they'll have an average age of forty-five. Within twenty that average will be fifty-five. Communist China has patience and prefers to wait for the armies of republican China to die of old age in Taiwan."

### KHRUSHCHEV, STAR OF AMERICAN TV

Television viewers of the United States were just watching the news of the events in Taiwan on their domestic screens, when a completely bald head made an appearance and began to say a string of unintelligible things in Russian, which a moment later a newscaster began to translate into English. That unknown star on U.S. television was a man who provided more to talk about in 1957—personality of the year Nikita Khrushchev, secretary of the Communist Party of the Soviet Union. The fact that Nikita Khrushchev could have leaned into all the homes in the United States was not much less than a maneuver prepared by the Soviet espionage service. It was achieved, in a year of diplomatic steps, by the Columbia Broadcasting Corporation, and the clip had been filmed at his own desk in the Kremlin, where Khrushchev lent himself to everything the American journalists demanded, except for makeup. "It's not necessary," an official Soviet spokesman declared. "Mr. Khrushchev shaves every day and uses talcum powder." Inside their own American homes, Khrushchev's voice began the disarming offensive, the first in-depth step of a campaign that would last all year and that without doubt was the essence of the diplomatic and political activity of the Soviet Union in 1957.

After Khrushchev's interview, the world's attention inevitably turned toward the socialist hemisphere. In the preparations for the celebration of the fortieth anniversary of the revolution, the enigmatic Mr. Khrushchev—who practically didn't let a day go by without making his voice heard in the West—unfurled a colossal range of activities, as much on interior problems as on exterior policies. In a single day, after a stormy meeting of the central committee of the Soviet Communist Party, four of the highest-ranking personalities in the Soviet Union were knocked out of action: Molotov, Malenkov, Shepilov, and Kaganovich. A few days later, at the moment when the prime minister of Tunisia, M. Burguiba, ousted a decrepit and obsolete monarch and proclaimed the youngest republic in the world, the representatives of the four world powers were discussing in London the provisions for world disarmament. Mr. Stassen, representative of the United States, had to leave the sessions urgently to attend his son's wedding. He was drinking his first celebratory whiskey when he learned that the disarmament conference was not going to get anywhere, but that Mr. Khrushchev had released a piece of news of the heaviest caliber: the Soviet Union had at its disposal "the ultimate weapon," a long-distance rocket that could reach any objective on the planet. The West, anticipating the imminent delivery of Gina Lollobrigida's firstborn, did not pay much attention to the news. But it was true. From that moment on, the superiority of the Soviet Union's attack was accepted as an indisputable fact. The West tried to swallow that bitter blow with the consoling news that Gina Lollobrigida had had a baby girl in perfect health: six pounds and ninety-nine grams.

### THE ASIAN FLU: THE WORLD WITH A FEVER OF 102

The small, redheaded John A. Hale, professor at Malaysia University, in Singapore, peered into the microscope, in spite of the stultifying 104-degree heat, on May 4, to examine a sample of microbes he had been sent that morning from Hong Kong. Five minutes later, in shock, the professor telephoned BOAC airline and they told him that fifteen minutes later a plane was leaving for London. Professor Hale sent on that plane, urgently, a very carefully wrapped glass cylinder, to Dr. Christopher Andrews, director of the global influenza center, in London. The cylinder contained the samples of an extremely rare microbe that the frightened investigator in Singapore had just identified and that, in spite of his precautions, would provoke the illness of the year: the Asian flu. When the BOAC plane landed in London, several marines on a ship that had left Singapore forty-eight hours earlier began to sneeze. An hour later their bones began to hurt. Five hours later, they had temperatures of 104 degrees. One of them died. The others, hospitalized in Taiwan, contaminated the doctors, nurses, and the other patients. By the time the global influenza center in London raised the alarm, the Asiatic flu was arriving in Europe. Four months later, the night when Charlie Chaplin's latest film, *A King in New York,* premiered in London, it had gone all the way around the world.

President Eisenhower was too busy those days to think about the danger of microbes. He'd had to study the problems of the powder keg of the Orient, think about compromising solutions that would allow him to be on good terms with the Arab world without displeasing his European allies, trying to decipher the indecipherable remarks of the indecipherable Mr. Khrushchev, and he barely had three days to go and play golf in the tepid New England summer, at his house on Narragansett Bay. He hadn't even gotten down the stairs from his private airplane, *Columbine III,* when his press secretary Hagerty came to tell him that in Little Rock, Arkansas, where Governor Faubus opposed integration—black students attending schools with white students—the situation was taking on gravely dramatic proportions. The problem had begun a week earlier: Opposing a Supreme Court decision, Governor Faubus had stationed the Arkansas National Guard at the doors of Central High School, under the pretext that the presence of negro students would provoke disturbances among the population. The racist population, evidently an insignificant minority, gathered at the door to the building and made it understood, with impassioned screams and at some moments with physical actions, that Governor Faubus was right. President Eisenhower, an enemy of using force, tried by every means possible to dissuade the rebel governor. But, in spite of his dialogue with the president, Faubus persisted in his attitude. Comments on General Eisenhower's weakness flew around the world much faster than the Asiatic flu. The socialist world exploited the situation. "We need a Truman in the White House," they said in the United States, especially in the north, where the memory of the energy, dynamism, and decisive spirit of the former president had not been forgotten. Pressured by the seriousness of the circumstances, seeing his authority in danger, President Eisenhower decided, on September 24, at 12:30 in the morning, to send a thousand elite paratroopers to Little Rock to enforce compliance with the Supreme Court ruling. At 3:15 on the same day, the problem was resolved: protected by the soldiers urgently sent from Washington, the fifteen black students sat with the white students at Central High and absolutely nothing happened.

### SPUTNIK: THE WORLD LEARNS ASTRONAUTICS

Sofia Loren had dressed up as a bride, in Hollywood, to film a scene in a movie—on September 21—when a court in Mexico—three thousand miles away—declared her married by proxy to the Italian producer Carlo Ponti, who at that very instant was in Los Angeles talking business by phone with an impresario in New York. That marriage, which had something futuristic about it, a bit like an interplanetary legend, did not awake the expected interest in Italy. Nor did it in the United States, where the Italian actress has not managed to thoroughly interest the baseball stadium public. New York fans shoved each other to get the best seats in the stands for the most highly anticipated game of the season, on October 4, when the world had already forgotten to argue about the legitimacy or illegitimacy of Sofia Loren's marriage. At that very instant, "some place in the Soviet Union," an anonymous scientist pressed a button: the first artificial satellite of Earth: Sputnik 1 (which in Russian means "companion") was sent into orbit around the globe. The sphere, constructed using an as-yet-unknown material, but able to withstand the very elevated temperature provoked by the speed of the launch, weighing 184 pounds, with a diameter of 23 inches, four antennae, and two radio transmitters, was placed into orbit, at an altitude of 600 miles and a speed of 18,000 miles per hour, by a rocket with unimaginable precision and pushed by an unsuspected force. Due to the spectacular publicity this event earned, one of the most important in the history of humanity from the scientific point of view, readers of all the newspapers in the world did an intensive and complete course in astronautics over the next four days. The only thing not known about Sputnik 1, as well as the material it's made of, is the fuel used for the launch and the exact time it went into orbit. The Soviets had a reason to keep this secret: if they knew the launch time, scientists in the United States would have been able to calculate the exact launch site.

"It's an unimportant piece of junk," declared an American military officer when he heard that Earth had a Soviet-made satellite. But that "unimportant piece of junk," whose scientific significance is incalculable, was at the same time the demonstration that Khrushchev hadn't been lying when he said his country had a rocket able to reach anywhere on the planet. If the Russians were able to launch Sputnik, it was because, in reality, they had at their disposal the super rocket Khrushchev had threatened the West with two months earlier.

### CHRISTIAN DIOR'S LAST HAND OF CANASTA

A man had found the way to attend his journalistic astronautics course without ignoring his many occupations: the dressmaker Christian Dior, who in his gigantic establishment on Montaigne Avenue, in Paris, worked fifteen hours a day before taking his annual vacation. On October 18, Christian Dior finished work and drove to the Italian beach resort of Montecatini, accompanied by a seventeen-year-old girl called Maria Colle, and Madame Raymendo Zanecker, his closest collaborator. The most precious object in his luggage of seven cases is a briefcase of emergency medicines, to which the highest-earning designer of 1957 must have recourse in case of emergency. On the 23rd, at 10:35 at night, after playing canasta with a group of friends at the Hotel de la Pace, Christian Dior felt weary and retired to his room. An hour later, awakened by a premonition, Madame Zanecker knocked three times on his door, with the briefcase of medicine. It was too late. A French doctor, staying in the same hotel, in his pajamas, at twenty-three minutes past eleven, confirmed that Christian Dior, a man who didn't know how to do anything eleven years ago and who was now the best-known and richest designer in the world, had died of a heart attack.

In Moscow, where those in charge of fashion resolved six months ago to do everything possible to get the Soviet people—who dress very badly—to dress better, they were expecting a visit from Christian Dior at the beginning of the new year. The news of his death arrived at a moment when the Soviet people were preparing to celebrate the fortieth anniversary of the revolution. The Western world, in its turn, was preparing a spectacular revelation. They knew that the Soviets, when they launched the first Sputnik, had only released a trial, a free sample of the mysterious and colossal event they were saving for November 4. In the expectation, as if to keep world attention awake, the Soviets granted an indefinite leave to General Zhukov, the minister of defense, the conqueror of Berlin, and personal friend of President Eisenhower. "I have just seen Zhukov," Khrushchev said that night, laughing his head off, at a reception in the Turkish embassy in Moscow. "We were looking for a post that might be suited to his abilities." Seventy-two hours later, to the beat of the martial anthems with which the Soviet Union was celebrating the eve of the anniversary of the revolution, the second Sputnik—as big and heavy as an automobile—completed its first orbit around the Earth.

### IKE LOSES THE VANGUARD, BUT NOT HIS SENSE OF HUMOR

The United States, which had already had time to react to the public opinion commotion caused by the first satellite, parried the blow this time with a magisterial idea: almost officially, but without anyone claiming responsibility for its authenticity, the news was published that on November 4, at noon, a Soviet projectile would reach the moon. That propaganda maneuver meant that on November 4, while the first living being—the dog Laika—was circling the Earth every ninety-six minutes, the West was feeling a little disappointed: they had the impression that really absolutely nothing had happened.

On November 5, in his rose-colored office in the White House, President Eisenhower, dressed severely in gray, received the learned men of the United States. In that meeting, which lasted exactly one hour and forty-three minutes, the man who fabricated the first long-range missile, Werner von Braun, originally German, now naturalized, spoke most of the time. In 1932—when he was barely eighteen years of age—Von Braun was chosen by Hitler to design a rudimentary rocket, the precursor of the famous V-2 and the venerable grandfather of Sputnik. This enthusiastic, bald, and round-bellied man who shares a taste for bandit novels with President Eisenhower convinced the head of state that the United States has a system of defense and attack much more advanced than that of the Soviet Union, concretely in the control of long-range rockets. But the president was not very reassured. A few weeks later—when Ingrid Bergman and Roberto Rossellini severed by common accord their shaky matrimonial links—the president suffered a mild stroke when he returned to the Washington airfield, where he received the King of Morocco. In Paris, a commission of FBI detectives was studying every square inch of the hybrid Palais de Chaillot to be sure that nobody could shoot Mr. Eisenhower from behind the numerous pale statues, during the course of the imminent NATO conference. When the news of the president's ill health reached them, the detectives returned to Washington, sure they'd been wasting their time. Surrounded by the best doctors in the United States, prepared to find the strength to attend the NATO conference no matter what, Mr. Eisenhower suffered another blow. A blow that this time was not directed against his brain, but against his heart, and against the very heart of the American nation: the minuscule satellite of the United States, a grapefruit of heat-resistant metal the photograph of which had already been published by all the newspapers in the world, rolled melancholically over the dry, stony ground of Cape Canaveral after the enormous and costly launch device of the Vanguard rocket blew up in pieces in an ostentatious failure of smoke and disappointment. A few days later, with his extraordinary capacity to absorb shocks, with a wide smile of a good sport and his long and sure Johnnie Walker strides, President Eisenhower disembarked in Paris to inaugurate the final international event of the year: the NATO conference.

January 3, 1958, *Momento*, Caracas

# Only Twelve Hours to Save Him

I t had been a bad Saturday afternoon. Caracas was starting to get hot. The Avenida de Los Ilustres, not ordinarily overcrowded, was impossible because of the car horns, the stampede of scooters, the reverberation of the pavement under the sweltering February sun, and the many women with children and dogs who were searching without luck for a cool afternoon breeze. One of them, who left her house at 3:30 intending to go for a short walk, returned annoyed a minute later. She was expecting to give birth the next week. Because of her condition, the noise, and the heat, she had a headache. Her oldest son, eighteen months old, who was walking with her, kept crying because a playful and excessively mischievous little dog had given him a superficial nip on his right cheek. In the evening she dressed it with mercurochrome. The boy ate normally and went to bed in a good mood.

In her pleasant penthouse in the Emma building, Señora Ana de Guillén found out that same night that her dog had bitten a child on the Avenida de Los Ilustres. She knew Tony very well, the animal she had raised and trained herself, and she knew he was affectionate and harmless. She didn't think anything of the incident. On Monday, when her husband came home from work, the dog went to greet him. With unusual aggression, instead of wagging his tail, he tore his pant leg. Someone came up to tell her, in the course of the week, that Tony had tried to bite a neighbor in the stairwell. Señora de Guillén blamed the heat for her dog's behavior. She locked him in the bedroom during the day, to avoid problems with the neighbors. On Friday, without the slightest provocation, the dog tried to bite her. Before going to bed she locked him in the kitchen, until she could think of a better solution. The animal, scratching the door, whined all night. But when the housemaid went into the kitchen the next morning, she found him floppy and calm, with his teeth bared and covered in froth. He was dead.

### 6:00 A.M. A DEAD DOG IN THE KITCHEN

March 1st was just another Saturday for the majority of the inhabitants of Caracas. But for a group of people who didn't even know each other, who are not superstitious about Saturdays and who woke up that morning aiming to have an ordinary day, in Caracas, Chicago, Maracaibo, New York, and even at an altitude of twelve thousand feet, in a cargo plane crossing the Caribbean on its way to Miami, that date would be one of the most agitated, anguished, and intense of their lives. The Guilléns, having to confront the reality of the situation after the maid's discovery, got dressed as fast as they could and went out without breakfast. The husband went to the corner store, looked quickly through the telephone book, and called the Institute of Hygiene, in Ciudad Universitaria, where, he had heard, they examined the brains of dogs that died of unknown causes, to determine if the dogs had contracted rabies. It was still very early. A porter with a sleepy voice answered and said that nobody would be there until 7:30.

Señora de Guillén must have walked a long and complicated route before arriving at her destination. In the first place, she had to remember, at that hour, on the Avenida Los Ilustres, where the good and hardworking neighbors who had nothing to do with her anguish were just beginning to be out and about, who it was who had told her on Saturday last week that her dog had bitten a child. Before eight, in a store, she found a Portuguese maid who thought she had heard the story of the dog from one of her neighbors. It was a false lead. But later she got some approximate information that the bitten child lived very near to the San Pedro church, in Chaguaramos. At nine in the morning, a van from the nearby health center took the dog's corpse away for examination. At ten, after having gone through every building close to the San Pedro church one by one, asking if anyone knew anything about a child who'd been bitten by a dog, Señora de Guillén found another piece of evidence. The Italian bricklayers on a construction site, on Avenida Ciudad Universitaria, had heard people talking about this over the course of the week. The child's family lived a hundred yards from the place the anguished Señora de Guillén had been exploring inch by inch all morning: the Macuto building, apartment number 8. At the door there was a piano teacher's card. She had to ring the bell, to the right of the door, and ask the Galician maid for Señor Reverón.

Carmelo Martín Reverón had left that Saturday, as he did every day, except Sunday, at 7:35 in the morning. In his light blue Chevrolet, which he parked by the door to the building, he had driven to the corner of Velázquez. The dairy products company where he'd worked for four years was located there. Reverón is thirty-two years old and from the Canary Islands and surprises people who meet him for the first time with his spontaneity and good manners. He had no reason to worry that Saturday morning. He had a steady job and his colleagues' respect. He'd been married for two years. His son, Roberto, had reached eighteen months in good health. On Wednesday, he'd experienced another satisfaction: his wife had given birth to a baby girl.

As a scientific delegate, Reverón spends most of his day out in the streets, visiting clients. He arrives at the laboratory at eight in the morning, takes care of the most pressing matters, and doesn't come back again until the next day, at the same time. That Saturday, because it was Saturday, he returned to the laboratory, unusually, at eleven in the morning. Five minutes later he received a telephone call.

With four words, a voice he'd never heard before, but which was the voice of an anguished woman, transformed his peaceful day into the most desperate Saturday of his life. It was Señora de Guillén. Her dog's brain had been examined, and the result left no doubt: positive. The boy had been bitten seven days earlier. This meant that by then the rabies virus might have progressed throughout his organism. It had had time to incubate. Even more so in his son's case, since the bite had been on the most dangerous part of his face.

Reverón remembers the movements he made after hanging up the phone as if it had been a nightmare. At 11:35, Dr. Rodríguez Fuentes, from the health center, examined the boy, gave him an anti-rabies vaccination, but did not offer much hope. The anti-rabies vaccination that is manufactured in Venezuela, and that has shown only very good results, begins to act seven days after application. There is a danger that, in the next twenty-four hours, the child might succumb to rabies, an illness as old as the human race, but for which science has not yet discovered a cure. The only recourse is the use of morphine to soothe the terrible pains, until death arrives.

Dr. Rodríguez Fuentes was candid: the vaccination might be futile. The other thing to do would be to find, in the next twenty-four hours, three thousand units of hyperimmune, an anti-rabies serum made in the United States. Unlike the vaccine, the anti-rabies serum begins to act the moment of the first application. Three thousand units do not take up more space or weigh any more than a packet of cigarettes. It shouldn't cost more than thirty bolívares. But the majority of the pharmacies in Caracas that were consulted gave the same answer: "None here." Some doctors hadn't even heard of the product, in spite of it appearing for the first time in the manufacturer's catalogs in 1947. Reverón had just twelve hours to save his son. The redemptive medicine was three thousand miles away, in the United States, where offices were getting ready to close until Monday.

### 12:00 P.M. VÍCTOR SAUME SENDS OUT AN SOS

The uninhibited Víctor Saume interrupted the *Twelve O'clock Show* on Radio Caracas-Television to transmit an urgent message. "Please," he said, "any person who has ampoules of hyperimmune anti-rabies serum, please contact us urgently by telephone. We need it to save the life of an eighteen-month-old child." At that very instant, Carmelo Reverón's brother retransmitted a cable to his friend Justo Gómez, in

Maracaibo, thinking that one of the oil companies might have supplies of the drug. Another brother remembered a friend who lived in New York—Mr. Robert Hester—and sent him an urgent wire, in English, at 12:05, Caracas time. Mr. Robert Hester was just about to leave the gloomy atmosphere of the New York winter to spend the weekend in the suburbs, as a guest of family friends. He was closing up the office when an employee of the All American Cable Company read over the phone the cable that had just arrived from Caracas. The half-hour time difference between the two cities benefited that race against time.

A viewer in La Guaira, who was having lunch in front of the television, leapt out of his chair and called a doctor he knew. Two minutes later he put through a call to Radio Caracas, and that message provoked, in the next five minutes, four urgent phone calls. Carmelo Reverón, who didn't have a telephone at home, had taken the child to number 37 Calle Lecuna, Country Club, where one of his brothers lived. There he received the message from La Guaira at 12:32: the health center of that city informed him that they had hyperimmune. A patrol car, which showed up spontaneously, drove there in twelve minutes, through the snarled midday traffic, running red lights at seventy-five miles an hour. They were twelve wasted minutes. A calm nurse, lethargic in front of an electric fan, informed him that it had been an involuntary mistake.

"We don't have any hyperimmune," she said. "But we have large quantities of anti-rabies vaccine."

That was the only concrete response the message on the television brought. It was incredible that in Venezuela no one could find anti-rabies serum. A case like that of the Reverón boy, whose hours were counted, could happen at any moment. Statistics demonstrate that every year people died as a consequence of bites from rabid dogs. From 1950 to 1952, more than five thousand dogs bit eight thousand inhabitants of Caracas. Of two thousand animals placed under observation, five hundred were contaminated by bites.

In recent months, the public health authorities, worried by the frequency of rabies cases, have intensified the vaccination campaigns. Officially, they are vaccinating five hundred people per month. Dr.

Briceño Rossi, director of the Institute of Hygiene and international authority on the subject, had suspicious dogs submitted to a rigorous fourteen-day observation. Ten in a hundred turned out to be contaminated. In Europe and the United States, dogs, like cars, need a license. They are vaccinated against rabies and a little aluminum tag is hung on their collars with the expiry date of their immunity etched in it. In Caracas, in spite of Dr. Briceño Rossi's efforts, there is no such regulation. Stray dogs fight in the streets and transmit a virus to each other which they later transmit to humans. It was incredible that in those circumstances anti-rabies serum could not be found in the pharmacies and that Reverón should have had to turn to the solidarity of people he didn't even know, whom he still doesn't even know, to save his son.

## "MONDAY WILL BE TOO LATE"

Justo Gómez, in Maracaibo, received the cable almost at the same time as Mr. Hester in New York. Only one member of the Reverón family had a tranquil lunch that day: the boy. Until that moment he had enjoyed apparently perfect health. In the clinic, his mother had not the slightest suspicion of what was going on. But she got worried, at visiting hours, because her husband didn't show up. An hour later, one of her brothers-in-law, feigning a serenity he was far from feeling, went to tell her that Carmelo Reverón would come later.

Six telephone calls put Justo Gómez, in Maracaibo, on the trail of the drug. A petroleum company, which a month before had been obliged to bring hyperimmune from the United States for one of its employees, had one thousand units. It was an insufficient dose. The serum was administered according to the weight of the patient and the severity of the case. For a child of forty pounds, one thousand units were enough twenty-four hours after the bite. But the Reverón boy, who weighed thirty-five, had been bitten seven days ago, and not in a leg, but in the face. The doctor thought it necessary to use three thousand units. In normal circumstances, that is the dose for a 120-pound adult. But this was not the moment to refuse one thousand units, given for free by the petroleum company, but rather to get them, as quickly as possible, to Caracas. At 1:45 in the afternoon, Justo Gómez communicated by telephone that he was driving to the Grano de Oro airfield, in Maracaibo, to send the ampoule. One of Reverón's brothers checked what planes were arriving that afternoon at Maiquetía and found out that at 5:10 an L7 plane from Maracaibo was landing. Justo Gómez, at fifty miles per hour, went to the airfield, and looked for someone he knew who was going to Caracas, but didn't find anyone. Since there was space on the plane and not a minute to lose, he bought a ticket in the airfield and brought it personally.

In New York, Mr. Hester did not close the office. He canceled his weekend plans, requested a telephone call with the top authority on the subject in the United States, in Chicago, and collected all the information necessary on hyperimmune. It was not easy to acquire the serum there either. In the United States, due to the authorities' control over dogs, rabies is on its way to total eradication. It has been years since a case of rabies in a human being was last recorded. In the last year, they only recorded twenty cases of rabid animals in the whole territory, and all of them were in two states on the periphery, along the Mexican border: Texas and Arizona. Since it is a drug that doesn't sell, the pharmacies do not keep it in stock. It can be found at the laboratories that produce the serum. But the laboratories have closed at noon. Another telephone call, this one from Chicago, tells Mr. Hester where he can find hyperimmune in New York. He gets hold of three thousand units, but the direct plane to Caracas had taken off a quarter of an hour ago. The next regular flight—Delta 751—would leave on Sunday night and not arrive at Maiquetía until Monday. Nevertheless, Hester sent the vaccines in the care of the captain and sent an urgent cable to Reverón, with all the details, including the telephone number of Delta in Caracas—558488—so he could get in contact with their agents and pick up the drug at Maiquetía, at dawn on Monday. But it might be too late by then.

Carmelo Reverón had lost two precious hours when he ran, panting, into the Pan American offices, on Avenida Urdaneta. Carlos Llorente, the employee on duty at the ticket desk, attended to him. It was 2:35. When he heard what was involved, Llorente took the case as if it were happening to him and pledged to bring the serum, from Miami or New York, in less than twelve hours. He consulted the itineraries. He explained the case to the company's air traffic director, Mr. Roger Jarman, who was taking a siesta at home and thinking of going down to La Guaira at four. Mr. Jarman also took the problem on as if it were his own, phoned the PAA doctor, in Caracas, Dr. Herbig—Avenida Caurimare, Colinas de Bello Monte—and in a three-minute conversation in English learned everything there is to know about hyperimmune. Dr. Herbig, a typical European doctor who speaks German with his secretaries, was already worried about the problem of rabies in Caracas before hearing about the case of the Reverón child. The month before he had attended two cases of people with animal bites. Two weeks earlier, a dog died outside his office door. Dr. Herbig examined it, purely out of scientific curiosity, and had no doubt that the dog had died of rabies.

Mr. Jarman phoned Carlos Llorente and told him, "Use all resources necessary to get the serum here." That was the order Llorente was waiting for. By a special channel, reserved for airplanes in danger, he transmitted, at 2:50, a cable to Miami, New York, and Maiquetía. Llorente did so with a perfect knowledge of the itineraries. Every night, except Sundays, a cargo plane leaves Miami for Caracas arriving at Maiquetía at 4:50 the following morning. It is flight number 339. Three times a week—Monday, Thursday, and Saturday—Flight 207 leaves New York, arriving in Caracas the following morning, at 6:30. In Miami and in New York, they had six hours to find the serum. He informed Maiquetía, so they would be aware of the operation there. All the employees of Pan American received the order to remain on alert to messages arriving that afternoon from New York and Miami. A cargo plane, flying to the United States, picked up the message at an altitude of twelve thousand feet and retransmitted it to all the airfields in the Caribbean. Completely sure of himself, Carlos Llorente, whose shift would be finished at four that afternoon, sent Reverón home with a single instruction:

"Call me at 10:30 on 718750. That's my home phone number."

In Miami, R. H. Steward, the employee on duty at the ticket desk, received the message from Caracas almost instantaneously, through the office's teletypes. He telephoned Dr. Martín Mangels, medical director of the Latin American Division of the company, at home, but had to make two more calls before he tracked him down. Dr. Mangels took charge of the case. In New York, ten minutes after receiving the message, they found an ampoule of one thousand units, but by 8:35 they'd given up hope of finding the rest. Dr. Mangels, in Miami, having almost exhausted his last resources, turned to Jackson Memorial Hospital, which immediately communicated with all the hospitals in the region. At seven that night, Dr. Mangels, waiting at home, had still not received any response from Jackson Memorial Hospital. Flight 339 was leaving in two and a half hours. The airport was twenty minutes away.

### LAST MINUTE: A DEGREE AND A HALF OF FEVER

Carlos Llorente, a twenty-five-year-old Venezuelan bachelor, handed over his post to Rafael Carrillo at four, and left him precise instructions on what he should do in case any cables arrived from the United States. He went to wash his car, a green and black model 55, thinking that by that time, in New York and in Miami, a whole system was in motion to save the Reverón boy. From the gas station where he was getting his car washed, he called Carrillo, who told him that no news had arrived yet. Llorente started to get worried. He went to his house on Avenida La Floresta, in La Florida, where he lives with his parents, and ate without appetite, thinking that within a few hours Reverón would call and he wouldn't have an answer for him. But at 8:35, Carrillo called him from the office to read him a cable that had just arrived from New York: on Flight 207, which would arrive at Maiquetía on Sunday morning at 6:30, one thousand units of hyperimmune were on their way. By that time, one of Reverón's brothers had met Justo Gómez, who bounded down the steps of the Maracaibo plane with the first one thousand units, which were injected into the boy that very afternoon. They still needed another one thousand units, as well as the one thousand that were definitely coming from New York. Since Reverón had not left any telephone number, Llorente did not advise him of events, but he went out a little bit more calmly, at nine, on a personal errand. He left his mother a note:

"Señor Reverón will call at 10:30. Tell him to call Señor Carrillo at the PAA office immediately." Before going out, he called Carrillo himself and told him to, if possible, keep the central line free after 10:15, so Reverón wouldn't get a busy signal. But by that time, Reverón was feeling like the world was falling in on him. The boy, after the injection of the first dose of serum, did not want to eat. That night he was not as lively as usual. When he put him to bed he had a bit of a fever. In some cases, very infrequently, the anti-rabies serum entailed certain dangers. Dr. Briceño Rossi, from the Hygiene Institute, had decided not to produce it until he was absolutely convinced that the person who was injected would not run any risk. The fabrication of the ordinary vaccine did not present complications: for animals, it is a live virus in a chicken embryo that gives three years of immunity in a single dose. For humans, it is made from the brain of a sheep. The production of the serum is a more delicate operation. Reverón knew it. When he noticed that his child had a fever, he thought all hope was lost. But his doctor calmed him down. He said it could be a natural reaction.

Resolved not to let himself be broken by circumstances, Reverón called Llorente's house at 10:25. He wouldn't have done so if he had known that no answer had been sent by then from Miami. But the Jackson hospital told Dr. Mangels at 8:30 that they'd found five thousand units, after a lightning-fast operation, in a neighboring town. Dr. Mangels collected the ampoules personally and drove with them, at top speed, to the airport, where a DC-6B was beginning preparations for the nocturnal flight. The next day no plane flew to Caracas. If Dr. Mangels did not arrive on time, he'd have to wait until Monday night. Then it would be too late. Captain Gillis, veteran of the Korean War and father of two boys, received the ampoules and Dr. Mangels's handwritten instructions personally. They shook hands. The plane took off at 9:30, at the moment when the Reverón boy, in Caracas, had a degree and a half of fever. Dr. Mangels watched the plane's perfect takeoff from the chilly airport roof. Then he ran up the steps two at a time, to the control tower, and dictated a message to be transmitted to Caracas by the special channel. On Avenida Urdaneta, in a lonely office, submerged in the colored reflections of neon ads, Carrillo looked at his watch: 10:20. He didn't have time to despair. Almost immediately the teletype began to jump spasmodically, and Carrillo read, letter by letter, mentally deciphering the company's internal code, Dr. Mangels's cable: "We are sending with Captain Gillis on flight 339 five ampoules of serum under guide number 26-16-596787 stop obtained Jackson Memorial Hospital stop if more serum needed request urgently Lederle laboratories in Atlanta, Georgia." Carrillo pulled out the paper, ran to the telephone, and dialed 718750, the number of the Llorente residence, but the telephone was busy. It was Carmelo Reverón, who was talking to Llorente's mother. Carrillo hung up. A minute later, Reverón was dialing Carrillo's number, from a shop on La Florida. He answered instantly.

"Hello," said Carrillo.

With the calm that precedes a nervous breakdown, Reverón asked a question he doesn't remember precisely. Carrillo read him the cable, word for word. The plane would arrive at 4:50 in the morning. It was perfectly on time. There was no delay. There was a brief silence. "I have no words to thank you," murmured Reverón, at the other end of the line. Carrillo couldn't say anything. When he hung up the phone he felt that his knees wouldn't support the weight of his body. He was shaken by a sweeping emotion, as if the life of his own son had just been saved. By contrast, the boy's mother was sleeping peacefully: she didn't know of the drama her family had lived through that day. She still doesn't.

March 14, 1958, *Momento*, Caracas

# June 6, 1958:
## Caracas Without Water

*If a downpour falls this morning, this feature is telling a lie.*
*But if it does not rain before June, read it . . .*

After listening to the 7:00 a.m. radio news bulletin, Samuel Burkart, a German engineer who lives alone in a penthouse on Avenida Caracas, in San Bernardino, went to the corner store to buy a bottle of mineral water to shave with. It was June 6, 1958. Unlike every other day since Samuel Burkart arrived in Caracas, ten years ago, that morning seemed mortally calm. From the nearby Avenida Urdaneta, the noise of cars or the explosions of scooters could not be heard. Caracas seemed like a ghost town. The sweltering heat of recent days had eased a little, but in the high, dense blue sky, not a single cloud moved. In the gardens of the country houses, in the little island of the Plaza de la Estrella, the shrubs were dead. The trees of the avenues, ordinarily covered in red and yellow flowers at this time of year, stretched long bare branches up to the sky.

Samuel Burkart had to wait in line in the store to be served by the two Portuguese shopkeepers who were talking to their frightened clientele about the same topic, the only topic over the last forty days, which that morning had burst out of the radio and the newspapers like a dramatic explosion: Caracas had run out of water. The previous night they had announced dramatic restrictions imposed by INOS (National Institute of Sanitation Works) on the last 100,000 cubic meters stored in La Mariposa reservoir. As of that morning, as a consequence of the most intense summer Caracas has suffered for seventy-nine years, the water supply had been suspended. The last reserves were destined for strictly essential services. The government had been making arrangements of extreme urgency for the last twenty-four hours to keep the population from dying of thirst. To guarantee public order, they had taken emergency measures, which civic brigades composed of students and professionals would be in charge of fulfilling. Newspapers, reduced to editions of four pages, were allocated the task of disclosing official instructions to the civilian population about the way they should proceed to overcome the crisis and prevent panic.

One thing hadn't occurred to Burkart: his neighbors had to make coffee with mineral water and had used up the store's entire supply in an hour. As a precaution against what might happen over the following days, he decided to stock up on fruit juice. But the Portuguese shopkeeper told him that the sale of fruit juice and soft drinks was rationed by order of the authorities. Each customer had the right to a quota limited to one can of fruit juice and one soda per day, until further orders. Burkart bought a can of orange juice and opted for a bottle of lemonade to shave with. Only when he attempted it did he discover that lemonade curdles the soap and does not produce foam. So he declared a definitive state of emergency and shaved with peach juice.

### FIRST SIGN OF THE CATACLYSM:
### A LADY WATERING HER GARDEN

With his perfectly squared, German brain, and his experiences of war, Samuel Burkart knew how to calculate with due anticipation the reach of a piece of news. That's what he had done, three months earlier, exactly on March 28, when he read the following information in a newspaper: "There is only forty days' worth of water left in La Mariposa."

The normal capacity of La Mariposa reservoir, which supplies

Caracas's water, is 9,500,000 cubic meters. On that date, in spite of the reiterated recommendations from INOS to economize water use, the reserves were down to 5,221,854 cubic meters. A meteorologist declared to the press, in an unofficial interview, that it would not rain before June. A few weeks later the water supply was reduced to an already worrying quota, in spite of the population not giving it due importance: 130,000 cubic meters per day.

On his way to work, Samuel Burkart greeted a neighbor who had been sitting in her garden since eight in the morning, watering the grass. On one occasion he spoke to her of the need to save water. Wrapped in a red, flowered, silk housecoat, she shrugged. "The newspapers are lying to frighten us," she replied. "As long as there's water, I'll water my flowers." The German thought he should tell the police, as he would have done in his country, but he didn't dare, because he thought the Venezuelan mentality was completely different from his. He had always been struck by the fact that the coins in Venezuela are the only ones that don't have their value inscribed on them and thought it might obey a kind of logic that was inaccessible to a German. He convinced himself of that when he noticed that some public fountains, though not the most important, were still functioning when the newspapers announced, in April, that the water reserves were declining at a rate of 150,000 cubic meters every twenty-four hours. A week later it was announced that they were producing artificial downpours at the headwaters of the Tuy—the vital source for Caracas—and that this had given the authorities a certain optimism. But by the end of April it still had not rained. The poor neighborhoods were left without water. In the residential neighborhoods water was restricted to one hour a day. At his office, since he had nothing to do, Samuel Burkart used a slide rule to discover that if things went on as they were there would be water until May 22. He was wrong, maybe due to an error in the data published by the newspapers. At the end of May water use was still restricted, but some housewives were still insisting on watering their potted plants. In one garden, hidden among the shrubberies, he even saw a tiny fountain running during the single hour when water was supplied. In the same building where he lived a lady boasted of not having gone without her daily bath at any time. Every morning she collected water in every available receptacle. Now, unexpectedly, despite having been announced with appropriate anticipation, the news exploded across all the newspapers. The reserves in La Mariposa would last for mere hours. Burkart, who had a complex about shaving on a daily basis, could not even brush his teeth. He went to his office, thinking that maybe at no point in the war, not even when he was retreating with the Africa Korps, in the middle of the desert, had he felt so threatened by thirst.

### IN THE STREETS, RATS DIE OF THIRST. THE GOVERNMENT ASKS FOR CALM

For the first time in ten years, Burkart walked to his office, situated a few steps away from the Ministry of Communications. He didn't dare use his car out of fear it might overheat. Not all the inhabitants of Caracas were as cautious. At the first gas station he passed there was a line of cars and a group of vociferous drivers, arguing with the owner. They had filled their gas tanks in the hope they'd be provided with water like in normal times. But there was nothing to be done. There was simply no water for the cars. Avenida Urdaneta was unrecognizable: no more than ten vehicles at nine in the morning. In the middle of the street, there were some overheated cars, abandoned by their owners. The bars and restaurants were not opening their doors. Signs were hung on the metal shutters: "Closed due to lack of water." That morning they'd announced that the buses would provide regular service in the rush hours. At the stops, lines were several blocks long at seven in the morning. The rest of the avenue looked normal, with its sidewalks, but nobody was working in the buildings: everyone was in the windows. Burkart asked a Venezuelan colleague at the office what all the people were doing at the windows, and he answered:

"They're looking at the lack of water."

At noon, the heat slumped over Caracas. Only then did the uneasiness begin. All morning, INOS trucks, with capacities of up to twenty thousand liters, delivered water to the residential neighborhoods. With the petroleum companies' tanker trucks reconditioned as water tankers, they had three hundred vehicles to transport water to the capital. Each of them, according to official calculations, could make up to seven trips a day. But an unexpected problem hampered the project: the access roads were congested from ten in the morning. The thirsty population, especially in the poor neighborhoods, pounced on the tankers, and the intervention of the armed forces was needed to reestablish order. The inhabitants of the hills, desperate, sure that the supply trucks could not reach their houses, came down in search of water. The pickup trucks of the student brigades, with loudspeakers on top, managed to prevent panic. At 12:30, the president of the Government Council, over the airwaves of Radio Nacional, the only broadcaster whose programs had not been limited, asked the population to remain calm, in a four-minute speech. Right afterward, in very brief statements, various political leaders spoke, as well as the leader of the University Front and the head of the Patriotic Council. Burkart, who had witnessed the popular revolution against Pérez Jiménez five months earlier, had experience: the people of Caracas are particularly disciplined. Most of all, they are very sensitive to coordinated campaigns on the radio, in the press, on television, and in flyers. He did not have the slightest doubt that these people would also know how to respond to that emergency. So the only thing that worried him at that moment was his thirst. He went down the stairs of the old building where his office was situated, and on the landing he found a dead rat. He didn't give it a second thought. But that afternoon, when he went out on his balcony to get some fresh air after drinking a liter of water supplied by the tanker truck that passed by his house at two, he saw a commotion in the Plaza de la Estrella. Bystanders were watching a terrible spectacle: animals driven crazy by thirst were emerging from all the buildings. Cats, dogs, mice, were running out into the street in search of relief for their dry throats. That night, at ten, the government imposed a curfew. In the silence of the sweltering night all that could be heard was the sound of the street sweepers performing an extraordinary service: first in the streets, and then inside the buildings, they collected the corpses of the animals that had died of thirst.

### FLEEING TOWARD LOS TEQUES,
### A CROWD DIES OF SUNSTROKE

Forty-eight hours after the drought reached its climax, the city was completely paralyzed. The government of the United States sent, from Panama, a convoy of airplanes loaded with drums of water. The Venezuelan air force and the commercial companies that service the country substituted their normal activities for an extraordinary service of water transport. The Maiquetía and La Carlota airports were closed to international traffic and devoted exclusively to that emergency operation. But when they managed to organize the urban distribution, 30 percent of the transported water had evaporated because of the intense heat. In Las Mercedes, in Sabana Grande, the police seized, on the night of June 7, several pirate trucks, which were selling water clandestinely for twenty bolívares a liter. In San Agustín del Sur, the people found two more pirate trucks and shared out their contents, with exemplary order, among the children. Thanks to the people's discipline and feeling of solidarity, by the night of June 8 no one had died of thirst. But since dusk, a pungent smell invaded the city streets. By nighttime, the smell had become unbearable. Samuel Burkart went down to the corner with his empty bottle at eight at night, and stood in an orderly half-hour line to receive his liter of water from a tanker truck driven by boy scouts. He observed a detail: his neighbors, who up till then had taken things a little lightly, who had managed to convert the crisis into a sort of carnival, began to be seriously alarmed. Especially due to the rumors. Starting at noon, at the same time as the bad smell, a wave of alarmist rumors had spread throughout the region. It was said that because of the terrible drought, the neighboring hills, the parks of Caracas, were starting to burn. There would be nothing they could do when the fires broke out. The firefighters had no means to combat them. The next day, as Radio Nacional announced, there would be no newspapers. Since the radio stations had suspended their broadcasts and there were only three daily bulletins on Radio Nacional, the city was, in a way, at the mercy of the rumors. They were transmitted by telephone and in most cases were from anonymous sources.

Burkart had heard that whole families were leaving Caracas. Since there were no means of transport, the exodus was attempted on foot, especially toward Maracay. A rumor said that in the afternoon, on the old road to Los Teques, a terrified crowd that was trying to flee from Caracas had succumbed to sunstroke. The exposed corpses, left in the open air, it was said, were the source of the bad smell. Burkart found that explanation exaggerated, but noticed that, at least in his sector, there was the beginning of a panic.

One of the Frente Estudiantil pickup trucks stopped beside the tanker truck. The crowd rushed toward it, anxious to find out if the rumors were true. A student climbed up on the hood and offered to answer, in turn, all the questions. According to him, the news of the dead crowd on the road to Los Teques was absolutely false. Besides, it was absurd to think that could be the source of the bad smell. Bodies cannot decompose to that extent in four or five hours. He assured them that the forests and parks were patrolled to avoid fires, that public order was normal, that the population was collaborating in a heroic way, and that in a few hours a sufficient quantity of water to guarantee standards of hygiene would reach Caracas, coming from all over the country. He asked people to transmit this news by telephone, with the warning that the alarming rumors were sown by supporters of Pérez Jiménez.

### IN COMPLETE SILENCE, ONE MINUTE UNTIL ZERO HOUR

Samuel Burkart went home with his liter of water at 6:45, planning to listen to the Radio Nacional bulletin at seven. On his way he found his neighbor who, in April, had still been watering the flowers in her garden. She was indignant with the INOS for not having foreseen that situation. Burkart thought his neighbor's irresponsibility had no limits.

"People like you are to blame," he said indignantly. "The INOS asked us to economize our water use in good time. You paid no heed. Now we are paying the price."

The Radio Nacional bulletin did nothing but repeat the information supplied by the students. Burkart understood that the situation was reaching a critical point. In spite of the authorities trying to prevent demoralization, it was obvious that the state of things was not as reassuring as the authorities presented it. An important aspect was being ignored: the economy. The city was totally paralyzed. Provisions had been limited, and in the next few hours food would be scarce. Surprised by the crisis, the population did not have money in cash. Stores, businesses, and banks were closed. Neighborhood stores began to close their doors due to lack of supplies: they'd sold out of everything they'd had. When Burkart turned off the radio he understood Caracas was reaching its zero hour.

In the mortal silence of nine at night, the heat went up one unbearable degree. Burkart opened doors and windows, but he felt asphyxiated by the dryness of the atmosphere and the smell, increasingly overpowering. He measured out his liter of water meticulously and kept two cubic inches to shave with the next day. For him, that was the most important problem: his daily shave. The thirst produced by dry food was beginning to wreak havoc within his body. He had given up, as recommended by Radio Nacional, salty foods. But he was sure that the next day his body would begin to show symptoms of his growing weakness. He took off all his clothes, drank a sip of water, and lay facedown on his scorching bed, feeling in his ears the profound palpitation of the silence. At times, very far away, the siren of an ambulance tore into the torpor of the curfew. Burkart closed his eyes and dreamed he was sailing into the port of Hamburg, in a black boat, with a white strip painted on the gunwale, with bright, shiny paint. When the boat berthed, he could hear, in the distance, the uproar of the docks. Then he woke up with a start. He heard, from all the floors of the building, a human mob rushing out to the street. A flash, filled with warm, pure water, came in through his window. He needed several seconds to realize what was happening: it was pouring rain.

April 11, 1958, *Momento*, Caracas

# Misadventures of a Writer of Books

Writing books is a suicidal job. None other demands so much time, so much work, so much dedication in relation to its immediate benefits. I don't believe there are many readers who finish a book wondering how many hours of anguish and domestic calamities those two hundred pages have cost their author and how much he received for his work. To put it briefly, for those who don't know it should be said that the author only earns ten percent of what the customer pays for a book in a store. So the reader who bought a book for twenty pesos only contributed two pesos to the author's subsistence. The rest is taken by the publishers who ran the risk of printing it, and the distributors and booksellers. This seems even more unfair when you think that the best writers are the ones who tend to write less and smoke more, and so it's normal that they need at least two years and twenty-nine thousand cigarettes to write a book of two hundred pages. What that means in good arithmetic is that just on what they smoke they spend more than what they'll earn from the book. No wonder a writer friend said to me, "All those publishers, distributors, and booksellers are rich and all us writers are poor."

The problem is more critical in underdeveloped countries, where the book trade is less intense, but it's not exclusive to them. In the United States, which is the paradise of successful writers, for every writer who gets rich overnight through the lottery of paperback editions, there are hundreds of acceptable writers condemned to a life sentence of the icy drip of the ten percent. The latest spectacular case of justified enrichment in the United States is that of the novelist Truman Capote with his book *In Cold Blood,* which in its first weeks produced half a million dollars in royalties and a similar amount in film rights. Conversely, Albert Camus, who will still be in bookshops when nobody remembers the marvelous Truman Capote, was living off pseudonymous film scripts, in order to be able to keep writing books. The Nobel Prize—which he received not long before he died—was barely a momentary ease from his domestic calamities, bringing with it more or less forty thousand dollars, which in those days is what a house cost, with a backyard for the children. Better, though involuntary, was the business Jean-Paul Sartre drummed up by refusing it, for his attitude earned him a fair and deserved reputation for independence, which increased demand for his books.

Many writers yearn for an old-fashioned patron, a rich and generous gentleman who supported artists so they could work at ease. Patrons of the arts do still exist, though they look different these days. There are huge financial consortiums that sometimes in order to pay lower taxes, or to dissipate the image of sharks that public opinion has formed of them, and not very often to ease their guilty consciences, allocate considerable sums to sponsor the work of artists. But we writers like to do whatever we feel like, and we suspect, perhaps without grounds, that sponsorship compromises the independence of thought and expression, and causes undesirable concessions. In my case, I prefer to write with no subsidies of any sort, not only because I suffer from a stupendous persecution complex, but also because when I start to write I have absolutely no idea with whom I'll be in agreement when I finish. It would be unfair if in the end I disagreed with the sponsor's ideology, which is quite likely given most writers' conflictive spirit of contradiction, just as it would be completely immoral if by chance I were in agreement.

The system of patronage, typical of the paternalistic vocation of capitalism, seems to be a replica of the socialist offer of considering the writer as a salaried state worker. In principle the socialist solution is correct, because it liberates the writer from the exploitation of the intermediaries. But in practice so far and for who knows how much longer, the system has given rise to risks more serious than the injustices it was meant to correct. The recent case of two terrible Soviet writers who have been sentenced to forced labor in Siberia, not for writing badly but for disagreeing with their sponsor, demonstrates how dangerous the trade of writing can be under a regime that lacks the sufficient maturity to admit the eternal truth that we writers are a bunch of miscreants on whom doctrinaire straitjackets, and even legal arrangements, pinch us more than shoes. Personally, I believe that the writer, as such, has no other revolutionary obligation than to write well. Nonconformism, under any regime, is an essential condition that can't be helped, because a conformist writer is most likely a bandit, and most definitely a bad writer.

After this sad revision, it seems elementary to wonder why we writers write. The answer, necessarily, is more melodramatic the more sincere it is. You're a writer in the very same way you might be Jewish or black. Success is encouraging, support of readers is stimulating, but these are supplementary rewards, because a good writer will carry on writing anyway with worn-out shoes, and even if his books don't sell. It is a kind of occupational hazard that explains very well the social madness that so many men and women have starved themselves to death, in order to do something that, after all, and speaking completely seriously, serves no purpose whatsoever.

July 1966, *El Espectador,* Bogotá

# I Can't Think of Any Title

Before the revolution I was never curious to see Cuba. Latin Americans of my generation imagined Havana as a scandalous brothel for gringos where pornography had reached its highest category of public spectacle long before it became fashionable in the rest of the Christian world: for the price of one dollar it was possible to see a woman and a man of flesh and blood making love in real life on a bed in a theater. That *pachanga* paradise exhaled a diabolical music, a secret language of the sweet life, a way of walking and of dressing, a whole culture of relaxation that exercised a cheerful influence on daily life on the Caribbean. However, those better informed knew that Cuba had been the most cultured colony of Spain, the only truly cultured one, and that the tradition of literary *tertulias* and poetic floral games remained incorruptible while the gringo marines pissed on the statues of their heroes and the president of the Republic's gunslingers held up the courts with weapons drawn to steal the proceedings. Next to *La Semana Comica*, an ambiguous magazine that married men read in secret in their bathrooms to hide it from their wives, one could find the most sophisticated arts and letters journals in all of Latin America. The radio drama serials that went on for interminable years, and kept the whole continent flooded in tears, had been engendered alongside Amalia Peláez's delirious flaming sunflowers and José Lezama Lima's mercurially hermetic hexameters. Those brutal contrasts helped to confuse much more than comprehend the reality of an almost mythical country whose risky independence war had still not ended, and whose political age, in 1955, was still an unpredictable enigma.

It was that year, in Paris, when I first heard the name of Fidel Castro. I heard it from the poet Nicolás Guillén, who was suffering a hopeless exile in the Grand Hôtel Saint-Michel, the least sordid on a street of cheap hotels where a gang of Latin Americans and Algerians awaited a return ticket eating rancid cheese and boiled cauliflower. Nicolás Guillén's room, as with almost all of them in the Latin Quarter, consisted of four fading and peeling walls, two chairs with worn upholstery, a sink and a portable bidet, a single bed for two, where mournful lovers from Senegal had been happy and had committed suicide. However, twenty years later, I can't really summon up the image of the poet in that room, but I do remember him in circumstances in which I never saw him: fanning himself in a wicker rocker, at siesta time, on the veranda of one of those big plantation houses out of a splendid Cuban painting of the nineteenth century. In any case, and even in the cruelest times of winter, Nicolás Guillén maintained in Paris the very Cuban custom of rising (without a rooster) at the crowing of the first roosters, and of reading the newspapers as he sipped his coffee lulled by the sweet wind of the sugar mills and the counterpoint of guitars in the clamorous dawns of Camagüey. Then he opened the window of his balcony, also as he would in Camagüey, and woke up the whole street by shouting the news from Latin America translated from French into Cuban slang.

The situation of the continent at that time was very well expressed by the official portrait of the conference of heads of state that had met the previous year in Panama: you can barely see a civilian in the midst of all the uproar of uniforms and war medals. Even General Dwight Eisenhower, who in the presidency of the United States usually hides the smell of gunpowder in his heart beneath the most expensive Bond Street suits, had put on his brasses of a warrior at rest for that historic photograph. So one morning Nicolás Guillén opened his window and shouted a single piece of news:

"The man has fallen!"

There was a commotion in the sleeping street because each of us believed the man who had fallen was his. The Argentinians thought it was Juan Domingo Perón, the Paraguayans thought it was Alfredo Stroessner, the Peruvians thought it was Manuel Odría, the Colombians thought it was Gustavo Rojas Pinilla, the Nicaraguans thought it was Anastasio Somoza, the Venezuelans thought it was Marcos Pérez Jiménez, the Guatemalans thought it was Castillo Armas, the Dominicans thought it was Rafael Leónidas Trujillo, and the Cubans thought it was Fulgencio Batista. It was Perón, actually. Later, talking about this, Nicolás Guillén painted a distressing panorama of the situation in Cuba for us. "The only thing I see for the future," he concluded, "is a kid who's getting a lot done over in Mexico." He paused like a clairvoyant, and concluded:

"His name is Fidel Castro."

Three years later, in Caracas, it seemed impossible that name had made its way in such a short time and with such strength to the top level of continental attention. But even then nobody had thought that the first socialist revolution of Latin America was gestating in the Sierra Maestra. Instead, we were convinced that it had begun to gestate in Venezuela, where an immense popular conspiracy had foiled General Marcos Pérez Jiménez's tremendous apparatus of repression in twenty-four hours.

Seen from outside, it had been an implausible action, for the simplicity of its approach and the speed and devastating efficacy of its results. The only order that had been imparted to the population was that at twelve noon on January 23, 1958, they should sound their car horns, stop working, and go out into the street to overthrow the dictatorship. Even from the editorial offices of a well-informed newsmagazine, where many of the staff were involved in the conspiracy, that seemed a juvenile order. Nevertheless, at the appointed hour, an immense clamor of unanimous horns exploded, an enormous traffic jam stopped traffic in a city where traffic jams were already legendary, and many groups of university students and workers took to the streets to confront the regime's forces with stones and bottles. From the surrounding hills, covered in colorful shacks that resembled Christmas nativity scenes, descended a devastating swarm of poor people who turned the whole city into a battleground. At nightfall, in the middle of dispersed gunshots and the howling of ambulances, a rumor of relief went round the newspaper offices: Pérez Jiménez's family had hidden in tanks and sought asylum in an embassy. Shortly before dawn the sky fell abruptly silent, and then an earsplitting shout of crowds exploded and the church bells rang and the factory sirens and car horns sounded, and out of every window Venezuelan folk songs poured out and went on almost ceaselessly for two years of false illusions. Pérez Jiménez had fled his stolen throne with his closest accomplices, and was flying in a military plane to Santo Domingo. The plane had its engines warmed up since noon at La Carlota airport, a few miles from the Miraflores presidential palace, but nobody had thought to move a staircase up to it when the fugitive dictator arrived closely followed by a patrol of taxis that were a very few minutes from catching him. Pérez Jiménez, who looked like a big baby in tortoiseshell glasses, was hoisted up into the cabin by rope with great difficulty, and in the extravagant maneuver he forgot his briefcase on the ground. It was an ordinary black leather briefcase, which contained the money he had hidden for his out-of-pocket expenses: thirteen million dollars.

Since then and during the whole of 1958, Venezuela was the freest country in the entire world. It seemed like a real revolution: each time the government glimpsed some danger, it immediately consulted the people by direct channels, and the people took to the streets against any attempt at regression. The most delicate official decisions were made in the public arena. There was no matter of state of a certain size that was not resolved with the participation of the political parties, with the communists at the forefront, and at least in the first months the parties were aware that their power was based on the pressure in the streets. If that were not the first socialist revolution in Latin America, it must have been due to the black arts of conjurers, but not in any case because the social conditions had not been most favorable.

The government of Venezuela and the Sierra Maestra established an undisguised complicity between them. The men of the 26th of

July Movement stationed in Caracas spread propaganda by all possible means, organized massive collections and sent aid to the guerrillas with official endorsement. Venezuelan university students, who'd been hardened by their involvement in the battle against the dictatorship, sent a pair of women's underpants in the mail to Havana university students. The Cuban students concealed very well the impertinence of that triumphalist package, and in less than a year, when the revolution triumphed in Cuba, returned them to the senders with no comment. The Venezuelan press, more from the pressure of internal conditions than from the will of the owners, was the legal press of the Sierra Maestra. It gave the impression that Cuba was not another country, but a piece of free Venezuela that had not yet been freed.

The New Year of 1959 was one of the few Venezuela celebrated without a dictatorship in its entire history. Mercedes and I, who had gotten married during those joyful months, returned to our apartment in the neighborhood of San Bernardino at the first light of dawn and found that the elevator was out of order. We walked up the six flights of stairs, pausing to rest on the landings, and we were barely inside the apartment when we were shaken by the absurd feeling that an instant we'd already lived through last year was repeating itself: the shouts of frenzied crowds suddenly rose up from the sleepy streets, and the church bells rang and the factory sirens and car horns sounded, and from all the windows came a torrent of harps and four-stringed guitars and braided voices singing of the glory of popular victories. It was as if time had been running backward and Marcos Pérez Jiménez had been toppled for a second time. Since we didn't have a telephone or a radio, we bounded back down the stairs, wondering what kind of hallucinogenic alcohol they'd given us at the party, and someone who ran past in the early-morning glow stunned us with the latest incredible coincidence: Fulgencio Batista had fled his stolen throne with his closest accomplices and flown in a military plane to Santo Domingo.

Two weeks later I arrived in Havana for the first time. The occasion presented itself sooner than I expected but in the least expected circumstances. On January 18, when I was tidying my desk to leave for home, a man from the 26th of July Movement arrived panting in the magazine office in search of journalists who wanted to go to Cuba that very night. A Cuban airplane had been sent for that purpose. Plinio Apuleyo Mendoza and I, who were the most resolute supporters of the Cuban Revolution, were the first to be chosen. We barely had time to go home and grab a bag, and I was so used to thinking that Venezuela and Cuba were the same country that I didn't remember to look for my passport. It didn't matter: the Venezuelan immigration agent, more Cuba-loving than any Cuban, asked me to show him any identity document I had on me, and the only piece of paper I found in my pockets was a laundry receipt. The agent stamped it on the back, killing himself laughing, and wished me a pleasant flight.

The serious problem showed up at the end, when the pilot discovered that there were more journalists than seats on the plane, and that the weight of the teams and baggage was above the acceptable limit. Nobody wanted to stay behind, of course, and nobody wanted to leave any of what they were bringing, and the airport official was determined to send the overloaded plane on its way. The pilot was a mature and serious man, with a graying moustache, in a blue uniform with golden trimming of the former Cuban air force, and for almost two hours he impassibly resisted all kinds of reasons. Finally one of us found the lethal argument:

"Don't be a coward, Captain," he said, "the *Granma* was overloaded too."

The pilot looked at him, and then he looked at all of us in muted fury.

"The difference," he said, "is that none of us is Fidel Castro."

But he was mortally wounded. He reached over the counter, ripped the page of flight regulations off the pad, and crumpled it into a ball in his hand.

"Alright," he said, "we'll go like this, but I'm not leaving a record that the plane's overloaded."

He put the paper in his pocket and motioned for us to follow him.

As we were walking toward the plane, trapped between my congenital fear of flying and my desire to see Cuba, I asked the pilot with a thread of a voice:

"Captain, do you think we'll make it?"

"We might," he answered, "with the help of Our Lady of Charity of El Cobre."

IT WAS a rickety old twin-engine plane. The legend circulated among us that it had been seized and flown to the Sierra Maestra by a pilot who deserted from Batista's air force, and sat abandoned to the sun and the dew until that night of my misfortune when they sent it to look for suicidal journalists in Venezuela. The cabin was narrow and badly ventilated, the seats were broken, and there was an intolerable smell of sour urine. Everybody made themselves comfortable however they could, some even sitting on the floor of the narrow aisle between the luggage and the film and television equipment. I felt airless, cornered against a little window in the tail, but I was comforted a little by my comrades' self-assurance. All of a sudden, someone among the most tranquil ones murmured in my ear between clenched teeth, "Lucky you not having a fear of airplanes." Then I reached the extreme of horror, for I understood they were all as frightened as I was, but they were also all pretending like me with a face as undaunted as mine.

In the center of the fear of flying there is an empty space, a sort of eye of the hurricane where one achieves a fatalistic unawareness, and which is the only thing that allows us to fly without dying. On my never-ending and sleepless nocturnal flights I only achieve that state of grace when I see that little orphaned star that accompanies airplanes over lonely oceans appear in the window. In vain I searched for it on that terrible Caribbean night from the soulless twin-engine that cut through stony clouds, crosswinds, abysses of lightning, flying blindly on just the breath of our startled hearts. At dawn we were taken by surprise by a burst of ferocious rain showers, the plane turned sideways with an interminable grinding of a capsizing sailboat, and landed trembling with shivers and with its engines bathed in tears at an emergency airport in Camagüey. Nevertheless, as soon as the rain stopped a spring day burst forth, the air became glass, and we flew the final stretch almost level with the perfumed sugar-cane plantations and marine pools with striped fish and hallucinatory flowers in the depths. Before noon we landed between the Babylonian mansions of the richest of the rich of Havana: in the Campo Columbia airport, then baptized with the name Ciudad Libertad, the former Batista fort where a few days earlier Camilo Cienfuegos had camped with his column of astonished peasants. The first impression was rather comical, for we were greeted by members of the former military air force who at the last minute had gone over to the revolution and were keeping to their barracks while their beards grew enough to look like old revolutionaries.

For those of us who had lived in Caracas for all of the previous year, the feverish atmosphere and creative disorder of Havana at the beginning of 1959 was not a novelty. But there was a difference: in Venezuela an urban insurrection promoted by an alliance of antagonistic parties, and with the support of a broad sector of the armed forces, had brought down a despotic coterie, while in Cuba it had been a rural avalanche that had defeated, in a long and difficult war, a salaried armed forces who fulfilled the functions of an occupation army. It was a deep distinction, which maybe contributed to defining the diverging future of the two countries, and which at noon on that splendid January day was noticeable at first glance.

To give his gringo associates proof of his dominion of power and of his confidence in the future, Batista had made Havana into an unreal city. The patrols of recently shod peasants, smelling like tigers, with archaic rifles and war uniforms too big for their age, strolled like sleepwalkers between astonishing skyscrapers and marvelous automobiles, and the almost naked gringas who arrived on the ferry from New Orleans captivated by the legend of the bearded ones. At the main entrance of the Hotel Habana Hilton, which had barely been inaugurated those days, there was a gigantic blond man in a uniform with tassels and a helmet with a crest of feathers of an invented marshal. He spoke a blend of slangy Cuban crossed with Miami English, and carried out his sad custodian's job without any qualms. One of the journalists of our delegation, who was a black Venezuelan, picked him up by the lapels and threw him into the middle of the street. The

Cuban journalists had to intervene with the hotel management so they'd allow free entry to those invited who were arriving from all over the world without distinctions of any kind. That first night, a group of kids from the rebel army, dying of thirst, went into the first door they found, which was that of the bar of the Hotel Habana Rivera. They only wanted a glass of water, but the bar manager, with the best manners he was capable of, turned them back out into the street. The journalists, with a gesture that then seemed demagogical, made them come back in and sit down at our table. Later, the Cuban journalist Mario Kuchilán, who heard about the incident, communicated his embarrassment and rage:

"This can't be cured except with a real revolution," he told us, "and I swear to you we're going to have one."

January 1977, *Revista de Casa de las Américas,* Havana

# The Sandinista Heist.
# Chronicle of the Assault
# on the "Hog House"

The plan seemed like overly simple insanity. The idea was to take the Palacio Nacional in Managua in broad daylight and with only twenty-five men, hold the members of the Chamber of Deputies hostage, and obtain as ransom the liberation of all the political prisoners. The National Palace, a dull, old building with monumental pretensions, occupies an entire city block with numerous windows on its sides and a façade with the columns of a banana-republic Parthenon facing the city's desolate central square, the Plaza de la República. As well as the Senate on the main floor and the Chamber of Deputies on the second, the Treasury Department, the Interior Ministry, and the Revenue Department are all headquartered there, so it is the most public and most populous of all official buildings in Managua. That's why there is always an armed police officer at every door, two more at the stairs up to the second floor, and lots of pistol-packing ministers and parliamentarians everywhere. During office hours, between employees and the public, in the basement, offices, and corridors, there are never fewer than three thousand people there. Nevertheless, the leadership of the Frente Sandinista de Liberación Nacional (FSLN) did not consider that the assault on that bureaucratic market was actually overly simple insanity, but just the opposite, a masterly piece of madness. In reality, the veteran militant Edén Pastora had conceived and proposed the plan back in 1970, but they only put it into practice this hot August, when it became too obvious that the United States had resolved to help Somoza remain on his bloody throne until 1981.

"Those who speculate about my health should not be mistaken," the dictator had said after his recent trip to Washington. "Others have it worse," he'd added, with very characteristic arrogance. Three loans of forty, fifty, and sixty million dollars were announced shortly afterward. Finally, President Carter, in his own handwriting, went even further overboard, with a personal letter of congratulations to Somoza for a supposed improvement in respect for human rights in Nicaragua. The national direction of the FSLN, stimulated by the noticeable rise in popular agitation, then considered that an emphatic reply was urgent and ordered the frozen plan, so often postponed during the last eight years, to be thawed out and put into action. Since it meant kidnapping parliamentarians of the regime, they gave the exploit the code name Operation Chanchera. That is: the attack on *the hog house*.

### ZERO, ONE, AND TWO

The responsibility for the operation fell to three well-tried members. The first was the man who had come up with the plan and would command it, and whose real name sounded like a poet's pseudonym in the land of Rubén Darío: Edén Pastora. He is forty-two years old, twenty of them spent in very intense militancy, and with a decisiveness of command that does not manage to hide his stupendous sense of humor. Son of a conservative household, he studied with the Jesuits and then did three years of medical school at the University of Guadalajara, in Mexico. Three years in five, because he interrupted his classes several times to return to the guerrilla battles of his country, and only when they were defeated did he return to medical school. His oldest memory, at the age of seven, was the death of his father, murdered by

Anastasio Somoza García's National Guard. As the commander of the operation, according to a traditional custom of the FSLN, he would be distinguished with the name of Zero.

Second in command was Hugo Torres Jiménez, a thirty-year-old veteran guerrilla fighter, with a political training as efficient as his military training. He had participated in the famous kidnapping of a party of Somoza's relatives in 1974, had been sentenced in absentia to thirty years in prison, and since then lived in Managua in absolute clandestinity. His name, as in the previous operation, was Number One.

Number Two, the only woman in the commando team, is Dora María Téllez, twenty-two years old, a very beautiful, shy, and committed young woman, with an intelligence and good judgment that would have served her well for any great project in life. She also studied three years of medicine, in León. "But I gave up in frustration," she says. "It was very sad spending so much work on curing malnourished children, only for them to come back into the hospital three months later, even more malnourished than before." Stationed on the northern Carlos Fonseca Amador Front, she had been living in clandestinity since January of 1976.

### NO LONG HAIR OR BEARDS

Another twenty-three *muchachos* completed the commando unit. The leaders of the FSLN chose them very rigorously from among the most resolved operatives with proven records in guerrilla warfare from all the regional committees of Nicaragua, but the most surprising thing about them is their youth. Omitting Pastora, the average age in the commando was twenty. Three of its members are eighteen.

The twenty-six members of the commando got together for the first time at a Managua safe house just three days before the anticipated date of the action. Apart from the top three numbers, none of them knew each other, or had the least idea of the nature of the operation. They had only been warned that it was an audacious act entailing an enormous risk to their lives, and they'd all accepted.

The only one of them who had ever been inside the National Palace once was Comandante Zero, when he was a very young boy accompanying his mother when she went to pay their taxes. Dora María, Number Two, had an idea of the Blue Room where the Chamber of Deputies met, because she'd seen it on television occasionally. The rest of the group not only didn't know the National Palace, even from the outside, but the majority of them had never even been to Managua. However, the three leaders had a perfect map, drawn with scientific skill by an FSLN doctor, and several weeks before the action they knew the details of the building by heart as if they had lived in it for half their lives.

The day chosen for the action was Tuesday, August 22, because the debate on the national budget assured a high attendance. At 9:30 on the morning of that day, when the surveillance services confirmed that there would be a meeting of the Chamber of Deputies, the twenty-three *muchachos* were informed of all the secrets of the plan, and they were each assigned a precise mission. Divided into six squads of four, by means of a complex but efficient system, each one was designated by a number, which allowed them to know which squad they belonged to and what their corresponding position was within it.

The ingenuity of the action consisted of passing for a patrol of the National Guard Basic Infantry Training School. So they dressed in olive-green uniforms made by clandestine seamstresses in different sizes, and they put on military boots purchased the previous Saturday in different stores. Each was given a campaign bag with a red and black FSLN bandanna, two pocket handkerchiefs in case of injury, a flashlight, gas masks and protective glasses, plastic bags to store drinking water in case of emergency, and a bag of bicarbonate of soda to help them face up to tear gas. In the commando's general supplies there were also ten five-foot lengths of nylon rope to tie up hostages and three chains with locks to secure all the National Palace doors from inside. They didn't take medical equipment because they knew there were medical services and emergency medicines in the Blue Room. Last of all, they distributed the weapons that in no way could be any different from those used by the National Guard, because almost all of them had been captured in combat. Their complete arsenal consisted of two Uzi submachine guns, a G3, an M3, an M2, and twenty Garand rifles, a Browning pistol, and fifty grenades. Each of them had three hundred rounds.

The only resistance they all put up came at the moment of cutting their hair and shaving off their beards, which had been so carefully grown on the front lines. However, no member of the National Guard could wear their hair long or not shave, and only officers were allowed moustaches. There was no choice but to cut it all off, and anyway, since the FSLN didn't have a trustworthy barber, at the last minute they had to cut each other's hair. A resolute *compañera* sheared off Dora María's beautiful combat mane in two snips, so no one would notice that she was a woman under her black beret.

At eleven fifty that morning, with its customary delay, the Chamber of Deputies commenced the session in the Blue Room. Only two parties take part: the Liberal Party, which is Somoza's official party, and the Conservative Party, which plays the game of loyal opposition. From the huge glass door of the main entrance, the liberal benches are on the right, and the conservative benches on the left, and at the back, on a platform, the long presidential desk. Behind each bench there is a balcony for each party's supporters and a press box, but the balcony for the Conservative supporters has been closed for a long time, while the Liberals' balcony is open and always very crowded with salaried followers. That Tuesday it was more crowded than usual and there were also about twenty journalists in the press box. Sixty-seven deputies were in attendance, and two of them were worth their weight in gold for the FSLN: Luis Pallais Debayle, Anastasio Somoza's first cousin, and José Somoza Abrego, son of General José Somoza, who is the dictator's half-brother.

### HERE COMES THE CHIEF!

The budget debate had begun at 12:30, when two Ford trucks painted a military green, with green canvas tarps and wooden benches in the back, stopped at the same time in front of the two side doors of the National Palace. At each of the doors, as expected, was a policeman armed with a rifle, and both were accustomed enough to their routine to notice that the green of those trucks was much brighter than that of the National Guard. Rapidly, in strict military order, three squadrons of soldiers descended from each of the trucks.

The first to get out was Commander Zero, in front of the eastern door, followed by three squads. The last was commanded by Number Two: Dora María. As soon as he jumped to the ground, Zero shouted with his loud voice full of authority:

"Stand aside! Here comes the chief!"

The policeman at the door immediately stepped to one side, and Zero left one of his men standing guard beside him. Followed by his men, he ran up the wide staircase to the second floor, with the same frightful shouts as the National Guard's when Somoza is approaching, and got to where the other two policemen were stationed with their revolvers and truncheons. Zero disarmed one and Number Two disarmed the other with the same paralyzing shout: "Here comes the chief!"

Two other guerrillas stayed posted there. By then, the crowds in the corridors had heard the shouts, had seen the armed guards, and had tried to escape. In Managua, it's almost a social reflex: when Somoza arrives, everyone flees.

Zero had the specific mission of entering the Blue Room and keeping the deputies at bay, knowing that all the Liberals and many of the Conservatives were armed. Commander Two had the mission of covering that operation in front of the big glass door, from where she could see down to the building's main entrance. On both sides of the glass doors they had expected to find two policemen with revolvers. Below, at the main entrance, which was a wrought iron gate, there were two men armed with a rifle and a submachine gun. One of them was a captain of the National Guard.

Zero and Two, followed by their squads, made their way through the terrified crowd to the door to the Blue Room, where they were surprised that one of the policemen had a rifle. "Here comes the chief!" Zero shouted again, and snatched the weapon away from him. Number Four disarmed the other, but the agents were the first to comprehend that this was a deception, and escaped down the stairs and outside.

Then, the two guards at the entrance fired on Number Two's men, and they returned fire. The National Guard captain was killed on the spot, and the other guard was wounded. The main entrance, for the moment, was unguarded, but Two left several armed men lying on the floor to cover it.

### EVERYBODY ON THE GROUND

When they heard the first shots, as planned, the Sandinistas who were guarding the side doors chased the disarmed police officers away, closed the doors with the chains and locks, and ran to reinforce their comrades among the crowd running in all directions, hounded by panic.

Commander Two, meanwhile, went around the front of the Blue Room to the end of the corridor, where the deputies' bar was. When she pushed open the door with the M1 rifle, ready to fire, all she saw was a heap of men crowded together lying on the blue carpet. The deputies there had thrown themselves to the ground as soon as they heard the first shots. Their bodyguards, believing it really was the National Guard, surrendered without any resistance.

Zero then pushed open the big frosted glass door of the Blue Room with the barrel of the G3, and found himself facing a fully paralyzed Chamber of Deputies: sixty-two livid men looking at the door with an expression of astonishment. Fearing that he might be recognized, because some of them had been classmates of his at the Jesuit College, Zero unleashed a burst of lead into the ceiling, and shouted:

"National Guard! Everybody on the floor!"

All the deputies threw themselves to the floor behind their desks, except for Pallais Debayle, who was speaking on the telephone at the presidential desk, and froze. Later they would explain the reason for their terror: they thought the National Guard had staged a coup and overthrown Somoza, and were coming to shoot them.

In the east wing of the building, Number One heard the first shots when his men had neutralized the two police agents on the second floor, and he was heading to the end of the corridor, where the Ministry of the Interior had its offices. Unlike Zero's squads, Number

One's entered in military formation, and stopped in their assigned positions to carry out their missions. The third squad, commanded by Number Three, pushed open the door of the Ministry of the Interior, at the moment when Zero's burst of gunfire resonated throughout the building. In the ministry's anteroom they met with a captain and a lieutenant of the National Guard, the minister's bodyguards, who were preparing to leave the room having heard the shots. Number Three's squad didn't give them time to fire. Then they pushed open the door at the back, and found a padded and air-conditioned office, and saw behind the desk a very tall and somewhat cadaverous fifty-two-year-old man, who raised his hands before anyone told him to. He was the agronomist José Antonio Mora, minister of the interior and Somoza's designated successor in the Congress. He surrendered without knowing to whom he did so, even though he had a Browning pistol on his belt and four full magazines in his pockets. Number One, meanwhile, had reached the back door of the Blue Room, jumping over the masses of men and women lying on the floor. The same thing happened to Number Two, who entered at that moment through the glass door, bringing in the deputies she'd found in the bar with their hands up. It took an instant before they realized that the hall looked deserted, because the deputies were all on the floor behind their desks.

Outside, at that instant, a brief exchange of gunfire was heard. Zero left the room again and saw a patrol of National Guard, under the command of a captain, who were shooting from the main door of the building at the guerrillas posted in front of the Blue Room. Zero threw a fragmentation grenade at them and put an end to the attack. A bottomless silence fell over the interior of the enormous building closed with thick steel chains, where no fewer than twenty-five hundred persons, chests to the ground, wondered about their fate. The whole operation, as planned, had lasted exactly three minutes.

### ENTER THE BISHOPS

Anastasio Somoza Debayle, the fourth of the dynasty that had oppressed Nicaragua for more than forty years, heard the news as he was sitting down to lunch in the air-conditioned cellar of his private stronghold. His immediate reaction was to order an indiscriminate barrage against the National Palace.

That was done. But the National Guard patrols could not get close, because the Sandinista squadrons, as planned, held them back with intense fire from the windows of all four sides. For fifteen minutes, a helicopter flew over firing bursts of machine gunfire at the windows, and wounded one guerrilla in a leg: Number Sixty-Two.

Twenty minutes after he ordered the siege, Somoza received the first direct call from inside the National Palace. It was his cousin Pallais Debayle, who transmitted the first message from the FSLN: either cease fire, or they would start to execute hostages, one every two hours, until he decided to discuss the terms. Somoza then ordered the siege halted.

A short while later, another call from Pallais Debayle informed Somoza that the FSLN proposed three Nicaraguan bishops as intermediaries: Monsignor Miguel Obando Bravo, archbishop of Managua, who had already been an intermediary when the Somocista party was attacked in 1974; Monsignor Manuel Salazar y Espinosa, bishop of León; and Monsignor Leovigildo López Fitoría, bishop of Granada. All three of them, by chance, were in Managua for a special meeting. Somoza accepted.

Later, also at the suggestion of the Sandinistas, the ambassadors of Costa Rica and Panama joined the bishops. The Sandinistas, for their part, entrusted the tough job of negotiating to the tenacity and good judgment of Number Two. Her first mission, carried out at two forty-five in the afternoon, was to submit the list of conditions to the bishops: immediate liberation of the political prisoners on the attached list, diffusion over all media of a communiqué and extensive political declaration, all guards pulled back three hundred meters from the National Palace, immediate acceptance of the demands of the striking hospital workers, ten million dollars and safe passage for the commando and liberated prisoners to travel to Panama. So the conversations began that same Tuesday, continued all night, and culminated on Wednesday toward six in the evening. In this space of time, the negotiators were in the National Palace five times, one of them at three in the morning on the Wednesday, and there didn't really seem to be any glimpses of an accord at all in the first twenty-four hours.

The request that all the military reports and a long political communiqué that the FSLN had prepared earlier be read over the radio was unacceptable to Somoza. But another was impossible: the liberation of all the prisoners on the list. In fact, on that list they had included, very intentionally, twenty Sandinista prisoners who had undoubtedly died in prison, victims of torture and summary executions, which the government refused to admit.

### SOMOZA'S AFFRONT

Somoza sent three replies to the National Palace, all unsigned and written in an informal style plagued with astute ambiguities but impeccably typed on an electric typewriter. He never made any counterproposals, but tried to evade the guerrillas' conditions. From the first message it was obvious he was trying to gain time, convinced that twenty-five adolescents would not be capable of holding at bay more than two thousand people suffering from anxiety, hunger, and exhaustion for very long. That's why his first response, at nine on Tuesday night, was an utterly contemptuous affront asking for twenty-four hours to think.

In his second message, however, at 8:30 on Wednesday morning, he had exchanged that arrogance for threats, but he was beginning to accept conditions. The reason seemed clear: the negotiators had walked through the National Palace at three in the morning, and had verified that Somoza was mistaken in his calculations. The guerrillas had evacuated at their own initiative the few children and pregnant women, had handed over the wounded and dead soldiers to the Red Cross, and the atmosphere in the interior was orderly and tranquil. On the first floor, in whose offices they'd found auxiliary employees, many were sleeping peacefully in their chairs and on their desks, and others were involved in invented pastimes. There was not the slightest sign of hostility, rather the exact opposite, against the uniformed *muchachos* who inspected the place every four hours. Even more: in some of the public offices they'd made coffee for them, and many of the hostages expressed sympathy and solidarity, even in writing, and had asked to remain there in any case as voluntary hostages.

In the Blue Room, where the most valuable hostages were concentrated, the negotiators had been able to observe that the atmosphere was as serene as it was on the first floor. None of the deputies had offered the slightest resistance, they'd been disarmed without difficulty, and as the hours went by they noticed growing rancor among them against Somoza for the slowness of the agreements. The guerrillas, for their part, were polite and sure of themselves, but also resolute. Their reply to the ambiguities of the second document was categorical: if there were no definitive responses within four hours, they would begin to execute hostages.

Somoza must have then understood that his calculations were in vain, and conceived the fear of a popular insurrection, the symptoms of which were beginning to be seen in different places around the country. So at 1:30 on Wednesday afternoon, in his third message, he accepted the most bitter of the conditions: the reading of the FSLN's political document over all the airwaves of the country. At six in the evening, two and a half hours later, the transmission was over.

### FORTY-FIVE HOURS WITHOUT SLEEP

Although they had still not arrived at any accord, the truth seemed to be that Somoza was ready to capitulate from noon on Wednesday. In fact, by then the prisoners in Managua had received orders to pack their bags to travel. The majority of them had been informed of the action by the prison guards, and many of these, in different jails, expressed their secret sympathies. In the interior of the country, the political prisoners were being driven to Managua long before any accord was in sight.

At the same time, the security services of Panama told General Omar Torrijos that a mid-level Nicaraguan bureaucrat wanted to know if he was prepared to send a plane for the guerrillas and liberated prisoners. Torrijos agreed. Minutes later he received a call from the president of Venezuela, Carlos Andrés Pérez, who was very well informed about the negotiations and considerably worried about the fate of the Sandinistas, and wanted to coordinate the transport operation with his colleague in Panama. That afternoon, the Panamanian government rented an Electra commercial airplane from the COPA company, and Venezuela sent an enormous Hercules. Both planes, ready to take off, waited for the end of the negotiations at the Panama airport.

Negotiations culminated, in fact, at four on Wednesday afternoon, and at the last minute Somoza tried to impose on the guerrillas a three-hour deadline to leave the country, but they refused, for obvious reasons, to leave at night. The ten million dollars were reduced to five hundred thousand, but the FSLN decided not to argue anymore, first because the money was a secondary condition anyway, but especially because members of the commando were beginning to show dangerous signs of tiredness after two days without sleep under such intense pressure. Commander Zero noticed the first serious symptoms in himself, when he discovered he could not think where in the city of Managua the National Palace was located. A short time later Number One confessed that he'd been the victim of hallucination: he thought he could hear unreal trains passing through the Plaza de la República. Finally, Zero observed that Number Two had begun to nod off and in the blink of an eye she was on the brink of dropping her rifle. Then he understood that it was urgent they conclude that drama that would end up lasting, one minute at a time, forty-five long hours.

### JUBILANT FAREWELL

On Thursday morning at 9:30, twenty-six Sandinistas, five negotiators, and four hostages left the National Palace for the airport. The hostages were the most important ones: Luis Pallais Debayle, José Somoza, José Antonio Mora, and the deputy Eduardo Chamorro. At that hour, sixty political prisoners from all over the country were already on board the two planes that had arrived from Panama, where they would all request asylum a few hours later. The only ones missing, of course, were the twenty they never could have rescued.

The Sandinistas had put as final conditions that there should be no military presence in sight or any traffic on the road to the airport. Neither of the conditions was honored, because the government sent the National Guard into the streets to prevent any demonstration of popular sympathy. It was a vain attempt. A standing ovation accompanied the passage of the school bus, and people took to the streets to celebrate the victory, and a long line of cars and motorcycles, growing increasingly numerous and more enthusiastic, followed it all the way to the airport. Deputy Eduardo Chamorro was amazed by that explosion of popular jubilation. Commander One, who was traveling beside him, told him with the good humor of relief:

"You see: this is the only thing you can't buy with money."

September 1978, *Alternativa*, Bogotá

# The Cubans Face the Blockade

That night, the first of the blockade, in Cuba there were 482,560 automobiles, 343,300 refrigerators, 549,700 radios, 303,500 television sets, 352,900 electric irons, 286,400 fans, 41,800 washing machines, 3,510,000 wristwatches, 63 locomotives, and 12 merchant ships. All these things, except for the wristwatches, which were Swiss, had been made in the United States.

It seems that a certain amount of time had to pass before the Cubans realized what those mortal numbers meant to their lives. From the point of view of production, Cuba soon found that it was not actually a distinct country but rather a commercial peninsula of the United States. As well as the sugar and tobacco industries depending entirely on *yanqui* consortiums, everything consumed on the island was made by the United States, whether in its own territory or in the territory of Cuba. Havana and two or three more cities inland gave the impression of the happiness of abundance, but in reality there was nothing that didn't belong to someone else, from the toothbrushes to the twenty-story glass hotels on the Malecón. Cuba imported from the United States almost thirty thousand useful and useless articles for daily life. Including the best clients of that market of illusions, who were the same tourists who arrived on the ferry boat from West Palm Beach or the sea train from New Orleans, for they too preferred to buy the items imported from their own country duty-free. Papayas, which Christopher Columbus discovered in Cuba on his first voyage, are sold in air-conditioned stores with the yellow sticker of the growers in the Bahamas. The artificial eggs that housewives spurn for their languid yolks and pharmacy taste have the brand symbol of a North Carolina factory farm stamped on their shells, but some savvy grocers wash them with solvent and daub them with chicken poop to sell them at a higher price, as if they were local.

There was no consumer sector that was not dependent on the United States. The few factories making simple goods that had been set up in Cuba to take advantage of cheap labor were put together out of secondhand machinery that had gone out of fashion in its country of origin. The best-qualified technicians were Americans, and the majority of the few Cuban technicians gave in to the luminous offers their foreign bosses made and went with them to the United States. There were no storehouses of replacement parts, either, for Cuba's illusory industry rested on the foundation of having replacement parts just ninety miles away, and a simple phone call was all it took to have the most difficult piece arriving on the next plane without any taxes or delays through customs.

In spite of such a state of dependence, the inhabitants of the cities carried on spending immeasurably when the blockade was a brutal reality. Even many Cubans who were ready to die for the revolution, and some who in fact did die for it, continued consuming with childish joy. More than that: the first measures the revolution took had immediately increased the buying power of the poorest classes, and they did not then have any other notion of happiness than the simple pleasure of consumption. Many dreams postponed for half a lifetime or even for entire lifetimes were realized all of a sudden. Only the things that sold out at the market were not replaced immediately, and some would not be replaced for many years, so the department stores that had been stunningly well stocked a month before were soon left stripped to the bone.

Cuba in those initial years was the kingdom of improvisation and disorder. Lacking a new moral—which would still need a long time to form in the conscience of the populace—Caribbean machismo had found its raison d'être in that general state of emergency. The national sentiment was so excited by that irrepressible gale of novelty and autonomy, and at the same time the threats of the wounded reaction were just as true and imminent, that many people confused one thing with the other and seemed to think that the shortage of milk could be resolved by gunfire. The impression of a phenomenal *pachanga* dance party that the Cuba of those days stirred up in the visiting foreigners had a true basis in reality and in the Cuban spirit, but it was also an innocent rapture on the edge of disaster. In fact, I had returned to Havana for the second time at the beginning of 1961, in my capacity of roving correspondent for Prensa Latina, and the first thing that caught my attention was that the visible appearance of the country had changed very little, but the social tension was beginning to get unbearable. I had flown from Santiago to Havana on a splendid March afternoon, looking out the window at the miraculous fields of that riverless country, the dusty villages, the hidden coves, and all through the long trip I had perceived signs of war. Giant red crosses within white circles had been painted on the rooftops of hospitals to keep them safe from predicted bombardments. Also on the schools, the churches, and retirement homes there were similar signs. In the civilian airports of Santiago and Camagüey there were Second World War antiaircraft guns disguised under the canvas of transport trucks, and the coasts were patrolled by speedboats that had been recreational and were now destined to prevent the landing of troops. Everywhere you could see the havoc wreaked by recent sabotage: sugar-cane plantations torched by incendiary bombs dropped by planes sent from Miami, ruins of factories dynamited by the internal resistance, improvised military camps in difficult zones where the first groups hostile to the revolution were beginning to operate with modern armaments and excellent logistical resources. At the Havana airport, where it was obvious they were making an effort so the war atmosphere would go unnoticed, there was a gigantic announcement from one edge of the cornice to the other on the main building: "Cuba, free territory of the Americas." Instead of the bearded soldiers of last time, security was the job of very young militiamen and women in olive-green uniforms, and their weapons were still those from the old arsenals of the dictatorship. There were no others yet. The first modern weapons the revolution managed to buy despite the contrarian pressures from the United States had arrived from Belgium on March 4 last year, on board the French ship *La Coubre,* which exploded at the Havana docks due to sabotage with seven hundred tons of weapons and ammunition in its holds. The attack killed seventy-five people and injured two hundred workers at the port, but was not claimed by anyone and the Cuban government attributes it to the CIA. It was at the funeral of the victims that Fidel Castro proclaimed the motto that would turn into the divisive maxim of the new Cuba: "*Patria o muerte.*" I had seen it written for the first time in the streets of Santiago, I'd seen it painted with a broad brush over the enormous billboards advertising North American airlines and toothpaste along the dusty highway to the Camagüey airport, and I found it again repeated without respite on little improvised pieces of cardboard in the windows of the tourist shops in the Havana airport, in the waiting rooms and at the counters, and painted with white lead on the mirrors of hair salons, and in lipstick on the windshields of taxis. It had achieved such a level of social saturation that there was no place and no moment when that furious motto was not written, from the drums of the sugar mills to the bottoms of official documents, and the papers, radio, and television repeated it pitilessly for entire days and interminable months, until it was incorporated into the very essence of Cuban life.

In Havana, the party was at its peak. There were splendid women who sang on the balconies, luminous birds in the sea, music everywhere, but beneath the joy you could feel the creative conflict of a way of life already forever condemned, that was struggling to prevail against another different way of life, still ingenuous, but inspired and devastating. The city continued to be a sanctuary of pleasure, with slot machines even in the pharmacies and aluminum automobiles too big for the colonial corners, but the appearance and behavior of the people was changing in an incredible way. All the sediment of the social subsoil had come to light, and an eruption of human lava, dense and steamy, scattered without control into all the twists and turns of the liberated city, and spread with a tumultuous vertigo to its last traces. The most noticeable was how naturally poor people sat in the seats of the rich in public places. They had invaded the lobbies of the luxury hotels, were eating with their fingers on the terraces of the Vedado cafés, and baking in the sun at the swimming pools with luminous colored water in the formerly exclusive clubs of Siboney. The blond porter at the Hotel Havana Hilton, which was starting to be called the Habana Libre, had been replaced by obliging militia kids who spent the day convincing the *campesinos* that they could come in without fear, showing them that there was one entrance door and another to exit, and that they didn't run any risk of catching tuberculosis from entering the air-conditioned lobby while sweating. A swaggering dude from Luyanó, very dark and slim, in a shirt with painted butterflies and patent leather shoes with Andalusian dancer heels, had tried to enter backward through the revolving glass doors of the Hotel Riviera, just when the succulent, dolled-up wife of a European diplomat was trying to leave. In a flash of instantaneous panic, the husband of the latter tried to force the door in one direction while the flustered militiamen outside tried to force it the opposite way. The white woman and the black man were stuck for a fraction of a second in the crystal trap, squashed in a space meant for a single person, until the door began to spin again and the confused and blushing woman ran, without even waiting for her husband, and hopped into the limousine that was awaiting her with the door open and which took off instantly. The black man, without really knowing what had just happened, was left confused and quivering.

"*Coño!*" he sighed. "She smelled of flowers!"

There were frequent setbacks. And this was understandable because the buying power of the urban and rural population had increased by a considerable extent in one year. Electricity, telephone, transport, and general public service rates had been reduced to humanitarian levels. The prices of hotels and restaurants, as with transport, had been lowered drastically, and special excursions were organized from the countryside to the city and from the city to the countryside, which were often free. Besides, unemployment was going down by leaps and bounds, wages were going up, and urban reform had alleviated the monthly anxiety of rent, and education and school supplies cost nothing. The twenty leagues of marble flour on the beaches of Varadero, which used to have just one owner and the enjoyment of which was reserved for the excessively wealthy rich, were opened without conditions for everyone, including the rich. Cubans, like Caribbean people in general, had always believed that money was only for spending, and for the first time in the history of their country they were proving it in practice.

I think very few of us were aware of the stealthy but irreparable way shortages were gradually intruding on our lives. Even after the Bay of Pigs landing the casinos were still open, and some little hookers without tourists hung around hoping some guy who got lucky at roulette might save their night. It's obvious that as conditions were changing, those solitary swallows were getting gloomier and cheaper all the time. But in any case, the nights of Havana and Guantánamo were still long and sleepless, and the music from parties for rent went on till dawn. Those vestiges of the old life kept up the illusion of normalcy and abundance that neither the nocturnal explosions nor the constant rumors of vile aggression, or even the real imminence of war, managed to extinguish, but it's been a long time since they were true.

Sometimes there was no beef in the restaurants after midnight, but we didn't care, because there might be chicken. Sometimes there were no plantains, but we didn't care, because there might be yams. The musicians from the neighboring clubs, and the undaunted pimps who awaited the night's yield in front of a glass of beer, seemed as distracted as we were at the uncontainable erosion of daily life.

At the shopping center the first lines had appeared, and an incipient but very active black market began to control industrially produced articles, but no one thought very seriously that this was happening because things were lacking; rather the opposite, they thought it was because there was a surplus of money. At that time, someone needed an aspirin after we'd been to a movie and we couldn't find one in three drugstores. We found one at the fourth, and the pharmacist explained without alarm that aspirin had been in short supply for three months. The truth is that not just aspirin but many essential things had been scarce for a while, but nobody seemed to think that they would run out completely. Almost a year after the United States decreed a total embargo on trade with Cuba, life continued without very notable changes, not as much in reality as in the spirit of the people.

I became aware of the blockade in a terrible, but at the same time a bit of a lyrical, way, as I'd become aware of almost everything in life. After a night shift at the Prensa Latina office I left alone and slightly sluggish to look for something to eat. Dawn was breaking. The sea was in a tranquil mood, and a yellow breach separated it from the sky on the horizon. I walked down the middle of the deserted avenue, against the salty wind of the Malecón, looking for some open place to eat under the corroded and seeping stone arcades of the old city. Finally I found a small restaurant with the metal shutters down but unlocked, and I tried to raise them to go in because there was light inside and a man polishing glasses at the counter. I had barely attempted it when I heard the unmistakable sound of a rifle being cocked behind me, and a very sweet but steadfast voice.

"Hold it, comrade," she said. "Hands up."

She was an apparition in the morning mist. She had a very beautiful face, with her hair tied back in a ponytail at the nape of her neck, and a military shirt drenched by the wind off the sea. She was startled, no doubt, but she had her heels separated and well fixed on the ground, and she held her rifle like a soldier.

"I'm hungry," I said.

Maybe I said it with too much conviction, because only then did she understand that I hadn't been trying to break into the place, and her distrust turned into pity.

"It's very late," she said.

"Just the opposite," I replied. "The problem is that it's too early. What I want is breakfast."

Then I made hand signals through the glass and convinced the man to serve me some food, even though it was two hours before he was going to open. I ordered eggs and ham, coffee with milk, bread and butter, and fresh fruit juice, whatever kind he had. The man told me with a suspicious precision that there hadn't been any eggs or ham in a week and no milk for three days, and the only thing he could serve me was black coffee and bread without butter, and maybe a bit of reheated macaroni from last night. Surprised, I asked him what was going on with foodstuffs, and my surprise was so innocent that it was he who felt surprised.

"Nothing's going on," he told me. "Just that this country has gone to hell."

He was no enemy of the revolution, as I imagined at first. Just the opposite: he was the last of a family of eleven who had all fled to Miami. He had decided to stay, and indeed he stayed forever, but his trade allowed him to decipher the future with more realistic elements than a sleepless journalist. He was thinking that in less than three months he'd have to close his diner due to lack of food, but he didn't mind too much because he already had very well defined plans for his personal future.

It was a very accurate prediction. On March 12, 1962, when three hundred and twenty-two days had passed since the beginning of the blockade, drastic rationing was imposed on foodstuffs. Each adult was assigned a monthly ration of three pounds of beef, one of fish, one of chicken, six of rice, two of lard, one and a half of beans, four ounces of butter, and five eggs. It was a ration calculated so that every Cuban could consume a normal quota of calories daily. There were special rations for children, according to age, and everyone under fourteen had the right to a liter of milk a day. Later there began to be shortages of nails, detergent, light bulbs, and many other urgent household articles, and the authorities' problem was not regulating them but acquiring them. The most admirable thing was seeing to what extent that scarcity imposed by the enemy was strengthening social morale. The same year that rationing was established saw the October Crisis, which the British historian Hugh Thomas has qualified as the gravest crisis in the history of humanity, and a huge majority of the Cuban people remained in a state of alert for a month, immobile in their combat sites until the danger seemed to have been warded off, and prepared to confront the atomic bomb with shotguns. In the midst of that massive mobilization, which would have been enough to unhinge any well-positioned economy, industrial production reached unusual figures, absenteeism ended in factories, and obstacles, which in less dramatic circumstances would have been fatal, were avoided. A New York telephone operator said to a Cuban colleague on one occasion that in the United States they were very frightened about what might happen.

"Whereas here we're very calm," the Cuban operator answered. "After all, the atomic bomb doesn't hurt."

The country then produced enough shoes so that every Cuban could buy a new pair every year, so distribution was channeled through the schools and workplaces. Only in August 1963, when almost all the stores were closed because there was absolutely nothing to sell, was the distribution of clothing regulated. They began by rationing nine articles, among them men's trousers, underwear for both sexes, and certain kinds of textiles, but within a year they had to increase it to fifteen.

That was the first Christmas of the revolution celebrated without suckling pig and *turrón*, and the first time toys were rationed. However, and thanks precisely to rationing, it was also the first Christmas in the history of Cuba when every single child, with no distinction whatsoever, had at least one toy. In spite of the intense Soviet aid and the help from the People's Republic of China, which was no less generous in those days, and in spite of the assistance of numerous socialist and Latin American specialists, the blockade was then an unavoidable reality that would contaminate the most recondite cracks of daily life and hasten the new irreversible course of Cuban history. Communications with the rest of the world had been reduced to the essential minimum. The five daily flights to Miami and twice-weekly Cubana de Aviación flights to New York stopped with the October Crisis. The few Latin American airlines that flew to Cuba gradually canceled them as their countries suspended diplomatic and commercial relations, and only a weekly flight from Mexico remained that for many years served as the umbilical cord to the rest of the Americas, though it was also a channel for infiltration for the services of subversion and espionage of the United States. Cubana de Aviación, with its fleet reduced to the epic Bristol Britannias, which were only maintained by way of special accords with the English manufacturers, provided an almost acrobatic flight over the polar route to Prague. A letter from Caracas, less than a thousand miles from the Cuban coast, had to go halfway around the world to get to Havana. Telephone connections with the rest of the world had to go through Miami or New York, under the control of the United States secret services, by way of a prehistoric undersea cable, which was broken on one occasion by a Cuban ship that left Havana harbor dragging the anchor it had forgotten to weigh. The only source of energy were the five million tons of petroleum that Soviet tankers transported every year from the ports of the Baltic, eight thousand miles away, and at a rate of one ship every fifty-three hours. The *Oxford*, a CIA boat equipped with all the latest espionage equipment, patrolled Cuban territorial waters for several years to make sure no capitalist country, apart from the very few who dared, contravened the will of the United States. It was also a calculated provocation in everybody's sight. From the Malecón in Havana or the higher neighborhoods of Santiago, people could see the luminous silhouette of that ship of provocation anchored in territorial waters.

Maybe very few Cubans remembered that on the other side of the Caribbean sea, three centuries earlier, the inhabitants of Cartagena de Indias had suffered a similar drama. The hundred and twenty best ships of the British navy, under the command of Admiral Vernon, had besieged the city with thirty thousand select soldiers, many of them recruited from the American colonies that would later become the United States. A brother of George Washington, the future liberator of those colonies, was one of the chiefs of staff of the assault troops. Cartagena de Indias, which was famous in the world then for its military fortifications and the frightful amount of rats in its sewers, resisted the siege with an invincible ferocity, despite its inhabitants eventually having to eat what they could find, from the bark of trees to the leather of stools. After several months, crushed by the bravery of the besieged, and decimated by yellow fever, dysentery, and the heat, the English retired in defeat. The inhabitants of the city, on the other hand, were healthy and full, but they'd eaten everything down to the last rat.

Many Cubans, of course, knew about this drama. But their rare sense of history prevents them from thinking it could be repeated. Nobody could have imagined in the uncertain New Year of 1964 that there were still worse times to come with that tight and heartless blockade, and that they'd reach such extremes as running out of drinking water in many homes and in almost all public establishments.

November–December 1978, *Alternativa,* Bogotá

# The Specter of the Nobel Prize

Every year, around these days, great writers are unsettled by a specter: the Nobel Prize for Literature. Jorge Luis Borges, who is one of the greatest and also one of the most assiduous candidates, once protested in an interview about the two months of anxiety he had to undergo due to the conjectures. It's inevitable: Borges is the writer of the highest artistic merits in the Spanish language, and they can't expect him to be excluded, if only for pity's sake, from the annual predictions. The bad thing is that the final result does not depend on the candidate's own right, and not even on the justice of the gods, but on the inscrutable will of the members of the Swedish Academy.

I don't remember an accurate prediction. The prizewinners, in general, seem to be the most surprised. When the Irish playwright Samuel Beckett received a telephone call informing him of his prize, in 1969, he exclaimed in consternation, "Oh God, what a catastrophe!" Pablo Neruda, in 1971, found out three days before the news was made public, by way of a confidential message from the Swedish Academy. But the following night he invited a group of friends for dinner in Paris, where he was then the ambassador for Chile, and none of us found out the reason for the party until the evening papers published the news. "I just don't believe in anything until I see it in print," Neruda told us later with his invincible laughter. A few days later, while we were having lunch in a clamorous restaurant on the Boulevard Montparnasse, he remembered he hadn't yet written his speech for the presentation ceremony, which would be held forty-eight hours later in Stockholm. So he turned over a page of the menu, and without a single pause, without worrying about the human uproar, as naturally as he breathed and with his usual, implacable green ink, in which he wrote his poetry, he wrote his stunning coronation speech right there.

The most common version among writers and critics is that the Swedish academics reach their agreement in May, when the snow begins to melt, and they study the work of the few finalists during the heat of the summer. In October, still bronzed from the southern sunshine, they issue their verdict. Another version claims that Jorge Luis Borges was the chosen one in May of 1976, but not in the final vote of November. Actually, the prizewinner that year was the magnificent and depressing Saul Bellow, quickly chosen at the last moment, in spite of the fact that the prizewinners for other subjects were also North Americans.

The truth is that on September 22 of that year—a month before the vote—Borges had done something that had nothing to do with his masterful literature: he visited Augusto Pinochet in a formal setting. "It is an undeserved honor to be received by yourself, *señor presidente*," he said in his ill-fated speech. "In Argentina, Chile, and Uruguay liberty and order are being saved," he continued, without anyone having asked him to. And he concluded impassively: "This is happening on an anarchized continent undermined by communism." It was easy to think that so many successive verbal atrocities were only possible to pull Pinochet's leg. But the Swedes did not understand the Buenos Aires sense of humor. Since then, Borges's name has disappeared from the predictions. Now, at the end of an unjust penance, it has reappeared, and nothing would please those of us who are his insatiable readers at the same time as his political adversaries more than knowing him at last freed from his annual anxiety.

His two most dangerous rivals are two English-language novelists. The first, who had figured without much noise in previous years, has now been the object of a spectacular promotion by the magazine

*Newsweek,* who put him on their August 18 cover as the great maestro of the novel; and rightly so. His full name is no less than Vidiadhar Surajprasad Naipaul, he's forty-seven years old, was born over here, next door to us, on the island of Trinidad, of an Indian father and Caribbean mother, and he is considered by some very severe critics the greatest living writer in the English language. The other candidate is Graham Greene, four years younger than Borges, with as many merits and as many years of delay in receiving that senile laurel.

In the autumn of 1972, in London, Naipaul did not seem very aware of being a Caribbean writer. I reminded him during a friendly gathering, and he was a little disconcerted; he reflected for a moment, and a new smile illuminated his taciturn face. "Good claim," he said. Graham Greene, on the other hand, who was born in Berkhamstead, didn't even blink when a journalist asked him if he was conscious of being a Latin American novelist. "Of course," he answered. "And I'm very happy about it, because Latin America is where the best novelists are these days, such as Jorge Luis Borges." A few years ago, talking about everything, I expressed to Graham Greene my perplexity and disgust that an author such as himself, with such a vast and original body of work, had not been given the Nobel Prize.

"They'll never give it to me," he said to me with absolute seriousness, "because they don't consider me a serious writer."

The Swedish Academy, which is in charge of awarding the Nobel Prize for Literature—just this one*—was founded in 1786, without any greater pretensions than to resemble the Académie Française. Nobody then imagined, of course, that in time it would come to acquire the biggest consecrating power in the world. It is composed of eighteen lifetime members of venerable ages, selected by the academy itself from among the most distinguished figures of Swedish letters. There are two philosophers, two historians, three specialists in Nordic languages, and only one woman. But that's not the only male chauvinist symptom; in the eighty years of the prize, it has only been awarded to six women,

---

* The other four prizes are for: Physics and Chemistry, awarded by the Royal Academy of Sciences; Medicine or Physiology, awarded by the Nobel Assembly at the Karolinska Institute, and Peace, granted by the Nobel Committee of the Norwegian Parliament.

as opposed to sixty-nine men. This year it will be awarded by an odd-number decision, since one of the most eminent academy members, Professor Lindroth Sten, died on September 3: fifteen days ago.

How they proceed, how they reach an agreement, what real compromises determine their designs, is one of the best-kept secrets of our times. Their criteria is unpredictable, contradictory, immune even to omens, and their decisions are secret, mutually binding, and final. If they weren't so serious, one might think they were animated by the prank of misleading the predictions. Nobody resembles death more than they do.

Another well-guarded secret is where the capital that produces such abundant dividends is invested. Alfred Nobel (with a stress on the *e* and not on the *o*) created the prize in 1895 with a capital of $9.2 million, the annual interest on which should be shared out each year, by November 15 at the latest, among the five prizewinners. The sum, therefore, is variable, depending on the year's harvest. In 1901, when the prizes were awarded for the first time, each laureate received 30,160 Swedish kroner. In 1979, which was the year with the most succulent interest rates, each received 160,000 kroner.

Rumormongers say the capital is invested in South African gold mines and that, therefore, the Nobel Prize lives off the blood of black slaves. The Swedish Academy, which has never made a public clarification or responded to any grievance, might defend itself with the argument that it is the Bank of Sweden, not the academy, that administers the cash. And banks, as everybody knows, have no heart.

The third enigma is the political criteria prevailing at the heart of the Swedish Academy. On several occasions, the prizes have led people to believe that its members are idealistic liberals. Its biggest, and most honorable, blunder was in 1938, when Hitler banned Germans from receiving the Nobel Prize, with the risible argument that their instigator was Jewish. Richard Kuhn, a German scientist who had been granted the Nobel Prize for Chemistry that year, had to refuse it. Out of conviction or prudence, none of the prizes were awarded during the Second World War. But as soon as Europe recovered from its afflictions, the Swedish Academy committed what seems to be its only regrettable blunder: they awarded the Literature Prize to Sir Winston Churchill only because he was the most prestigious man of his times, and it was not possible to give him any of the other prizes, much less the Peace Prize.

Maybe the Swedish Academy's most difficult relations have been with the Soviet Union. In 1958, when the prize was awarded to the very eminent Boris Pasternak, he refused it out of fear of not being allowed to return to his country. The Soviet authorities considered the prize to be a provocation. Nonetheless, in 1965, when the prizewinner was Mikhail Sholokhov, the most official of official Soviet writers, his country's authorities celebrated with jubilation. On the other hand, five years later, when it was granted to the foremost dissident, Alexander Solzhenitsyn, the Soviet government blew its top and went so far as to say that the Nobel Prize was an instrument of imperialism. I have it on good authority, however, that the warmest congratulations Pablo Neruda received came from the Soviet Union, and some of them from very high-level officials. "For us," a Soviet friend told me, smiling, "the Nobel Prize is good when it's given to a writer we like, and bad when the opposite happens." The explanation is not as simplistic as it appears. Deep down in our hearts we all have the same view.

The only member of the Swedish Academy who reads in Spanish, and very well, is the poet Artur Lundkvist. He is the one who knows the work of our writers, who proposes their candidacy, and who wages secret battles for them. This has converted him, very much to his chagrin, into a remote and enigmatic deity, on whom to a certain extent the universal destiny of our literatures depends. However, in real life he is a youthful old man, with a slightly Latin sense of humor, and with such a modest house that it's impossible to think that anyone's destiny might depend on him.

Some years ago, after a typical Swedish dinner in that house—with cold meats and warm beer—Lundkvist invited us to have coffee in his library. I was astonished. It was incredible to find such a quantity of books in Spanish, the best and worst all mixed up together, and almost all of them signed by their once hopeful authors whether living, expiring, or dead. I asked the poet's permission to read some of the dedications, and he granted it with a kind and complicit smile. Most of them were so affectionate, and some so direct and heartfelt, that when the time came to write my own I thought a mere signature would be indiscreet. A guy could get a complex, damn it!

October 8, 1980, *El País*, Madrid

# Telepathy Without Strings

A noted French neurologist, a full-time researcher, told me the other night that he had discovered a function of the human brain that seemed to be of great importance. He only had one problem: he hadn't been able to establish what it was for. I asked him, with a certain hopefulness, if there wasn't any possibility that it might be the function that regulates premonitions, portentous dreams, and the transmission of thoughts. His only response was a pitying look.

I had seen that same look eighteen years earlier, when I asked a similar question of a very dear friend, who was also investigating the human brain, at the University of Mexico. My opinion, already by then, was that telepathy and its diverse means are not the stuff of sorcerers, as some incredulous people seem to believe, but simple organic faculties that science repudiates, because it does not know them, just as it repudiated the theory that the Earth is round when they believed it to be flat. My friend admitted, if I remember correctly, that the area of the brain whose functions are fully verified is very small, but he refused to admit that in the rest of those shadows there might be a place to anticipate the future.

I made telepathic jokes that he disqualified as pure coincidences, in spite of some of them seeming too obvious. One night I phoned him to invite him to our house for dinner, and only afterward did I realize there wasn't enough food in the kitchen. I called him back to ask him to bring a particular and unusual bottle of wine, and a piece of Iberian sausage. Mercedes shouted from the kitchen to ask him to pick up some dish soap as well. But he'd already left his house. However, at the moment of hanging up the phone, I had the clear impression that, by an impossible to explain marvel, my friend had received the message. Then I wrote it down on a piece of paper, so he wouldn't doubt my version, and out of pure poetic virtuosity I added that he would also bring a rose. A little while later, he and his wife arrived with the things we'd requested, including the same brand of dish soap we used. "The supermarket happened to be open, and we decided to bring you these things," they said, almost apologizing. Only the rose was missing. That day my friend and I began a different dialogue that still hasn't finished. The last time I saw him, six months ago, was entirely devoted to establishing in which part of the brain the conscience is found.

Life, more than one believes, is embellished by this mystery. The night before the assassination of Julius Caesar, his wife Calpurnia saw with terror all the windows of the house suddenly opened at the same time, with no wind and no noise. Centuries later, the novelist Thornton Wilder attributed to Julius Caesar a phrase that is not in his war memoirs or in the fascinating chronicles of Plutarch and Suetonius, but defines better than anything the human condition of the emperor: "I govern innumerable men, but must acknowledge that I am governed by birds and thunderclaps." The history of humanity—since young Joseph deciphered dreams in Egypt—is full of these fabulous flashes. I know identical twins who had pain in the same molar at the same time in different cities, and who when they're together have the sensation that the thoughts of one interfere with those of the other. Many years ago, in a tiny village on the Caribbean coast, I knew a healer who prided himself on curing animals from a distance if he was given a precise description and the place where it was. I saw it with my own eyes: an infected cow, whose live maggots were falling out of ulcers, while the healer was reciting a secret prayer several leagues away. However, I only remember one experiment that had taken these faculties seriously in current history. The U.S. Navy, which didn't have a means to communicate with the nuclear submarines navigating beneath the polar ice cap, decided to try telepathy. Two compatible people, one in Washington and another on board a submarine, tried to establish a system for exchanging thought messages. It was a failure, of course, for telepathy is unpredictable and spontaneous, and does not allow for any kind of systemization. That's its defense. Every prediction, from a morning's foreboding to the prophecies of Nostradamus, comes coded from its conception and is only comprehended when it comes true. If it were not like that, it would defeat itself in advance.

I speak of this with such propriety because my maternal grandmother was the most lucid adept I ever knew in the science of portents. She was an old-school Catholic, so she repudiated as artifices of the black arts anything that pretended to be a methodical divination of the future. Whether they were cards, the lines in a palm, or the evocation of spirits. But she was a master of her omens. I remember her in the kitchen in our big house in Aracataca, watching over the secret signs of the fragrant breads she was taking out of the oven.

Once she saw 09 written in the leftover flour, and she moved heaven and earth until she found a lottery ticket with that number. She lost. However, the following week she won an Italian coffeepot in a raffle, with a ticket my grandfather had bought and forgotten in the pocket of his jacket the week before. It was number 09. My grandfather had seventeen children of the kind they then called "natural"—as if the ones from marriage were artificial—and my grandmother treated them as her own. They were spread out all over the coast, but she talked to all of them at breakfast time, and found out about the health of each one and how their businesses were going as if she kept up an immediate and secret correspondence. It was the tremendous era of telegrams that arrived when they were least expected and entered the house like a gust of panic. A telegram would be passed from one hand to the next with nobody daring to open it, until the providential idea occurred to someone to get a small child to open it, as if innocence had the virtue of changing the evil of bad news.

This happened once in our house, and the bewildered adults decided to leave the telegram without opening it until later, when my grandfather arrived. My grandmother didn't bat an eyelid. "It's from Prudencia Iguarán to let us know she's on her way," she said. "Last night I dreamed she was coming to visit." When my grandfather came home he didn't even have to open the telegram. He came home with Prudencia Iguarán, whom he'd met by chance at the train station, in a dress covered in painted birds and with a massive bouquet of flowers, and convinced that my grandfather was there due to the infallible magic of her telegram.

My grandmother died when she was almost a hundred years old without ever having won the lottery. She had gone blind, and in her final years she raved in a way that made it impossible to follow the thread of her reason. She refused to get undressed to go to sleep while the radio was on, in spite of our explanations every night that the announcer was not inside the house. She thought we were tricking her, because she could never believe in a diabolical machine that allowed us to hear someone who was talking in another faraway city.

November 25, 1980, *El País*, Madrid

# The New Oldest Profession

The Parisian autumn began suddenly and late this year, with a glacial wind that plucked the last golden leaves from the trees. The café terraces closed at midday, life became unsettled, and the radiant summer that had lasted longer than it should have turned into a fickleness of memory. It seemed as if several months had passed in a few hours. Dusk was premature and gloomy, but nobody really complained, for this misty weather is natural to Paris, what most often and best suits this city.

The most beautiful of the women for rent who routinely stroll the alleys of the Quartier Pigalle was a splendid blonde who in a less obvious place would have been mistaken for a movie star. She was wearing a black pantsuit, which was the height of fashion, and when the icy wind began to blow put on a real mink coat. There she was, offering herself for two hundred francs in front of an hourly rate hotel on Rue Duperré, when a car pulled up in front of her. From the driver's seat, another beautiful and well-dressed woman shot straight at her seven times with a rifle. That night, when the police caught the murderer, that outskirts drama had already echoed through the newspapers, because it had two new elements that made it different. In fact, neither the victim nor the killer was blond or lovely, but were two fully grown men, and both were from Brazil.

The news did nothing but demonstrate what is already well known in Europe: street prostitution in the big cities is now a job for men, and the most sought after among them, the most expensive and best dressed, are young Latin Americans disguised as women. According to press reports, of the two hundred cross-dressing street workers in France, at least half of them have come from Brazil. In Spain, England, Switzerland, or West Germany, where the trade seems to be even more lucrative, the number is much higher and the nationalities more varied. The phenomenon has different nuances in each country, but in all of them it presents itself as a fundamental change in the oldest and most conservative profession in the world.

When I was in Europe for the first time, twenty-five years ago, prostitution was a prosperous and orderly industry, with precise categories and very well shared out territories. I was still clinging to my idyllic image of Caribbean brothels, those courtyards full of dancing with colored garlands in the almond trees, undaunted hens wandering around pecking the ground amid the music and the lovely untamed mulatas who sold themselves more for the fiesta than for the money and who sometimes committed the enormous naïveté of lovelorn suicide. Sometimes, I would stay with them, not so much for straying—as my mother would say—but for the pleasure of hearing them breathe in their sleep. Breakfasts there were more homey and affectionate than at home, and the real party started at eleven in the morning, under the dull almond trees.

Brought up in such a human school, I couldn't help but be depressed by the commercial rigor of the Europeans. In Geneva they prowled the lakeshore, and the only thing that distinguished them from the upstanding wives were the colorful open parasols they carried rain or shine, day or night, like a stigma of their class. In Rome I heard them whistle like birds among the trees of the Villa Borghese, and in London they became invisible in the fog and had to turn on lights that seemed like ship's lanterns so one could find their course. The ones in Paris, idealized by the *maudit* poets and bad French films of the 1930s, were the harshest. Nevertheless, in the all-night bars of the Champs-Élysées one suddenly discovered their human side: they cried like girlfriends over the despotism of their pimps, unsatisfied with the night's takings. It was hard to understand such meekness of heart in women hardened by such a brutal job. So great was my curiosity that, years later, I met a pimp and asked him how it was possible to dominate with an iron fist such rough women, and he answered impassively, "With love." I didn't ask anything else, in fear of understanding even less.

The irruption of transvestites in that world of exploitation and death has only managed to make it more sordid. Their revolution consists of carrying out two jobs at once: that of prostitutes and that of their own pimps. They are autonomous and fierce. Many nocturnal territories that women have left as too dangerous have been taken over by them and their concealed weapons. But in most cities they have confronted the women and their pimps with hammer blows, and are exercising their right of conquest over the best street corners in Europe. The fact that many Latin Americans are participating in this apotheosis of machismo is nothing to boast of. It is yet another proof of our social disturbances and shouldn't alarm us any more than other weightier ones.

The majority, of course, are homosexuals. They have splendid silicon busts, and some of them end up realizing the gilded dream of a drastic operation that leaves them forever installed in the opposite sex. But many are not, and they have taken to the life with their weapons—borrowed or usurped by force—because it is a bad way to earn a good living. Some are peaceful family men who spend the day in charitable work and at night, when the children are asleep, take to the streets in their wives' Sunday dresses. Others are poor students who are thus able to pay for their studies. The most able make up to five hundred dollars on a good night. Which—according to my wife, here at my side—is a better wage than writing earns.

December 2, 1980, *El País*, Madrid

# Yes, Nostalgia Is the Same as It Ever Was

It has been a worldwide victory for poetry. In a century in which the winners are always those who hit hardest, who take the most votes, who score the most goals, the richest men and the most beautiful women, the commotion caused all over the world by the death of a man who has done nothing but sing to love is encouraging. It's the apotheosis of those who never win.

For forty-eight hours no one has talked of anything else. Three generations—ours, that of our children, and that of our oldest grandchildren—have for the first time the impression of living through a collective catastrophe, and for the same reasons. The reporters on television asked an eighty-year-old woman in the street what her favorite John Lennon song was, and she answered, as if she were fifteen, "Happiness Is a Warm Gun." A boy who was watching the program said, "I like them all." My younger son asked a girl his age why John Lennon was killed, and she answered, as if she were eighty years old, "Because the world is ending."

That's how it is: the only nostalgia you can have in common with your children are Beatles songs. Each for different reasons, of course, and with different pain, as always happens with poetry. I'll never forget that memorable day in 1963, in Mexico, when I heard a Beatles song for the first time in a conscious way. From that moment on I discovered they had infested the whole world. In our house in San Ángel, where we barely had room to sit down, there were only two records: a selection of Debussy preludes and the Beatles' first album. In every city, at all hours, crowds were heard shouting, "Help, I need somebody." Someone brought up the old idea that all the best musicians began with the second letter of the catalog: Bach, Beethoven, Brahms, and Bartók. Someone said with the same silliness as usual that Mozart had to be included. Álvaro Mutis, who like all great erudites of music has a weakness for symphonic bricks, insisted on including Bruckner. Someone else tried to repeat again the battle in favor of Berlioz, which I waged on the opposing side because I couldn't overcome the superstition that he's a *oiseau de malheur*, that is, a bad-omen bird. Whereas I insisted, ever since then, on including the Beatles. Emilio García Riera, who agreed with me and is a film critic and historian of almost supernatural lucidity, especially after the second drink, said to me back in those days, "I listen to the Beatles with a certain amount of fear, because I think I'm going to remember them for the rest of my life." It's the only case I know of someone clairvoyant enough to realize he's witnessing the birth of his own nostalgias. We used to walk into Carlos Fuentes's study and find him typing with a single finger of one hand, as he always has, in the middle of a dense cloud of smoke and isolated from the horrors of the universe by the music of the Beatles at full blast.

As always happens, we thought we were very far from being happy then, and now we think the opposite. It's the trick of nostalgia, removing bitter moments from their place and painting them another color, and putting them back where they no longer hurt. As in old portraits, which seem illuminated by the illusory brilliance of happiness, and where we only see with astonishment how young we were when we were young, and not only those of us who were there, but also the house and the trees in the background, and even the chairs we were sitting on. Che Guevara, talking with his men around the fire on an empty wartime night, once said that nostalgia begins with food. It's true, but only when you're hungry. However, it always starts with music. Actually, our personal past moves away from us starting from the moment we're born, but we only feel it when a record ends.

This afternoon, thinking all of this while watching snow fall outside a mournful window, more than fifty years old and still not knowing very well who I am, or what the hell I'm doing here, I have the impression that the world was the same from my birth until the Beatles started to sing. Everything changed then. Men let their hair and beards grow, women learned to take their clothes off naturally, styles of dressing and loving changed, and thus the liberation of sex and of other drugs for dreaming began. They were the clamorous days of the Vietnam War and university rebellion. But, most of all, it was a tough apprenticeship of a different relationship between parents and their children, the beginning of a new dialogue that had seemed impossible for centuries.

The symbol of all this—at the front of the Beatles—was John Lennon. His absurd death leaves us a different world populated by beautiful images. In "Lucy in the Sky with Diamonds," one of their most beautiful songs, newspaper dogs wear looking-glass ties. In "Eleanor Rigby"—with an obstinate bass line of baroque cellos—a desolate girl is left to pick up the rice in a church where a wedding has been. "All the lonely people, where do they all come from?" is the unanswered question. Father McKenzie is also left writing sermons that no one will hear, wiping his hands as he walks from a grave, and a girl takes off her face and leaves it in a jar by the door when she goes in the house and puts it back on again when she goes out. These creatures have caused people to say that John Lennon was a surrealist, which is something said too easily of everything that seems odd, as people who don't know how to read him tend to say of Kafka. For others, he is the visionary of a better world. Someone who let us understand that old people aren't those of us who've lived for many years, but those who didn't get on board their children's train in time.

December 16, 1980, *El País*, Madrid

# Horror Story for New Year's Eve

We arrived in Arezzo a little before noon, and we wasted almost two hours looking for the medieval castle that the writer Miguel Otero Silva had bought at that idyllic bend in the Tuscan countryside. It was a burning and bustling Sunday near the beginning of August, and it was not easy to find anyone who knew anything in the streets invaded by tourists. After many futile attempts we went back to the car, left the city by an unsignposted track, and an old woman who was herding geese showed us precisely where the castle was. Before she said goodbye she asked us if we were planning to sleep there, and we answered—as we had planned—that we were only going there for lunch. "Thank goodness," she said, "because that house is full of frights." My wife and I, who do not believe in apparitions in broad daylight, made fun of her credulity. But the children were delighted at the idea of meeting a ghost in the flesh.

Miguel Otero Silva, who as well as a good writer is a splendid host and an exacting gourmet, was waiting for us with an unforgettable lunch. Since we were late, we didn't have time to see the interior of the castle before sitting down at the table, but from outside it didn't look at all terrifying, and any concern was mitigated by a view of the entire city from the summer terrace where we had lunch. It was difficult to believe that on that crowded hill of houses piled on top of each other, with barely enough room for ninety thousand people, so many of lasting genius had been born, such as Guido d'Arezzo, who invented musical notation, or the splendid Giorgio Vasari and the foul-mouthed Pietro Aretino, or Julio II and Gaius Cilnius Maecenas himself, the two great patrons of the arts and literature of their day. However, Miguel Otero Silva told us with his habitual sense of humor that such high historical figures were not the most distinguished of Arezzo. "The most important," he told us, "was Ludovico." Just like that, without need of any surnames: Ludovico, the great gentleman of the arts and of war who had constructed that castle of his misfortune.

Miguel Otero Silva told us about Ludovico during the whole lunch. He told us about his immeasurable power, his unhappy love, and his dreadful death. He told us how it was that, in a heartbeat of madness, he had stabbed his lady in the bed where they had just been making love, and then sicked on himself his ferocious war dogs, who tore him to pieces. He assured us, very seriously, that after midnight the specter of Ludovico wandered through his castle in darkness, trying to get a moment's serenity from his purgatory of love. Nevertheless, in the light of day, with a full stomach and contented heart, that could not seem like anything other than a joke, like so many others that Miguel Otero Silva told to entertain his guests.

The castle, in reality, was immense and somber, as we discovered after a siesta. Its two upper floors and eighty-two rooms had suffered all kinds of alterations by its successive owners. Miguel Otero Silva had restored the whole ground floor and had a modern bedroom constructed with marble floors and a sauna and exercise facilities, as well as the terrace with its intense flowers where we'd had lunch. "They're things from Caracas to mislead Ludovico," he told us. I had heard it said, in fact, that the only thing that confuses ghosts are labyrinths of time.

The second floor was untouched. It had been the one most used over the course of the centuries, but now it was a succession of characterless rooms, with abandoned furniture from different eras. The top floor was the most abandoned of all, but one room was conserved intact, where time had forgotten to pass. It was Ludovico's bedchamber. It was a magic moment. There was the canopy bed, with its curtains embroidered with golden thread and the bedspread with its marvelous trimmings still spattered with the blood of his slaughtered lover. There was the fireplace with the cold ashes and the petrified last log, the wardrobe with its well-primed weapons, and the portrait in oils of the pensive gentleman, painted by one of the Florentine masters who was not fortunate enough to survive his times. However, what most struck me was the scent of fresh strawberries that lingered, with no possible explanation, in the room's air.

Summer days are long and unhurried in Tuscany, and the horizon stays in its place until nine at night. After showing us the interior of the castle, Miguel Otero Silva took us to see the frescos of Piero della Francesca, in the Church of San Francisco; then we lingered over a very conversational coffee under the trellises of the market square enhanced by the early-evening breezes, and when we returned to the castle to pick up our luggage we found dinner on the table. So we stayed to eat. While we did so, the boys lit some more torches in the kitchen and went to explore the darkness upstairs. From the table we heard them galloping like wild horses up the stairs, the mournful creaking of door hinges, the happy shouts calling Ludovico in the abandoned rooms. They were the ones who came up with the bad idea that we should stay the night. Miguel Otero Silva encouraged them with delight, and we didn't have the heart to say no.

Contrary to what I feared, we slept very well; my wife and I in a bedroom on the ground floor, and my sons in an adjacent room. While I was trying to get to sleep I counted twelve insomniac chimes from the pendulum clock in the sitting room, and for an instant I remembered the woman with the geese. But we were so tired that we fell asleep very quickly, and slept soundly and continuously, and I woke up, after seven, to bright sunshine. At my side, Mercedes was sailing on the peaceful sea of the innocent. "How silly," I said to myself, "that some people still believe in ghosts these days." Only then did I realize—with a slash of horror—that we were not in the room where we'd laid down last night, but in Ludovico's bedroom, lying in his bloody bed. Someone had changed our room while we slept.

December 30, 1980, *El País,* Madrid

# Magic Caribbean

Surinam—as not everyone knows—is an independent country on the Caribbean Sea, which was until a few years ago a Dutch colony. It covers 64,000 square miles and has just over 384,000 inhabitants of multiple origins: Indians from India, local Indians, Indonesians, Africans, Chinese, and Europeans. Its capital, Paramaribo—which they pronounce with a stress on the antepenultimate syllable—is a clamorous and sad city, with a spirit more Asian than South American, where four languages and numerous aboriginal dialects, as well as the official tongue—Dutch—are spoken and six religions professed: Hinduism, Roman Catholicism, Islam, Moravian, Dutch Reform, and Lutheran. Currently, the country is governed by a regime of young military officers, about whom very little is known, even in the neighboring countries, and nobody would remember it if it weren't for a weekly stopover by a Dutch plane that flies from Amsterdam to Caracas.

I had heard of Surinam since I was very small, not as Surinam—which was then called Dutch Guyana—but because it was on the border with French Guyana, in whose capital, Cayenne, was until recently the terrible penal colony known, in life and in death, as Devil's Island. The few who managed to escape that hellhole, who might be vicious criminals as easily as political idealists, scattered across the numerous islands of the West Indies until they managed to return to Europe or establish themselves with new identities in Venezuela or the Caribbean coast of Colombia. The most famous of all was Henri Charrière, author of *Papillon,* who prospered in Caracas as a restaurant promoter and in other less clear jobs, and who died a few years ago at the crest of an ephemeral literary glory, as deserving as it was undeserved. That glory, in reality, belonged to another French fugitive, with better qualifications, who described the horrors of Devil's Island long before Papillon, but who does not figure anywhere in the literature today, not even his name can be found in the encyclopedias. He was called René Belbenoît, and had been a journalist in France before being sentenced to life for a cause no journalist today can remember, and he continued to be one in the United States, where he was granted asylum and where he died at a venerable old age.

Some of those fugitives found refuge in the Caribbean Colombian town where I was born, in the times of the banana fever, when cigars were not lit with matches but with five-peso bills. Several of them assimilated into the population and became very respectable citizens, always distinguished by their difficult speech and the hermeticism of their past. One of them, Roger Chantal, who had arrived with no other trade than pulling teeth without anesthesia, became a millionaire overnight with no explanation whatsoever. He held Babylonian parties—in an implausible town that had very little to begrudge Babylonia—would get deadly drunk, and shout in his happy agony, *"Je suis l'homme le plus riche du monde."* In the midst of his delirium he would fancy himself a benefactor, an aspect no one had seen up till then, and presented the church with a full-size clay saint, who was enthroned with three days of revelry. One ordinary Tuesday three secret agents arrived on the eleven o'clock train and went straight to his house. Chantal wasn't home, but the agents performed a thorough search in the presence of his native wife, who put up no resistance, except when they wanted to open the enormous wardrobe in the bedroom. Then the agents broke the mirrors and found more than a million dollars in counterfeit bills hidden between the glass and the wood. Nothing more was ever heard of Roger Chantal. Later the legend circulated that the million fake dollars had entered the country inside the clay saint, which no customs agent had been curious enough to inspect.

All this came back to my memory in a sudden jolt just before Christmas of 1957, when I had to make a stopover in Paramaribo. The airport was a flattened runway with a palm-thatch hut, on the central prop of which was a telephone like the ones in cowboy movies, with a crank handle you have to turn with great effort and many times before getting a response. The heat was searing, and the air, dusty and still, had the smell of a sleeping caiman by which one recognizes the Caribbean when arriving from another world. On a stool leaning against the telephone post was a very beautiful, well-built, young black woman, with a multicolored turban like the ones women wear in some African countries. She was pregnant, about to give birth, and was smoking a cigar in silence and in a way I've only seen people do in the Caribbean: with the lit end inside her mouth and puffing smoke out the stub end, like a tugboat funnel. She was the only human being in the airport.

After a quarter of an hour a decrepit jeep arrived surrounded by a cloud of burning dust, from which descended a black man in shorts and a cork helmet with the papers to dispatch the plane. While he completed the formalities, he was talking on the phone, shouting in Dutch. Twelve hours earlier I was on a seaside terrace in Lisbon, in front of the enormous Portuguese ocean, watching the flocks of seagulls going inside the port saloons fleeing from the glacial wind. Europe was then a decrepit land covered in snow, daylight lasted no more than five hours, and it was impossible to imagine that a world of hot sun and rotting guavas, like the one where we'd just landed, truly existed. However, the only image that persists from that experience, which I still conserve intact, was that of the beautiful, aloof black woman, who had a basket of ginger roots on her lap to sell to the passengers.

Now, traveling again from Lisbon to Caracas, I've landed again in Paramaribo, and my first impression was that we'd landed in the wrong city. The airport terminal is now a luminous building, with big glass windows, very faint air conditioning, smelling of children's medicine, and that canned music that's repeated pitilessly in all the public places in the world. There are shops selling duty-free luxury items, as abundant and well stocked as in Japan, and a crowded cafeteria where the seven races of the country, their six religions, and uncountable languages are found scrambled and boiling all together.

My professor Juan Bosch, author of, among many other things, a monumental history of the Caribbean, said once in private that our magic world is like those invincible plants that are reborn under the concrete, until they split and shatter it and flower again in the same place. I understood this more than ever when I walked out an unexpected door of the Paramaribo airport and found a line of old women sitting impassively, all black, all wearing colorful turbans and all smoking with the lit end inside their mouths. They were selling local fruit and handicrafts, but none of them made the slightest attempt to convince anyone. Only one of them, who wasn't the oldest, was selling ginger root. I recognized her instantly. Not knowing where to start or what to do in reality with that find, I bought a handful of ginger. While I was doing so, remembering her state the first time, I asked her without preambles how her son was. She didn't even look at me. "It wasn't a son, but a daughter," she said, "and at twenty-two years old she's just given me my first grandchild."

January 6, 1981, *El País*, Madrid

# Poetry, in Children's Reach

A literature teacher warned the youngest daughter of a great friend of mine last year that her final exam would be on *One Hundred Years of Solitude*. The girl was frightened, with every reason, not only because she hadn't read the book, but because she was concentrating on other, more important subjects. Luckily, her father has a very serious literary education and a poetic intuition like few others, and he subjected her to such an intense preparation that, undoubtedly, she arrived at the exam better armed than her teacher. However, he asked her an unexpected question: What is the meaning of the backward letter in the title *Cien años de soledad*? He was referring to the Buenos Aires edition, the cover of which was designed by the painter Vicente Rojo with one letter turned backward, because his absolute and sovereign inspiration instructed him to. The girl, of course, did not know how to answer. Vicente Rojo said when I told him that he wouldn't have known either.

That same year, my son Gonzalo had to answer a literature questionnaire prepared in London for an entrance exam. One of the questions purported to establish what the rooster symbolized in *No One Writes to the Colonel*. Gonzalo, who is very familiar with our house style, could not resist the temptation to pull the leg of that distant scholar, and answered, "It is the rooster of the golden eggs." We later learned that the person who received the highest grade was the student who answered, as the teacher had taught him, that the colonel's rooster was the symbol of the repressed power of the people. When I found that out, I was again glad of my tactful lucky star, for the end of the book I had planned, and which I changed at the last minute, was to have the colonel wring the rooster's neck and make out of him a soup of protest.

For years I've been collecting these pearls bad teachers of literature use to pervert children. I know one who in very good faith believes the heartless, fat, and voracious grandmother who exploits the naive Eréndira to collect a debt is the symbol of insatiable capitalism. A Catholic teacher taught that Remedios the Beauty's ascent to the sky is a poetic transposition of the Virgin Mary's ascension in body and soul. Another taught a whole class on Herbert, a character from some story of mine who resolves problems for everyone and gives away money hand over fist. "He is a lovely metaphor for God," said the teacher. Two Barcelona critics surprised me with the discovery that *The Autumn of the Patriarch* has the same structure as Béla Bartók's third piano concerto. That caused me great joy because of the admiration I have for Béla Bartók, and especially for that concerto, but I still haven't been able to understand those two critics' analogies. A literature professor at the Havana School of Letters spent many hours on an analysis of *One Hundred Years of Solitude* and reached the conclusion—flattering and depressing at the same time—that it offered no solution. Which completely convinced me that the interpretive mania eventually ends up being a new form of fiction that sometimes gets stranded on a foolish remark.

I must be a very ingenuous reader, because I've never thought that novelists mean to say more than what they say. When Franz Kafka says that Gregory Samsa woke up one morning transformed into a gigantic insect, it doesn't strike me as a symbol of anything, and the only thing that has always intrigued me is what kind of creature he might have been. I believe that in reality there was a time when carpets flew and genies were imprisoned in bottles. I believe Balaam's ass spoke—as the Bible tells us—and the only regrettable thing is that his voice was not recorded, and I believe that Joshua destroyed the walls of Jericho with the power of his trumpets, and the only regrettable thing is that no one transcribed the demolition music. I believe, indeed, that the lawyer of glass—by Cervantes—really was made of glass, as he believed in his madness, and I truly believe in the joyful truth that Gargantua pissed in torrents over the cathedrals of Paris. Even more: I believe other similar wonders are still happening, and if we don't see them it is in large measure because we are impeded by the obscurantist rationalism inculcated in us by bad literature teachers.

I have great respect, and most of all great affection, for the job of teacher, and that's why it hurts me that they too are victims of a system of learning that leads them to spout nonsense. One of my unforgettable beings is the teacher who taught me to read at the age of five. She was a lovely and wise girl who didn't pretend to know more than she knew, and she was also so young that with time she has ended up being younger than me. She was the one who read to us in class the first poems that rotted my brain forever. I remember with the same gratitude my high school literature teacher, a modest and prudent man who led us through the labyrinth of good books without farfetched interpretations. This method allowed his students a more personal and free participation in the wonder of poetry. In short, a course in literature should not be much more than a good reading guide. Any other pretension is no use for anything but frightening children. That's what I think, here in the back room.

January 27, 1981, *El País,* Madrid

# The River of Life

The only reason I'd like to be a child again would be to travel once more by boat up the Magdalena River. Those who didn't do so back then cannot even imagine what it was like. I had to do it twice a year—once up and once down—during my six years of secondary school and two of university, and every time, I learned more about life than at school, and better than at school. When the water level was high, the upstream voyage took five days from Barranquilla to Puerto Salgar, where we caught the train up to Bogotá. In times of drought, which were more frequent and more fun to travel, it could take up to three weeks.

The train from Puerto Salgar climbed as if crawling up rock cornices for a whole day. In the steepest sections it would back down as if to gather momentum and try the ascent again puffing like a dragon, and on occasion it was necessary for the passengers to get off and walk up to the next cornice, to lighten the load. The villages along the way were freezing and sad, and through the carriage windows, the lifelong peddlers offered big, yellow chickens, cooked whole, and snowy potatoes that tasted like hospital food. The train reached Bogotá at six in the evening, which since then has been the worst hour to live. The city was mournful and bitter, with noisy streetcars that spat out sparks at the corners, and a rain of water mixed with soot that never let up. The men, dressed in black, walked quickly and stumbling as if they were running urgent errands, and there was not a single woman in the street. But there we had to stay all year round, pretending to study, although in reality we were only waiting for it to be December again so we could travel once more down the Magdalena River.

These were the times of three-story boats with two funnels, which passed through the night like an illuminated village, and left a trail of music and fanciful dreams in the sedentary villages on the banks. Unlike the boats on the Mississippi, the drive wheels of ours were not outboards but in the stern, and nowhere in the world have I ever again seen ones like them. They had easy and immediate names: *Atlántico, Medellín, Capitán de Caró, David Arango.* Their captains, like Conrad's, were authoritarian and kindhearted, ate like barbarians, and never slept alone in their isolated cabins. The crew members were called *mariners,* by extension, as if they sailed the sea. But in the canteens and brothels of Barranquilla, where they mixed with the mariners of the sea, they were distinguished by an unmistakable name: *vaporinos,* steamshippers.

The trips were slow and surprising during the day; we passengers sat on the balconies to watch life go by. We saw alligators that looked like tree trunks at the river's edge, with their jaws wide open, waiting for something to eat to fall in. You could see throngs of cranes taking off startled by the boat's wake, flocks of wild ducks from the marshes inland, interminable schools of fish, manatees that nursed their young and cried as if singing on the empty beaches. Sometimes a nauseating stink would interrupt our siesta, and it was the cadaver of an immense drowned cow, floating downstream almost immobile with a solitary vulture standing on its belly. All through the voyage, one would wake up at dawn, bewildered by the racket of the monkeys and the scandal of the parrots.

It's unusual nowadays to meet someone on an airplane. On the Magdalena riverboats passengers ended up resembling a single family, for we would make arrangements every year to sail on the same voyage. The Eljaches embarked at Calamar, the Peñas and the Del Toros—paisanos of the legendary alligator-man—embarked at Plato;

the Estorninos and Viñas, at Magangué; the Villafañes, at Banco. As the trip advanced, the party grew bigger. Our life was linked in an ephemeral, but unforgettable, way, to the stopover villages, and many got tangled up forever in their destiny. Vicente Escudero, who was a medical student, went into a wedding dance without being invited in Gamarra, danced without permission with the most beautiful woman in town, and her husband killed him with one shot. Pedro Pablo Guillén, on the other hand, got married during a Homeric drunken binge to the first girl he fancied in Barrancabermeja, and is still happy with her and their nine children. The irretrievable José Palencia, who was a congenital musician, entered a drumming contest in Tenerife and won a cow, which he sold on the spot for fifty pesos: a fortune back then. Sometimes the boat would get stranded for up to fifteen days on a sandbar. Nobody worried, for the party went on, and a letter from the captain sealed with his friend's coat of arms was a valid justification for arriving late to school.

One night, on my last voyage in 1948, we were awakened by a heart-rending wail coming from the riverbank. Captain Clímaco Conde Abello, who was one of the greats, gave the order for the searchlights to look for whatever was making that distressing sound. It was a female manatee that had gotten trapped in the branches of a fallen tree. The *vaporinos* dove into the water, tied a winch rope around her, and managed to unstrand her. It was a fascinating and touching animal, almost fourteen feet long, and her pale and smooth skin, and her womanly torso, with big breasts of a very loving mother, and from her enormous and sad eyes sprung human tears. It was also Captain Conde Abello who I first heard say that the world was going to end if people kept killing the animals of the river, and he banned shooting from the boat. "Anyone who wants to kill someone should go kill him at home," he shouted. "Not on my boat." But nobody heeded him. Thirteen years later—on January 19, 1961—a friend phoned me at home in Mexico to tell me that the steamship *David Arango* had been set alight and burned to ashes in the port of Magangué. I hung up the telephone with the horrible impression that my youth had ended that day, and all that was left of our river of nostalgia had just gone to hell.

It had indeed. The Magdalena River is dead, with its waters poisoned and its animals exterminated. The recuperation work that the government has begun to talk about since a concentrated group of journalists made the problem trendy is a distracting farce. The rehabilitation of the Magdalena will only be possible with the continued and intense effort of at least four conscientious generations: an entire century.

People speak too easily of reforestation. This actually means planting 59,110 million trees on the banks of the Magdalena. I'll repeat that just to be clear: fifty-nine thousand, one hundred and ten million trees. But the biggest problem is not planting them, but where to plant them. Almost all the useful land on the riverbanks is private property, and complete reforestation would have to occupy ninety percent of it. It would be worth asking which property owners would be kind enough to cede ninety percent of their lands for tree planting and renounce ninety percent of their current profits.

The pollution, moreover, does not just affect the Magdalena River, but all its tributaries. They are the sewer systems of the riverside cities and towns that drag and accumulate industrial, agricultural, animal, and human waste and flow into the immense world of national filth called Bocas de Ceniza. In November of last year, in Tocaima, two guerrillas dove into the Bogotá River while fleeing from the armed forces. They managed to escape, but were on the verge of death from infections contracted from the water. So the people who live on the Magdalena, especially in the lower reaches, have not been drinking or using pure water or eating healthy fish for a very long time. They only receive—as the ladies say—pure shit.

The task is enormous, but that is perhaps the best thing about it. The complete project of what must be done is in a study carried out by a joint Dutch and Colombian commission, the thirty volumes of which sleep the sleep of the unjust in the archives of the Institute of Hydrology and Meteorology (IMAT). The deputy director of that monumental study was a young engineer from Antioquia, Jairo Murillo, who dedicated half his life to it, and before it was finished he relinquished what was left of it: he drowned in the river of his dreams. On the other hand, no presidential candidate in recent years has run the risk of drowning in those waters. The inhabitants of riverside towns—which in the coming days are going to be in the front lines of the national intention with the voyage of the *Caracola*—should be aware of that. And remember that between Honda and Bocas de Ceniza, there are enough votes to elect a president of the republic.

March 25, 1981, *El País*, Madrid

# María of My Heart

A couple of years ago I told the Mexican film director Jaime Humberto Hermosillo about a real-life episode, in the hopes that he would turn it into a movie, but it didn't seem to have captured his attention. Two months later, however, he came to tell me without warning that he had the first draft of a script, so we continued working on it together until it was in its definitive form. Before structuring the characteristics of the central protagonists, we agreed which two actors could best embody them: María Rojo and Héctor Bonilla. This also allowed us to be able to count on the collaboration of both of them when writing certain dialogues, and we even left some of them barely sketched out so they could improvise them in their own language during filming.

The only thing I had written of the story—since hearing it many years ago in Barcelona—were a few random notes in a school notebook, and a projected title: "No, I only came to use the phone." But when it came time to register the script project we thought it wasn't the most appropriate title, and put a different provisional one: *María of My Love*. Later, Jaime Humberto Hermosillo decided on the definitive title: *María de mi corazón—María of My Heart*. It was the one that best suited the story, not only its nature but also its style.

The film was made with everyone's contributions. Artists, actors, and technical specialists all contributed our work to the production, and the only ready money we had at our disposal was two million pesos from the University of Veracruz; that is, about eighty thousand dollars, which, in movie terms, is barely even pocket change. It was filmed on 16 mm color film, and in ninety-three days of hard labor in the feverish atmosphere of the Colonia Portales, which strikes me as one of the most characteristic neighborhoods of Mexico City. I already knew it well, because more than twenty years ago I worked as a pressman for a printer in that *colonia,* and at least one night a week, after we finished work, I'd go out with those good artisans and better friends to drink everything up to and including the alcohol in the lamps in the neighborhood cantinas. We thought that was the natural setting for *María of My Heart.* I have just seen the finished movie, and I'm pleased to see that we weren't wrong. It's excellent, at once tender and brutal, and as I walked out of the screening room I felt shaken by a gust of nostalgia.

María—the protagonist—was in real life a twenty-five-year-old woman, recently married to a public service employee. One afternoon of torrential rain, when she was driving alone on an empty road, her car broke down. After an hour of futile signals to passing vehicles, a bus driver felt sorry for her. He wasn't going very far, but María just needed a telephone to ask her husband to come and pick her up. It would never have occurred to her that on this rented bus, completely occupied by a group of lethargic women, an absurd and unwarranted drama had begun that would change her life forever.

At nightfall, still under a persistent rain, the bus entered the cobbled courtyard of an enormous, gloomy building, situated in the middle of a nature reserve. The woman responsible for the others made them disembark with slightly childish instructions, as if they were schoolgirls. But they were all grown-ups, faded and absent, and they moved in a way that did not seem of this world. María was the last to get out, without worrying about the rain, since she was soaked to the skin anyway. The woman in charge of the group then handed them over to others, who came out to receive them, and left in the bus. Until that moment, María had not noticed that those women were thirty-two placid patients being transferred from some other city, and that where she actually found herself was a mental asylum.

Inside the building, María separated from the group and asked an employee where there was a telephone. One of the nurses who was guiding the patients made her get back in line while saying in a very sweet voice, "This way, honey, there's a phone down this way." María followed, along with the other women, down a dark corridor, and finally entered a dorm room where the nurses began to assign beds. They assigned one to María as well. Rather amused by the mistake, María explained then to the nurse that her car had broken down on the highway and she just needed to use the telephone to let her husband know. The nurse pretended to listen to her attentively, but took her back to her bed, trying to calm her with soft words.

"Sure, sweetie," she said, "if you behave yourself you can call who-ever you want. But not now, tomorrow."

Understanding all of a sudden that she was about to fall into a lethal trap, María ran out of the dormitory. But before she reached the gate, a corpulent guard caught up to her and got her in a headlock, and two others helped to put her in a straitjacket. A short time later, since she didn't stop shouting, they injected her with a sedative. The next day, since she persisted in her insurrectional attitude, they transferred her to the ward for the violent patients, and subdued her until she was exhausted with a ice-cold water from a high-pressure hose.

María's husband reported her disappearance just after midnight, when he was sure she wasn't at the house of anyone they knew. The car—abandoned and dismantled by thieves—was recovered the next day. After two weeks, the police declared the case closed, and took it for granted that María, disappointed with her brief matrimonial experience, had run off with another man.

At that time, María had not yet adapted to sanatorium life, but her spirit had been crushed. She was still refusing to participate in outside games with the patients, but no one forced her. After all, the doctors said, they all start out like that, and sooner or later they end up joining the life of the community. Toward the third month of her confinement,

María finally managed to gain the confidence of a social visitor, who offered to get a message to her husband.

María's husband visited her the following Saturday. In the reception room, the director of the sanatorium explained in very convincing terms the state María was in and how he could best help her to recover. He warned him of her dominant obsession—the telephone—and instructed him on how to treat her during the visit, to prevent her from having a relapse into one of her frequent crises of rage. It was all a matter, as they say, of going along with her.

In spite of him following the doctor's instructions to the letter, the first visit was dreadful. María tried to leave with him at any cost, and they had to resort to the straitjacket again to restrain her. But little by little she grew more docile on subsequent visits. So her husband carried on visiting her every Saturday, bringing her a pound box of chocolates every time until the doctors told him it wasn't the most suitable gift for María, because she was gaining weight. From then on, he only brought her roses.

May 5, 1981, *El País*, Madrid

# Like Souls in Purgatory

I t was many years ago now that I first heard the story of the old gardener who killed himself at Finca Vigía, the beautiful house among huge trees, in a suburb of Havana, where Ernest Hemingway spent a large part of his writing life. Since then I have continued to hear it many times in numerous versions. According to the most common one, the gardener made the extreme decision after the writer decided to discharge him, because he insisted on pruning the trees despite instructions not to. One hoped that in his memoirs, if he wrote them, or in any of his posthumous writings, Hemingway would tell the real version. But it seems he did not.

All the variations concur that the gardener, who had been there since before the writer bought the house, disappeared all of a sudden without any explanation. After four days, following the unequivocal signals from the vultures, they discovered the body at the bottom of a well that supplied Hemingway and his then wife, the lovely Martha Gelhorn, with drinking water. However, the Cuban writer Norberto Fuentes, who has meticulously scrutinized Hemingway's life in Havana, published a little while ago another different and maybe more well-founded version of such a controversial death. The former house steward told him that the well where the man had died did not supply drinking water but just water for the swimming pool. And, according to the steward's version, they frequently put chlorine tablets in it, though perhaps not enough to disinfect it of an entire dead body. In any case, the latest version belies the oldest version, which was also perhaps the most literary, and according to which the Hemingways had been drinking drowned man's water for three days. They say the writer had said, "The only difference we noticed was that the water had become sweeter."

This is one of so many fascinating stories—written or told—that stay with a person forever, more in the heart than in the memory, and which fill up everyone's lives. Maybe they are the souls in purgatory of literature. Some are legitimate pearls of poetry that we've come to know on the fly without really registering who the author was, because they seemed unforgettable; or that we'd heard someone telling without asking who, and after a certain while we no longer know for sure if they were stories we dreamt. Of all of them, undoubtedly the most lovely, and the best known, is that of the newborn baby mouse who met a bat the first time he went outside of the family cave, and returned astonished, shouting, "Mother, I've seen an angel." Another, also from real life, but outdoing fiction by leaps and bounds, is that of the Managua amateur radio enthusiast who, at daybreak on December 22, 1972, tried to communicate with anyone anywhere in the world to let people know of the earthquake that had erased his city from the map. After an hour of fiddling with the dial and hearing nothing but sidereal whistles, a more realistic companion convinced him to desist. "It's useless," he said, "this happened all over the world." Another story, as truthful as the previous ones, was suffered by a symphony orchestra in Paris, which ten years ago was about to liquidate itself due to an inconvenience that hadn't occurred to Franz Kafka: the building they'd been assigned as a rehearsal space only had one hydraulic elevator with a maximum capacity of four persons, so the eighty musicians began going upstairs at eight in the morning, and four hours later, by the time the last of them got up there, they had to start going down for lunch.

Among the written stories that dazzled me from the first reading, which I reread again every chance I get, the best to my taste is "The Monkey's Paw" by W. W. Jacobs. I only remember two short stories that seem perfect to me: this one, and "The Facts in the Case of M. Valdemar" by Edgar Allan Poe. However, while we can identify everything up to the quality of the latter writer's undergarments, what is known of the former is very little. I don't know very many scholars who can say what his double initials stand for without looking it up once more in the encyclopedia, as I have just done: William Wymark. He was born in London, where he died in 1943, at the modest age of eighty, and his complete works in eighteen volumes—though the encyclopedia does not say so—occupy twenty-five inches of library shelf space. But his glory rests completely on a masterpiece five pages long.

Finally, I wish I could remember—and I know some charitable reader is going to tell me in the coming days—who the authors are of two stories that profoundly incited the literary fever of my youth. The first is the drama of the disappointed man who threw himself off a tenth-story balcony, and as he fell was looking through the windows into the private worlds of his neighbors, the small domestic tragedies, the furtive loves, the brief instants of happiness, news of which had never reached the communal stairwell, so that by the moment his head split open on the sidewalk his conception of the world had completely changed, and he had reached the conclusion that the life he was leaving forever by the back door was worth living. The other story is that of two explorers who manage to take shelter in an abandoned cabin, after having endured three anguished days lost in the snow. After another three days, one of them died. The survivor digs a grave in the snow, a hundred yards from the cabin, and buries the corpse there. The next day, however, when he wakes from his first restful sleep, he finds him back inside the house again, dead and frozen stiff, but sitting like a formal visitor in front of his bed. He buries him again, maybe in a more distant grave, but when he wakes up the next day he finds him sitting in front of his bed again. Then he loses his mind. The truth of his story is found in the pages of the diary he has kept up till then. Among the many explanations that tried to clear up the enigma, one seemed to be the most plausible: the survivor felt so deeply affected by his solitude that he sleepwalked and dug up the corpse that he had buried in his waking hours.

The story that made the strongest impression on me in my life, the most brutal and at the same time the most human, was told to Ricardo Muñoz Suay in 1947, when he was imprisoned in Ocaña in the province of Toledo, Spain. It is the real story of a Republican prisoner who was executed in the early days of the Spanish Civil War in the Ávila prison. The firing squad took him from his cell at dawn on an icy morning, and they all had to walk across a snow-covered field to reach the execution spot. The Civil Guards were well protected from the cold in their capes and gloves and tricorn hats, but even so they were shivering as they crossed the frozen wasteland. The poor prisoner, wearing only a fraying wool jacket, didn't stop rubbing his freezing body, while he complained out loud about the deadly cold. At a certain point, the commander of the squad, exasperated with the complaints, shouted:

"For fuck's sake, stop playing the martyr about the goddamn cold. Spare a thought for those of us who have to go back."

May 12, 1981, *El País,* Madrid

# Something Else on Literature and Reality

A very serious problem that our disproportionate reality poses for literature is the insufficiency of words. When we speak of a river, the furthest a European reader can go is imagining something as big as the Danube, which is 1,700 miles long. It is difficult to imagine, if it is not described, the reality of the Amazon, 3,500 miles in length. From the riverbank in Belem, in the Brazilian state of Pará, you cannot see the other side, and the river is wider than the Baltic Sea. When we write the word "storm," Europeans think of thunder and lightning, but it's not easy for them to conceive of the same phenomenon that we want to depict. The same happens, for example, with the word "rain." In the Andes mountain range, according to the description a Frenchman called Javier Marimier wrote for his countrymen, there are storms that can last for five months. "Those who have not seen those storms," he says, "cannot imagine the violence with which they develop. For hours on end the lightning strikes follow each other in rapid succession like cascades of blood and the atmosphere trembles under the continual shaking of thunder, the blasts of which echo off the immensity of the mountains." The description is very far from being a masterwork, but would suffice to give horrified shudders to the least credulous European.

So it would be necessary to create a whole system of new words for the size of our reality. The examples of that necessity are interminable. F. W. Up de Graff, a Dutch explorer who traveled the upper Amazon at the beginning of the century, says that he found a stream of boiling water that made hard-boiled eggs in five minutes, and had passed through a region where people couldn't speak out loud because it would trigger torrential downpours. Somewhere on the Caribbean coast of Colombia, I saw a man recite a secret prayer in front of a cow with maggots in her ear, and I saw the maggots fall to the ground dead as the prayer went on. That man assured me he could apply the same cure from a distance, as long as he had a description of the animal and was told where it could be found. On May 8, 1902, the Mont Pelée volcano, on the island of Martinique, destroyed in a few minutes the port of Saint Pierre and killed and buried in lava all of its thirty thousand inhabitants. Except for one: Ludgar Sylvaris, the town's only prisoner, who was protected by the invulnerable structure of the individual cell they'd constructed for him so he couldn't escape.

Just in Mexico many volumes would have to be written to express its incredible reality. After almost twenty years there, I could still spend entire hours, as I have so many times, contemplating a bowl of Mexican jumping beans. Benevolent nationalists have explained that their mobility is due to a living larva they have inside, but the explanation seems poor: the marvelous thing is not that the beans move because they have a larva inside, but that they have a larva inside so they can move. Another of the strange experiences of my life was my first encounter with an ajolote (*axolotl*). Julio Cortázar tells in one of his stories about meeting an axolotl in the Jardins de Plantes in Paris, one day when he wanted to see the lions. When he passed through the aquariums, Cortázar says, "I glanced at a lot of ordinary-looking fish until I unexpectedly came across the axolotl." And he concludes: "I stayed there staring at them for an hour, and left, unable to think of anything else." The same thing happened to me, in Pátzcuaro, only I didn't watch them for an hour, but for a whole afternoon, and I returned several times. But there was something that impressed me more than the animal itself, and it was the sign nailed to the door of the house. "Axolotl syrup for sale."

That incredible reality reaches its maximum density in the Caribbean, which, strictly speaking, extends (northward) to the southern United States, and south to Brazil. Don't think that's an expansionist's delirium. No: it's that the Caribbean is not just a geographical area, as geographers of course believe, but a very homogeneous cultural area.

In the Caribbean, the original elements of the primal beliefs and magical conceptions previous to the discovery are joined by the profuse variety of cultures that came together in the years following it in a magic syncretism the artistic interest and actual artistic fecundity of which are inexhaustible. The African contribution was forced and infuriating, but fortunate. In that crossroads of the world, a sense of endless liberty was forged, a reality with neither God nor laws, where each person felt it was possible to do what they wanted without limits of any kind, and bandits woke up converted into kings, fugitives into admirals, prostitutes into governors. And the opposite, too.

I was born and raised in the Caribbean. I know it country by country, island by island; maybe my frustration that nothing has ever occurred to me, and that I could never do anything more surprising than reality, springs from there. The furthest I've been able to go is to transpose it with poetic resources, but there is not a single line in any of my books that does not have its origin in a real event. One of those transpositions is the stigma of the pig's tail that so worries the Buendía lineage in *One Hundred Years of Solitude*. I could have resorted to any image, but I thought the fear of the birth of a child with a pig's tail was the one that had the fewest possibilities of coinciding with reality. However, as soon as the novel began to become known, confessions surfaced from men and women in different parts of the Americas who had something resembling a pig's tail. In Barranquilla, a young man showed his in the newspapers: he had been born and raised with that tail, but he had never revealed it, until he read *One Hundred Years of*

*Solitude*. His explanation was more astonishing than his tail. "I never wanted to tell anyone I had it because I was ashamed," he said, "but now, reading the novel and hearing from people who have read it, I've realized that it's a natural thing." A little while later, a reader sent me the clipping of a photo of a baby girl in Seoul, the capital of South Korea, who was born with a pig's tail. Contrary to what I thought when I wrote the novel, they cut the girl's tail off in Seoul and she survived.

Nevertheless, my most difficult experience as a writer was the preparation of *The Autumn of the Patriarch*. During almost ten years I read everything possible on the dictators of Latin America, especially the Caribbean, determined that the book I was planning to write would resemble reality as little as possible. Every step was a disappointment. Juan Vicente Gómez's intuition was much more penetrating than true foresight. Doctor Duvalier, in Haiti, had all the black dogs in the country exterminated because one of his enemies, trying to escape the tyrant's persecution, had slipped out of his human condition and turned into a black dog. Dr. Francia, whose prestige as a philosopher was so widespread that Carlyle wrote an essay on him, closed the Republic of Paraguay as if it were a house, and only left one window open so the mail could arrive. Antonio López de Santa Anna buried his own leg with splendid funeral rites. Lope de Aguirre's severed hand sailed downriver for several days, and those who saw it pass by recoiled in horror, thinking that even in that state the murderous hand could brandish a dagger. Anastasio Somoza García, in Nicaragua, had a zoo in the courtyard of his house with double cages: on one side were savage beasts, and on the other, scarcely separated by iron bars, his political enemies were locked up.

Martínez, the theosophist dictator of El Salvador, had all the street lighting in the country wrapped in red paper, to combat a measles epidemic, and he had invented a pendulum that he held over his food before eating, to make sure it wasn't poisoned. The statue of Morazán that still exists in Tegucigalpa is actually of Marshal Ney: the official commission that traveled to London to get it resolved that it would be cheaper to buy that forgotten statue in a warehouse than to commission an authentic one of Morazán.

In short, Latin American and Caribbean writers have to admit, hands on hearts, that reality is a better writer than we are. Our destiny, maybe our glory, is to try to imitate it with humility, and as best we can.

July 1, 1981, *El País,* Madrid

# My Personal Hemingway

I recognized him all of a sudden, walking with his wife, Mary Welsh, along Boulevard Saint-Michel, in Paris, one day in the rainy spring of 1957. He was walking on the opposite sidewalk in the direction of the Jardin du Luxembourg, and he was wearing some very well worn jeans, a checked shirt, and a baseball cap. The only thing that didn't seem like his were the tiny, metal-rimmed, round glasses, which gave him a premature grandfatherly look. He had turned fifty-nine, and he was enormous and too visible, but he didn't give the impression of brute strength he no doubt would have liked because his hips were a bit narrow and his legs didn't have much flesh on the bones. He looked so lively among the secondhand bookstalls and the youthful torrent from the Sorbonne that it was impossible to imagine he would be dead in barely four years.

For a fraction of a second—as has always happened to me—I found myself divided between my two rival trades. I didn't know whether to interview him for the press or just cross the avenue to express my unconditional admiration. For both intentions, however, there was a similar large disadvantage: back then I spoke the same rudimentary English I've always spoken, and I wasn't very sure of his *torero*'s Spanish. So I did neither of the two things that might have ruined the moment, but cupped my hands to my mouth, like Tarzan in the jungle, and shouted from one sidewalk to the other, "Maeeeestro!" Ernest Hemingway realized there could be no other maestro among the crowd of students, and turned with his hand raised, and shouted back to me in a slightly childish voice, "Adióóóós, amigo." It was the only time I ever saw him.

I was then a twenty-eight-year-old journalist, with one novel published and a literary prize back in Colombia, but I was stranded and aimless in Paris. My two greatest masters were the two North American novelists who seemed to have the least in common. I had read everything they had published so far, but not as complementary readings, but the exact opposite: as two different and almost mutually exclusive ways of conceiving of literature. One of them was William Faulkner, whom I never saw with my own eyes and whom I could only imagine as the farmer in rolled-up sleeves scratching his arm beside two little white dogs, in the famous portrait Henri Cartier-Bresson took of him. The other was that ephemeral man who just said *adiós* to me from the other side of the street, and had left me with the impression that something had happened in my life, and it had happened forever.

I don't know who said that novelists read other novels only to see how they're written. I believe it's true. We aren't content with the secrets exposed on the front of the page, but have to turn it over, to decipher the stitching. In some impossible-to-explain way we take the book apart into its essential pieces and put it back together again once we know the mysteries of its personal clockwork. That temptation is disheartening in Faulkner's books, because he didn't seem to have an organic system of writing, but wandered blindly through his biblical universe like a herd of goats loose in a glassworks. When you manage to dismantle one of his pages, you get the impression that there are extra springs and bolts and that it'll be impossible to put it back again into its original state. Hemingway, on the other hand, with less inspiration, with less passion, and less madness, but with a lucid rigor, left his bolts visible on the outside, like in railway cars. Maybe that's why Faulkner is a writer who has a lot to do with my soul, but Hemingway is the one who's had most to do with my trade.

Not only with his books, but also with his startling knowledge of the artisanal aspect of the science of writing. In the historic interview the journalist George Plimpton did for *The Paris Review,* he taught once and for all—against the romantic concept of creation—that economic comfort and good health are advantages for writing, that one of the biggest difficulties is organizing words well, that it's good to reread one's own books when the work is difficult to remember that it was always difficult, that you can write anywhere as long as there are no visitors or telephones, and that it's not true that journalism finishes off the writer, as so many have said, rather quite the contrary, as long as you give it up in time. "Once writing has become your major vice and greatest pleasure," he said, "only death can stop it." For all that, his lesson was the discovery that each day's work should only be interrupted when you know how you're going to start the next day. I don't think anyone has ever given a more useful piece of advice for writing. It is, no more, no less, the absolute remedy against the writer's most feared phantom: the morning agony facing the blank page.

All of Hemingway's work demonstrates that his spirit was brilliant, but of short duration. And it's understandable. An internal tension like his, submitted to such a severe technical control, is unsustainable within the vast and risky scope of a novel. It was a personal condition, and his mistake was to have tried to exceed his splendid limits. That's why everything superfluous is much more noticeable in him than in other writers. His novels seem like outsize stories overflowing with too many things. On the other hand, the best thing about his short stories is the impression they give of missing something, and that's precisely what bestows their mystery and their beauty. Jorge Luis Borges, who is one of the great writers of our time, has the same limits, but he has had the intelligence not to exceed them.

Francis Macomber's single shot at the lion teaches so much as a hunting lesson, but also as a summary of the science of writing. In some story he writes that a bull, after brushing past the chest of the bullfighter, turned "like a cat coming around a corner." I believe, in total humility, that this observation is one of those brilliant pieces of foolishness that are only possible in the most lucid writers. Hemingway's work is full of those simple and dazzling discoveries, which demonstrate up to what point he clung to his own definition that literary writing—like an iceberg—was only valid if it is sustained below the water by seven-eighths of its volume.

That technical awareness will no doubt be the reason that Hemingway does not reach the heights of glory with any of his novels, rather with his strictest short stories. Talking about *For Whom the Bell Tolls*, he said he did not have a preconceived plan while composing the book, but rather invented it each day as he was writing. He didn't have to say so: it shows. However, his instantaneously inspired stories are invulnerable. Like those three he wrote in an afternoon one May 16 in a pension in Madrid, when a snowfall forced the cancelation of the San Isidro bullfights. Those stories—as he himself told George Plimpton—were "The Killers," "Ten Indians," and "Today Is Friday," and all three are masterly.

Within that strand, to my taste, the story where his virtues are best condensed is one of his shortest: "Cat in the Rain." However, although it seems like a mockery of fate, I think his most beautiful and human work is his least successful: *Across the River and into the Trees*. It is, as he himself revealed, something that began as a short story and went astray in the mangrove swamp of a novel. It's difficult to understand so many structural cracks and so many errors of literary mechanics from such a wise technician, and some dialogues so artificial and so contrived from one of the most brilliant dialogue craftsmen in the history of literature. When the book was published, in 1950, the criticism was ferocious. Because it was not accurate, Hemingway felt wounded where it hurt most, and defended himself with a passionate telegram from Havana that did not seem worthy of an author of his stature. Not only was it his best novel, but also his most personal, for he had written it at the dawn of an uncertain autumn, with the irreparable nostalgia of the years lived and the nostalgic premonition of the few years he had left to live. In none of his books did he leave as much of himself nor manage to capture with such beauty and such tenderness the essential sentiment of his work and his life: the futility of victory. The death of his protagonist, so apparently natural and peaceful, was the coded prefiguration of his own suicide.

When you cohabit for so many years with the work of a beloved writer, you inevitably end up blending fiction with reality. I have spent many hours of many days reading in that café on the Place Saint-Michel that he considered such a good place to write, because he thought it pleasant, warm, clean, and friendly, and I have always hoped to encounter that girl again who he saw come into the café on a cold windy afternoon, and who was very pretty and fresh-faced, with her hair cut diagonally like a crow's wing. "You belong to me and all Paris belongs to me," he wrote for her, with that inexorable power of appropriation his literature had. Everything he described, every instant that was his, goes on belonging to him forever. I cannot pass number 112 on Rue de l'Odeón, in Paris, without seeing him talking to Sylvia Beach in a bookshop that's no longer the same, playing for time until six o'clock in case James Joyce comes by. On the plains of Kenya, just by seeing them once, he became the owner of its buffalos and lions, and of the most intricate secrets of the art of hunting. He made himself the owner of bullfighters and boxers, artists and gunfighters, who only existed for an instant, while they were his. Italy, Spain, Cuba, half the world is full of places he appropriated just by mentioning them. In Cojímar, a tiny village near Havana where the solitary fisherman of *The Old Man and the Sea* lived, there is a commemorative bandstand with a bust of Hemingway painted with gold varnish. At Finca Vigía, his Cuban refuge where he lived until shortly before he died, the house is intact among the shady trees, with his disparate books, his hunting trophies, his writing lectern, his enormous dead man's shoes, the countless knickknacks of his life from all over the whole world that were his until his death, and that go on living without him with the soul he instilled in them just by the magic of his dominion. Years ago I got into Fidel Castro's car—and he is a stalwart reader of literature— and saw a small, red, leather-bound book on the seat. "It's Hemingway, the master," he said. In reality, Hemingway is still where one least imagines him—twenty years after his death—as persistent and at the same time as ephemeral as that morning, which was perhaps in May, when he said *adiós, amigo,* to me from the other side of the Boulevard Saint-Michel.

July 29, 1981, *El País,* Madrid

# Ghosts of the Road

T wo boys and two girls who were traveling in a Renault 5 picked up a woman dressed in white who signaled to them at a crossroads just after midnight. The weather was clear, and the four kids—as was later verified ad nauseam—were all in their right minds. The lady traveled in silence for several miles, sitting in the middle of the back seat, until just before the Quatre Canaux bridge. Then she pointed ahead with a terrified index finger and yelled, "Careful, that curve is dangerous," and there and then she vanished.

This happened on May 20 on the Paris-Montpellier freeway. The police commissioner of the later city, whom the four kids woke up to tell of the frightening event, admitted that it was neither a joke nor a hallucination, but filed the case because he didn't know what to do with it. Almost all the press in France commented on it in the following days, and numerous parapsychologists, occultists, and metaphysical reporters gathered at the place of the apparition to study its circumstances, and exhausted the four chosen by the lady in white with rationalist questions. But after a few days, all was forgotten, and the press as well as the scientists took refuge in the analysis of an easier reality. The most understanding among them admitted that the apparition might be true, but still, faced with the impossibility of understanding her, they preferred to forget her.

For me—a convinced materialist—there is no doubt that it was one more episode, and one of the loveliest, in the rich history of the materialization of poetry. The only fault I find in it is that it happened at night, and, worse still, around midnight, like in the worst horror movies. Apart from that, there is not a single element that does not correspond to the metaphysics of roads we've all felt pass close by during the course of trip, but before the disturbing truth of which we refuse to surrender. We have ended up accepting the marvel of ghost ships that wander all the seas searching for their lost identities, but we refuse that right to so many poor souls in purgatory left scattered and aimless at the side of the road. In France alone they registered two hundred deaths a week a few years ago in the most frenetic summer months, so there's no reason to be surprised by such an understandable episode such as that of the lady in white, who will undoubtedly continue repeating herself until the end of the centuries, in circumstances that only heartless rationalists are incapable of understanding.

I have always thought, on my long road trips in so many parts of the world, that most of us human beings these days are survivors of a curve. Each one is a defiance of fate. All it takes is for the vehicle ahead of us to suffer a mishap after the curve for us to forever thwart our opportunity to tell the story. In the early years of the automobile, the English enacted a law—the Locomotive Act—which required all drivers to be preceded by a person on foot, carrying a red flag and ringing a bell, so pedestrians would have time to get out of the way. Often, at the moment of accelerating to immerse myself in the unfathomable mystery of a curve, I have regretted deep in my soul that the wise English arrangement has been abolished, especially once, fifteen years ago, when I was driving from Barcelona to Perpignan with Mercedes and the boys at sixty miles an hour, and suddenly had an incomprehensible intuition to slow down before taking a curve. The cars behind me, as always happens in these situations, overtook us. I'll never forget it: there was a white van, a red Volkswagen, and a blue Fiat. I even remember the shiny curly hair of the healthy-looking Dutch woman driving the van. After passing us in perfect order, the three cars disappeared around the curve, but we found them again an instant later one on top of the other, in a pile of smoking wreckage, embedded in an out-of-control truck in the oncoming lane. The only survivor was the Dutch couple's six-month-old baby.

I have passed that place many times since, and I have always thought of that beautiful woman who was reduced to a mound of pink flesh in the middle of the highway, completely naked due to the impact, and with her lovely Roman emperor's head dignified by death. It would not be surprising if someone found her one of these days in the place of her misfortune, alive and whole, making the conventional signs like the Montpellier woman in white, so she could be taken out of her stupor for an instant and given the opportunity to warn with the yell nobody let out for her: "Careful, that curve is dangerous."

The mysteries of the road are not more popular than those of the sea, because there is no one more distracted than amateur drivers. Professional ones, however—like the old mule drivers—are endless sources of fantastic stories. At roadside diners, as at the ancient inns along bridle paths, the weathered truckers, who seem not to believe in anything, tirelessly recount the supernatural episodes natural to their trade, especially those that happen in broad daylight and on the busiest routes. In the summer of 1974, traveling with the poet Álvaro Mutis and his wife along the same freeway where the lady in white now appeared, we saw a small car pull out of a long line of a traffic jam in the other direction, and drive straight toward us at a foolish speed. I barely had time to dodge it, but our car went over the edge and got embedded in the bottom of a ditch. Several witnesses managed to see the image of the fugitive car: it was a white Skoda, the license plate of which was noted down by three different people. We made the corresponding report at the police station in Aix-en-Provence, and after some months the French police had verified that the white Skoda with the designated license plate without a doubt existed in reality. However, they had also verified that at the time of our accident it was on the opposite side of France, parked in its garage, while its owner and sole driver was dying in a nearby hospital.

From these, and many other experiences, I have learned to have an almost reverential respect for roads. For all that, the most disturbing episode I remember happened in the very center of Mexico City, many years ago. I had been waiting for a taxi for almost half an hour, at two in the afternoon, and was about to give up when I saw one approaching that looked empty at first glance and also had its flag raised. But when it was a little bit closer I saw beyond doubt that there was a person beside the driver. Only when he stopped, without my having waved him down, did I realize my error: there was no passenger beside the driver. Along the way I told him of my optical illusion, and he listened with total openness. "It happens all the time," he said. "Sometimes I drive around all day, without anyone stopping me, because almost everyone sees that ghost passenger in the seat beside me." When I told this story to Luis Buñuel, he considered it as natural as the cab driver. "It's a good opening for a film," he said.

August 19, 1981, *El País*, Madrid

# Bogotá 1947

Back then everyone was young. But there was something worse: in spite of our implausible youth, we were always meeting others who were younger than we were, and that made us feel a sensation of danger and an urgency to finish things that were not letting us calmly enjoy our well-earned youth. The generations shoved one another, especially among the poets and the criminals, and just as soon as you'd done something, along came someone threatening to do it better. Sometimes I find by chance a photograph from those days and I can't suppress a shiver of pity, because I don't think those in the picture are actually us, but rather that we were our own children.

Bogotá was a remote, lugubrious city back then, where an inclement drizzle had been falling since the beginning of the sixteenth century. I suffered that bitterness for the first time on an ill-fated January afternoon, the saddest of my life, when I arrived from the coast just thirteen years old, in a black wool suit of my father's that had been tailored to fit me, with a vest and hat, and a metal trunk that had something of the splendor of the holy sepulcher. My lucky star, which has so rarely failed me, did me the immense favor of making sure no photo exists of that afternoon.

The first thing that caught my attention in that somber capital was that there were too many hastening men in the streets, that they were all dressed like me, in black suits and hats, and, conversely, I could not see any women. The huge Percheron horses that pulled the beer wagons in the rain caught my attention, as did the pyrotechnical sparks from the streetcars as they turned the corners under the rain, and the stopped traffic to let the interminable funerals pass by under the rain. They were the gloomiest funerals in the world, with high altar carriages and horses decked out in black velvet and feather hoods, and corpses of good families who think themselves the inventors of death. Under the fine drizzle of the Plaza de las Nieves, as a funeral pulled out, I saw a woman on the streets of Bogotá for the first time, and she was slender and stealthy, as poised as a queen in mourning, but I was left forever with half the illusion, because her face was covered by an impenetrable veil.

The image of that woman, which still flusters me, is one of my few nostalgic memories of that city of sin, in which almost everything was possible, except making love. That's why I have said on occasion that the only heroism of my life, and that of others of my generation, is having been young in the Bogotá of that time. My most salacious fun on Sundays was to take the blue-glassed streetcars, which for five centavos revolved unceasingly from Plaza de Bolívar to the Avenida de Chile, and spend those desolate afternoons there that seemed to drag the interminable tails of many more empty Sundays. The only thing I did during the journey in vicious circles was to read books of verses and verses and verses, at a rate perhaps of a block of poems for each city block, until the first streetlights came on in the eternal rain, and then I'd make my way through the taciturn cafés of the old city in search of someone who'd do me the charity of sharing conversations about the verses and verses and verses I'd just read. Sometimes I'd find someone, who was always a man, and we'd stay until after midnight drinking coffee and smoking the butts of the cigarettes we'd smoked ourselves, and talking of verses and verses and verses, while in the rest of the world all of humanity was making love.

One night as I was returning from my solitary poetic festivals on the streetcar, something happened to me for the first time that deserved to be told. It happened that at one of the stations in the north a faun had boarded the streetcar. That's what I said: a faun. According to the *Dictionary of the Real Academia Española,* a faun is "a demigod of the woodlands and countryside." Each time I reread that unhappy definition I regret that its author had not been there that night when a flesh-and-blood faun boarded the streetcar. He was dressed in the style of the day, like a chancellor on his way home from a funeral, but his bullock's horns and billy goat beard gave him away, and the well-groomed hooves under his fancy trousers. The air was pervaded by his personal fragrance, but no one seemed to notice that it was *eau de lavanda,* maybe because the same dictionary had repudiated the word "lavender" as a Gallicism that means *agua de espliego.*

The only friends I told such things were Álvaro Mutis, because he found them fascinating even though he didn't believe them, and Gonzalo Mallarino, because he knew they were true even if they weren't exactly factual. On one occasion, the three of us had seen in the atrium of the Church of San Francisco a woman who was selling toy turtles whose heads moved in a surprisingly natural way. Gonzalo Mallarino asked the woman if those turtles were alive or if they were plastic, and she replied:

"They're plastic, but they're alive."

Nevertheless, the night I saw the faun on the streetcar neither of the two answered their telephones, and I was suffocating from the urge to tell someone. So I wrote a short story—the story of the faun on the streetcar—and I mailed it to the Sunday supplement of *El Tiempo,* the editor of which, Don Jaime Posada, never published it. The only copy I kept burned in the boardinghouse where I was living on April 9, 1948, the day of the Bogotazo, and that's how national history did us a double favor: one for me and one for literature.

I couldn't avoid these personal memories as I was reading the delightful book Gonzalo Mallarino just published in Bogotá: *Historias de caleños y bogoteños.* Gonzalo and I were at the Faculty of Law at the Universidad Nacional at the same time, but we did not attend classes as regularly as we did the little university café, where we dodged the drowsiness of legal codes by exchanging verses and verses and verses of the vast universal poetry we both could recite by heart. At the end of classes, he went home to his family house, which was big and pleasant among eucalyptus trees. I went back to my gloomy boardinghouse on Calle Florián, with my friends from the coast, borrowed books, and tumultuous Saturday dances. Actually, it never occurred to me to ask Gonzalo Mallarino where the hell he was in the many hours we didn't spend at the university, while I went all around the whole city reading verses and verses and verses on the streetcars. It took me thirty years to find out, reading this exemplary book, where he reveals with so much simplicity and so much humanity the other half of his life in those times.

October 21, 1981, *El País,* Madrid

# Tales of the Road

**M**any years ago I was waiting for a taxi on a central avenue in downtown Mexico City, in broad daylight, when I saw one approach that I didn't think of flagging down, because there was someone sitting in the passenger seat. However, when it was closer I realized it was an optical illusion: the taxi was free.

Minutes later I told the driver what I'd seen, and he told me with absolute openness that it was by no means a hallucination of mine. "It happens all the time, especially at night," he told me. "Sometimes I'll be driving around the city for hours without anyone flagging me down, because they always see someone sitting beside me." In that comfortable and dangerous seat that in some countries is called "the dead man's position," because it is the most affected in accidents, and was never so worthy of the name as in the case of that taxi.

When I told Luis Buñuel this episode, he said, with great enthusiasm: "That could be the beginning of something really good." I've always thought he was right. For the episode is not in itself a complete story, but it is, undoubtedly, a magnificent takeoff point for a written or filmed story. With one serious drawback, of course, and that's that everything that happens next would have to be better. Maybe that's why I've never used it.

What interests me now, however, and after so many years, is that someone has just told me the same story again as if it just happened to him in London. It's strange, as well, that it should have been there, because London taxis are different from those in the rest of the world. They look like hearses, with little lace curtains and purple carpets, soft leather seats and supplementary ones to accommodate up to seven people, and an interior silence with something like a funereal oblivion to it. But in the dead person's place, which is not to the right but to the left of the driver, there is not a seat for another passenger, but a space for luggage. The friend who told me in London, assured me, however, that it was in that place where he saw the nonexistent person, but that the driver had told him—unlike what the Mexican one told me—that maybe it had been a hallucination. Now then: yesterday I told all this to a friend from Paris, and he was convinced that I was pulling his leg, because he says he was the one who it happened to. Besides, he told me, it happened to him in a more serious way, since he told the taxi driver what the person he'd seen at his side looked like, described the shape of his hat and the color of his bowtie, and the driver recognized him as the specter of a brother of his who'd been killed by the Nazis during the German occupation of France.

I don't think that any of these friends are lying, as I didn't lie to Luis Buñuel, I just want to point out that there are stories that happen all over the world, always in the same way, and without anyone ever being able to establish for sure whether they're true or whether they're fantasies, or to decipher their mystery. Of all of them, maybe the oldest and most recurring I heard for the first time in Mexico.

It is the eternal story of the family whose grandmother dies during their vacation at the beach. Few formalities are as difficult or as expensive or require more legal paperwork as that of transporting a cadaver from one state to another. Someone told me in Colombia that they had to sit their corpse up between two living persons in the back seat of their car, and even put a lit cigarette in his mouth when they were passing the highway controls, to deceive the countless barriers to legal transport. So the Mexican family rolled the dead grandmother up in a carpet, tied her with cords, and secured her to the roof rack of the car. During a break in the journey, while the family was having lunch, the car was stolen with the grandmother's body on top, and they never found any trace. The explanation they gave for the disappearance was that the thieves had maybe buried the body in a deserted spot and dismantled the car in order, literally, to get rid of a dead weight.

There was a time when that story was repeated all over Mexico, and always with different names. But the different versions had something in common: the one who was telling it always said he was a friend of the protagonists. Some, as well, gave their names and addresses. So many years later, I've heard the same story in the most distant parts of the world, including Vietnam, where an interpreter told me as if it had happened to a friend of his during the war. In every case the circumstances are the same, and if you insist, you'll get the names and addresses of those it happened to.

A third recurring story I've known for less time than the others, and those who have the patience to read this column every week might remember it. It is the chilling story of four young French people who last summer picked up a woman dressed in white on the Montpellier freeway. All of a sudden, the woman pointed ahead with a terrified index finger, and yelled, "Careful! That curve is dangerous!" And she vanished in that instant. I read the story in various French newspapers, and it made such an impression that I wrote an article about it. I thought it surprising that the French authorities hadn't paid attention to an event of such literary beauty, and also that they'd closed the case without finding a rational explanation for it. However, a journalist friend told me a few days ago in Paris that the reason for the official indifference was something else: in France, that story has been repeated for many years, even since long before the invention of the motorcar, when wandering ghosts on nocturnal roads requested the favor of a lift in the stagecoaches. This made me remember that also among the tales of the conquest of the west of the United States a legend is repeated of the solitary traveler who traveled all night in the passenger wagon, along with the old banker, the novice judge, and the pretty northern girl, accompanied by her governess, and the next morning at dawn only his place was empty. But what has most surprised me is discovering that the story of the lady in white, just as

I took it from the French press, and just as I told it in this column, was already told by the most prolific among us, and that's Manolo Vázquez Montalbán, in one of his few books that I hadn't read: *The Angst-Ridden Executive.* I discovered the coincidence from a photocopy a friend sent me, who also already knew the story from years ago and from a different source.

The copyright problem with Vázquez Montalbán doesn't worry me: we both have the same literary agent of all *els altres catalans,* and she will take care of distributing the rights to the story to whomever they belong. What does worry me is the other coincidence of this recurring tale, the third I've discovered: that it also takes place on a road. I've always known an expression, which I cannot now find in any of the many many useless dictionaries I have on my shelves, and it's an expression that surely has something to do with these stories: *"Son cuentos de caminos"*—They're tales of the road. The problem is that the expression means they're lies, and these three that haunt me are, without doubt, complete truths that happen ceaselessly over and over again in different places and to different people, so nobody forgets that literature too has its souls in purgatory.

January 27, 1982, *El País,* Madrid

# My Other Me

A short while ago, after waking up in bed in Mexico, I read in a newspaper that I had delivered a literary lecture the previous day in Las Palmas de Gran Canaria, on the other side of the ocean, and the conscientious correspondent had not only provided a detailed reckoning of the event, but also a very subtle synthesis of my exposition. But the most flattering thing for me was that the subjects of the review were much more intelligent than could ever have occurred to me, and the way in which they were laid out much more brilliant than I could have done. There was only one problem: I hadn't been in Las Palmas, neither the previous day nor in the previous twenty-two years, and I've never delivered a lecture on any subject in any part of the world.

It often happens that my presence is announced in places where I am not. I have told all the media that I don't participate in public acts, or pontificate at universities, or exhibit myself on television, or attend promotions of my books, or get involved in anything that might turn me into a spectacle. It's not out of modesty that I refuse, but something worse: shyness. And it's not hard for me, because the most important thing I've learned to do after forty years is to say no when I mean no. However, there's never a shortage of abusive promoters who announce in the press, or in private invitations, that next Tuesday, at six in the afternoon, I will be at some event I've never heard of. At the hour of truth, the promoter apologizes to the audience for the dereliction of the writer who promised to come and didn't come, adds a few drops of nastiness about sons of telegraph operators whose fame has gone to their heads, and ends up winning over the benevolence of the crowd and is able to do with them what he wishes. At the beginning of this ill-fated artist's life, that sort of evil trick began to cause me erosions in my liver. But I've consoled myself a little by reading the memoirs of Graham Greene, who complains of the same thing in his funny final chapter, and has made me understand that there's no remedy, that it's nobody's fault, because another me exists and is wandering loose out in the world, without any sort of control, doing everything I should do and don't do.

In that sense, the strangest thing that has happened to me was not the invented lecture in the Canary Isles, but the hard time I had a few years ago with Air France, due to a letter I never wrote. In reality, Air France had received an angry and bombastic protest, signed by me, in which I complained of the mistreatment I had been the victim of on that company's flight from Madrid to Paris, on a specific date. After a rigorous investigation, the firm had imposed sanctions on the flight attendant in question, and the public relations department sent me a very kind and contrite letter of apology to Barcelona, that left me perplexed, because I had never actually been on that flight. Even more: I always fly so frightened that I don't even notice how anyone treats me, and all my energy goes into gripping my seat with my hands to hold it up in order to help the plane stay up in the air, or trying to keep children from running in the aisles for fear they'll break through the floor. The only undesirable incident I remember was on a flight from New York in an airplane so overloaded and oppressive that it was hard to breathe. Midflight, the stewardess gave each passenger a red rose. I was so startled that I opened my heart to her. "Instead of giving us a rose," I said, "it would be better to give us a couple of inches more space for our knees." The beautiful girl, who was obviously descended from the brave lineage of conquistadors, answered me dauntlessly: "If you don't like it, you can get out here." It did not occur to me, of course, to write any letter of protest to an airline whose name I don't wish to recall, but rather I ate the rose, one petal at a time, chewing unhurriedly its medicinal fragrance against anxiety, until I caught my breath. So when I received the letter from Air France I felt so ashamed for something I had not done that I went in person to the offices to clear things up, and there they showed me the letter of protest. I wouldn't have been able to repudiate it, not just the style, but because it would have been very hard work for me to discover that the signature was fake.

The man who wrote that letter is, without doubt, the same one who gave the lecture in the Canary Isles, and the one who does so many things I only occasionally get wind of by chance. Often, when I go to a friend's home, I look for my books on their shelves with a distracted air, and write a dedication without their noticing. But more than twice I have found that my books are already signed, in my own handwriting, with the same black ink I always use, and in the same fleeting style, and signed with an autograph missing only one thing to make it mine, and that's for me to have written it.

I have been just as surprised to read in an improbable newspaper some interview I never gave, but that I could not in all honesty reprove, because it corresponds line for line with my thinking. Even more: the best interview with me that has been published to this day, the one that best expresses and in the most lucid way the most intricate nooks and crannies of my life, not only in literature, but also in politics, in my personal tastes, and in the joys and uncertainties of my heart, was published a couple of years ago in Caracas, and it was invented down to the last breath. It made me very happy, not just for being so accurate, but because it was signed with the full name of a woman I didn't know, but who must love me very much to know me so well even if only through my other me.

Something similar happens to me with enthusiastic and affectionate people I meet the world over. There's always someone who was with me in a place where I've never been, and who cherishes a fond memory of that encounter. Or who is a very good friend of some member of my family, who they don't really know, because the other me seems to have as many relatives as I do, although they're not real either, but rather the doubles of my relatives.

In Mexico I frequently meet someone who tells me of the Babylonian binges he goes on with my brother Humberto in Acapulco. The last time I saw him he thanked me for the favor I did through him, and I could say nothing but you're welcome, *hombre*, don't mention it, because I've never had the heart to confess that I don't have any brothers called Humberto or any who live in Acapulco.

Three years ago or so I had just finished lunch at home in Mexico when the doorbell rang, and one of my sons, laughing his head off, said, "Dad, you're wanted by yourself at the door." I leapt out of my chair, thinking with an uncontainable excitement, "Finally, here he is." But it wasn't the other, but rather the young Mexican architect Gabriel García Márquez, a calm and tidy man, who endures with great stoicism the misfortune of being listed in the telephone directory. He had been kind enough to find out my address to bring me the correspondence that had been accumulating in his office for years.

A short time ago, someone who was passing through Mexico looked up our number in the phone book, and was told that we were at the hospital, because *la señora* had just had a baby girl. What more had I ever desired! The fact is that the architect's wife must have received a splendid bouquet of roses, and very much deserved, as well, to celebrate the arrival of the daughter I've dreamed of all my life and never had.

No. The young architect is not my other me either, but someone much more respectable: a homonym. The other me, conversely, will never find me, because he doesn't know where I live, or what I'm like, nor could he conceive of how different we are. He'll go on enjoying his imaginary existence, dazzling and strange, with his own yacht, his private plane, and his imperial palaces where he bathes in champagne with his golden lovers and knocks out his main rivals. He will go on feeding off my legend, richer than anyone could be, young and handsome forever and happy until the last tear, while I continue growing old without remorse in front of my typewriter, far from his delusions and excesses, and going out to find my lifelong friends every night to drink the usual drinks and miss unconsoled the smell of guava. Because the most unfair thing is this: the other is the one who enjoys the fame, but I am the one who gets screwed by living it.

February 17, 1982, *El País,* Madrid

# Poor Good Translators

Someone said that translating is the best way to read. I think it's also the most difficult, the least appreciated, and the worst paid. *Traduttore, traditore,* says the tiresome Italian refrain, taking it for granted that whoever translates us betrays us. Maurice-Edgar Coindreau, one of the most intelligent and obliging translators in France, made some kitchen revelations in his memoirs that might lead us to think the opposite. "The translator is the novelist's ape," he said, paraphrasing Mauriac, and meaning that the translator should make the same gestures and assume the same postures as the writer, whether she wants to or not. His own French translations of then young and unknown writers from the United States—William Faulkner, John Dos Passos, Ernest Hemingway, John Steinbeck—are not only magisterial recreations, but also introduced to France a historic generation, whose influence among their European contemporaries—including Sartre and Camus—is more than evident. So Coindreau was not a traitor, but just the opposite: a brilliant accomplice. As all great translators always have been, though their personal contributions to the translated work tend to go unnoticed, while their defects get magnified.

When you read an author in a language that is not your own you feel an almost natural desire to translate it. This is understandable, because one of the pleasures of reading—like music—is the possibility of sharing it with your friends. Maybe that explains how Marcel Proust died without fulfilling one of his recurring desires, which was to translate into French someone as different from himself as John Ruskin. Two of the writers I would have liked to translate just for the pleasure of doing it are André Malraux and Antoine de Saint-Exupéry, neither of whom, by the way, enjoys the highest esteem of their current compatriots. But I have never gone any further than the desire. However, for a long time I have been translating drop by drop Giacomo Leopardi's *Cantos,* but I do so in hiding and in my very scant free time, and in the full knowledge that this will not be the path to glory for either Leopardi or myself. I just do it as one of those bathroom pastimes that the Jesuit fathers used to call solitary pleasures. But the mere attempt has been enough to lead me to realize just how difficult it is, and how self-sacrificing, to try to compete with professional translators for their daily broth.

It is unlikely that a writer could be satisfied with the translation of a work of his own. In each word, in each sentence, in each emphasis of a novel there is almost always a second secret intention that only the author knows. That's why it is undoubtedly desirable that the writer himself should participate in the translation as far as possible. A notable experience in that sense is the exceptional French translation of James Joyce's *Ulysses.* The basic first draft was done complete and alone by August Morell, who then worked toward the final version with Valery Larbaud and Joyce himself. The result is a masterpiece, barely improved on—according to those in the know—by the Brazilian Portuguese version by Antonio Houaiss. Whereas the only translation that exists into Spanish is almost nonexistent. But its history serves as an excuse. An Argentinian called J. Salas Subirat did it for himself, just as a distraction; in real life he was an authority on life insurance. The editor Santiago Rueda, of Buenos Aires, discovered it, unfortunately, and published it at the end of the 1940s. I met Salas Subirat a few years later in Caracas behind an anonymous desk in an insurance company and we spent a stupendous evening talking about English novelists, whom he knew almost by heart. The last time I saw him seems like a dream: he was dancing, quite old by then and more alone than ever, in the crazy parade of the Barranquilla carnival. It was such a strange apparition that I couldn't make up my mind to say hello.

Other historical translations are those that Gustav Jean-Aubry and Phillipe Neel did of Joseph Conrad's novels into French. This all-time great writer—who was really called Jozef Teodor Konrad Korzeniowski—had been born in Poland, and his father was a translator of English authors, including Shakespeare. Conrad's main language was Polish, but from a very early age he learned French and English, and he eventually became a writer in both those languages. Today we consider him, with reason or without it, as one of the masters of English literature. It is told that he made his French translators' lives unlivable trying to impose his own perfection on them, but he never chose to translate himself. It's odd, but not many bilingual writers do so. The closest case to us is Jorge Semprún, who writes in French and in Spanish, but always separately. He never translates himself. Stranger still is the Irish writer Samuel Beckett, Nobel Prize in Literature, who writes the same work twice in two different languages, but their author insists that one is not the translation of the other, but that they are two distinct works in two different languages.

Some years ago, in the scorching summer of Patelaria, I had an enigmatic experience as a translator. Count Enrico Cicogna, who was my translator into Italian until his death, was translating the novel *Paradiso,* by the Cuban writer José Lezama Lima, during that vacation. I am a devoted fan of Lezama Lima's poetry, as I also was of his strange personality, though I had few occasions to see him, and at that time I wanted to get to know his hermetic novel better. So I helped Cicogna a little, less in the translation than in the tough business of deciphering the prose. It was then I understood that, in fact, to translate is the most profound way to read. Among other things, we found a sentence whose subject changed gender and number several times in less than ten lines, to the point where by the end it was not possible to know who was who, or when, or where. Knowing Lezama Lima, it's possible that such disorder was deliberate, but only he could have said so, and we were never able to ask him. The question Cicogna wondered about was whether the translator had to respect those blunders of agreement in Italian or if he should render them with academic correctness. My opinion was that he should conserve them, so the work would pass into the other language just as it was, not only with its virtues, but also with its defects. It is a duty of loyalty to the reader in the new language.

For me there is no more boring curiosity than that of reading translations of my own books in the three languages it would be possible for me to do so. I don't recognize myself, except in Spanish. But I have read some of the books translated into English by Gregory Rabassa and I have to admit that I found some passages that I liked more than I did in Spanish. The impression Rabassa's translations give is that he memorized the book in Spanish and then went back and wrote the whole thing again in English: his fidelity is more complex than simple literalism. He never explains anything in a footnote, which is the least valid and unfortunately most well worn resource of bad translators. In this sense, the most notable example is that of the Brazilian translator of one of my books, who added a footnote to the word *astromelia:* "Imaginary flower invented by García Márquez." The worst of it is that I later read somewhere that astromelias not only exist, as everyone knows, in the Caribbean, but that their name comes from the Portuguese.

June 21, 1982, *El País,* Madrid

# Sleeping Beauty on the Airplane

She was beautiful and lithe, with soft skin the color of bread and eyes like green almonds, and her hair was straight and black and all the way down her back, and she had an aura of oriental antiquity that could just as easily have come from Bolivia as from the Philippines. She was dressed with subtle taste: a lynx jacket, a silk blouse with very faint flowers, natural linen slacks, and flat shoes the color of bougainvillea. "This is the most beautiful woman I've ever seen in my whole life," I thought, when I saw her in the boarding line for the New York flight from Paris in the Charles de Gaulle airport. I stepped aside for her, and when I arrived at the seat assigned by my boarding pass, I found her settling into the seat next to mine. Almost breathless I managed to wonder which of the two of us had the bad luck of that terrifying coincidence.

She settled in as if she were going to live there for several years, putting each thing in its place in a perfect order, until her personal space was arranged like an ideal home where everything is within reach. While she was doing this, the steward offered us a welcoming glass of champagne. She didn't want one, and she tried to explain something in rudimentary French. The steward then spoke to her in English, and she thanked him with a stellar smile, and asked for a glass of water, and not to be woken for any reason during the flight. Then she opened on her lap a large, square vanity case, with copper corners like our grandmothers' travel trunks, and she took two golden tablets from a box that contained more of many different colors. She did everything in a methodical and unhurried way, as if there had never been anything unforeseen for her since her birth.

Finally, she put the little pillow in the corner against the window, covered herself with the blanket up to her waist without taking her shoes off, and turned on her side in the seat, almost in a fetal position, and slept without a single pause, without a sigh, without the tiniest change in position, for the seven terrifying hours and the extra twelve minutes the flight to New York lasted.

I have always believed that there is nothing more beautiful in nature than a beautiful woman. So it was impossible for me to escape the spell of that fabulous creature sleeping at my side even for an instant. It was such a stable sleep that at a certain moment I was concerned that the tablets she'd taken were not for sleeping but for dying. I contemplated her many times inch by inch, and the only signs of life I could detect were the shadows of her dreams that passed across her forehead like clouds over water. She had a chain around her neck so fine it was almost invisible on her golden skin, perfect unpierced ears, and a plain band on her left hand. Since she looked no older than twenty-two, I consoled myself with the idea that it wasn't a wedding ring but just that of a happy and ephemeral engagement. She wasn't wearing any perfume: her skin exhaled a tenuous breath that could not be anything but the natural fragrance of her beauty. "You on your sleep and on the sea the ships," I thought, twenty thousand feet above the Atlantic Ocean, trying to remember in order Gerardo Diego's unforgettable sonnet. "Knowing that you sleep, certain, safe, faithful channel of abandonment, pure line, so close to my manacled arms." My reality so resembled that of the sonnet that within half an hour I had reconstructed it in my memory to the end: "What terrifying islander slavery, I sleepless, crazed, on the cliffs, the ships on the sea, you on your sleep." Nevertheless, after five hours of flight having contemplated the sleeping beauty so much, and with so much undirected anxiety, I suddenly understood that my state of grace was not in the

Gerardo Diego sonnet, but in another masterpiece of contemporary literature, *The House of the Sleeping Beauties,* by the Japanese writer Yasunari Kawabata.

I discovered this lovely novel by way of another long path, but which in any case concluded with this sleeping beauty on the airplane. Several years ago, in Paris, the writer Alain Jouffroy phoned to tell me that he wanted to introduce me to some Japanese writers who were at his house. The only thing I knew of Japanese literature at the time, apart from sad high school haikus, were a few stories by Junichiro Tanizaki that had been translated into Spanish. Actually, the only thing I knew for sure about Japanese writers was that all of them, sooner or later, ended up committing suicide. I had heard people talk about Kawabata for the first time when they gave him the Nobel Prize in 1968, and then I tried to read something of his, but I fell asleep. A short while later he disemboweled himself with a ritual saber, as another notable novelist, Osamu Dazai, had done in 1946, after several frustrated attempts. Two years before Kawabata, and also after several frustrated attempts, the novelist Yukio Mishima, who might be the best known in the West, had done a complete hara-kiri after directing a patriotic harangue to soldiers of the Imperial Guard. So when Alain Jouffroy called me on the phone, the first thing that came to mind was the cult of death that Japanese writers seemed to have. "I'll come over with great pleasure," I told Alain, "but on the condition that none of them commit suicide." They did not kill themselves, and instead we spent a charming night, during which the best thing I learned was that they were all mad. They agreed. "That's why we wanted to meet you," they told me. Finally, they convinced me that for Japanese readers there was no doubt that I was a Japanese writer.

Trying to understand what they meant, I went the next day to a specialist bookshop in Paris and bought all the books available by those authors. Shusaku Endo, Kenzaburo Oé, Yasushi Inoue, Akutagawa Ryonosuke, Masuji Ibusi, Osamu Dazai, as well as the obvious ones by Kawabata and Mishima. For almost a year I read nothing else, and now I am convinced: Japanese novels have something in common with mine. Something I could not explain, that I did not feel in the life of the country during my only visit to Japan, but that seems more than evident.

However, the only one I would have liked to have written is Kawabata's *The House of the Sleeping Beauties,* which tells the story of a strange mansion in the suburbs of Kyoto where elderly bourgeois men pay enormous sums to enjoy the most refined form of last love: to spend the night contemplating the city's most beautiful girls, who lie naked and tranquilized in the same bed. They cannot wake them, or even touch them, though nor do they try to, because the purest satisfaction of that senile pleasure was to be able to dream at their sides.

I lived this experience beside the sleeping beauty on the airplane to New York, but I was not pleased. On the contrary: the only thing I desired in the last hour of the flight was for the steward to wake her up so I could regain my freedom, and maybe my youth. But it didn't happen that way. She woke up on her own once the plane was already on the ground, fixed herself up, and stood without looking at me, and she was the first one off the plane and disappeared forever into the crowd. I stayed on the same flight to Mexico, pampering the first traces of nostalgia for her beauty beside the seat still warm from her sleep, unable to get what the crazy writers in Paris had said about my books out of my head. Before landing, when they gave me the customs card, I filled it out with a sense of bitterness. Profession: Japanese writer. Age: 92 years old.

September 20, 1982, *Proceso,* Mexico City

# Writer Wanted

I often wonder what is most lacking in my life, and I always answer with the truth: "A writer." The joke is not as silly as it seems. If I ever found myself with the unavoidable commitment of writing a fifteen-page story by tonight, I would turn to my countless notes going way back and I am sure I would make it to press in time. Maybe it would be a very bad story, but the commitment would be met, which after all is the only thing I meant to say with this nightmare example. However, I would not be able to write a telegram of congratulations or a letter of condolences without ruining my liver for a week. For those undesirable duties, as with so many others of social life, most writers I know wish they could appeal to the good offices of other writers. This column I write every week, and which on one of these October days is going to celebrate its first two years of solitude, is without doubt good proof of my almost barbarian sense of professional honor. Only once has this corner been missing my column, and it was not my fault: it was a last-minute failure of the transmission system. I write it every Friday, from nine in the morning until three in the afternoon, with the same will, the same conscience, the same joy, and often the same inspiration with which I should have written a masterpiece. When I don't have a well-defined topic I go to bed grumpy on Thursday night, but experience has taught me that the drama will resolve itself while I sleep and will begin to flow in the morning, as soon as I sit in front of the typewriter. However, I almost always have several topics planned in advance, and bit by bit I gradually collect and order the data from various sources and check them very rigorously, for I have the impression that readers are not as indulgent with my blunders as they might be with those of that other writer who I need. My first aim with these notes is that every week they should teach something to the average readers who are the ones that interest me, even if those teachings might seem obvious and maybe puerile to the wise university grads who already know everything. My other aim—the more difficult one—is that they should always be written as well as I am able without the help of the other, for I have always believed that good writing is the only happiness that is enough in and of itself.

I imposed this servitude on myself because I was feeling that between one novel and the next I was spending a lot of time not writing, and gradually—like pitchers—it was taking longer and longer to warm up my arm. Later, that artisanal decision turned into a commitment to readers, and now it's a labyrinth of mirrors I can't find my way out of. Unless I encountered, of course, the providential writer who would take my place. But I think it might already be too late, as the last three times I made the determination to stop writing these columns I was prevented, with his implacable authoritarianism, by the small Argentinian that I too have inside.

The first time I decided was when I tried to write the first one, after more than twenty years of not doing it, and I needed a week of galley slave work to finish it. The second time was more than a year ago, when I spent a few days of rest with General Omar Torrijos at the Farallón military base, and the day was so clear and the ocean so calm that I was more tempted to go sailing than to write. "I'll send the editor a telegram saying there's no column today, and that'll be that," I thought, with a sigh of relief. But I couldn't eat lunch for the weight of my guilty conscience, and, at six in the evening, I locked myself up in my room, wrote for an hour and a half about the first thing that came to mind, and gave the column to one of General Torrijos's aides-de-camp so he could send it to Bogotá by telex, with a plea that they would send it on to Madrid and Mexico. Only on the following day did I learn that General Torrijos had had to arrange the shipment in a military plane to the Panama airport, and from there, by helicopter, to the presidential palace, whence they did me the favor of distributing the text by some official channel.

The last time, six months ago now, when I discovered upon waking that I now had ripe in my heart the love novel I'd been longing to write for so many years, and that I had no choice other than never writing it or immersing myself in it immediately and full-time. However, at the hour of truth, I did not have enough guts to renounce my weekly captivity, and for the first time I'm doing something I always thought impossible: writing a novel every day, letter by letter, with the same patience, and I hope the same luck, as the hens who peck in the patios, and hearing the fearful footsteps closer every day of next Friday's large animal. But here we are again, as ever, and I hope forever.

I was already suspecting that I would never escape this cage since the afternoon when I started writing this piece at home in Bogotá and finished it the next day under the diplomatic protection of the Mexican embassy; I kept suspecting it at the telegraph office in Crete, one Friday last July, when I succeeded in communicating with the employee on duty to get the text transmitted in Spanish. I continued suspecting it in Montreal, when I had to buy an emergency typewriter because the voltage of mine was not the same as that in the hotel. I just suspected it again, forever, barely two months ago, in Cuba, when I had to change typewriters twice because they refused to get along with me. Finally, they brought me an electric one with such advanced customs that I ended up writing it by hand in a notebook with square ruled pages, like in the remote and happy times of primary school in Aracataca. Each time one of these setbacks happened to me I appealed with more anxieties to my wish for someone to take charge of my good luck: a writer.

All things considered, I've never felt that need in such an intense way as the day many years ago when I arrived at Luis Alcoriza's house, in Mexico, to work with him on a screenplay. I found him dismayed at ten in the morning, because his cook had asked him as a favor to write a letter to the director of social security. Alcoriza, who is an excellent writer, with a daily practice of a bank teller, who had been the most intelligent writer of the first scripts for Luis Buñuel and, later, for his own movies, had thought the letter would take him about half an hour. But I found him, mad with fury, in the midst of a pile of torn-up sheets of paper, on which there was not much more than all conceivable variations of the formulaic opening: "By means of the present document, herewith, I have the pleasure of addressing you for . . ." I tried to help him, and three hours later we were still writing drafts and crumpling them up, now half cut on gin and vermouth and stuffed with Spanish chorizos, but without having progressed beyond the first conventional letters. I'll never forget the compassionate face of the kind cook when she returned at three for her letter and we told her shamefaced that we hadn't been able to write it. "But it's very simple," she said, with all her humility, "Look, sir." And then she began to improvise the letter with such precision and such fluency that Luis Alcoriza found himself having trouble typing with the same fluidity with which she dictated it. That day—and still today—I was left thinking that maybe that woman, who was growing old without glory in the limbo of the kitchen, was perhaps the secret writer who was missing from my life that I needed in order to be a happy man.

October 6, 1982, *El País,* Madrid

# Obregón or the Boundless Vocation

Many years ago, a friend asked Alejandro Obregón to help him look for the body of the skipper of his boat, who had drowned at dusk, while they were fishing for twenty-pound *prochilos* in the swampy marshlands of Santa Marta. Both went over that immense paradise of wilted waters for the whole night, exploring the least likely bends with fishermen's lamps, following the drift of floating objects that tend to lead to pools where drowned people stay sleeping. All of a sudden, Obregón saw him: he was submerged to the crown, almost sitting in the water, and the only thing floating on the surface were the errant strands of his hair. "He looked like a medusa," Obregón told me. He grabbed the hair with both hands and, with his vast painter of toros and tempests strength, pulled the whole drowned man out, with his enormous eyes open, dripping mud of anemones and manta rays, and threw him like a dead fish in the bottom of the boat.

This episode, which Obregón tells me again because I ask him to every time we get lethally drunk—and which also gave me the idea for a story about drowning victims—might be the moment of his life that most closely resembles his art. That's how he paints, in fact, as if he's fishing for drowned men in the darkness. His paint with horizons of thunder spills out bullfighting minotaurs, patriotic condors, billy goats in heat, and impudent barracudas. In the midst of the tormented fauna of his personal mythology wanders a woman crowned with a garland of flowers, the same one as ever and as never, who prowls around his canvases with the clues switched, for in reality she is the impossible creature for whom this reinforced concrete romantic would have wished to die. Because he is as all we romantics are, and as we have to be: without any shame.

The first time I saw that woman was the same day I met Obregón, thirty-two years ago, in his studio on Calle de San Blas, in Barranquilla. It was two large, plain rooms through the widespread windows of which climbed the Babylonian uproar of the city. There she was in a different corner, among the latest Picassian still lifes and the first eagles of his heart, with her hanging lotus flowers, green and sad, holding her soul in her hand. Obregón, who had just come back from Paris and was running around as if dumbfounded by the fragrance of guava, was already identical to this self-portrait of his that watches me from the wall while I write, and which he tried to kill one crazy night with five heavy-caliber shots. Nevertheless, what most impressed me when I met him were not those diaphanous pirate's eyes that made the market fags sigh, but his big, tough hands, which we saw him use to knock down half a dozen Swedish sailors in a brothel fight. They are old Spanish hands, gentle and barbarous at the same time, like those of Don Rodrigo Díaz de Vivar, who fattened his hunting falcons on the doves of the woman he loved.

Those hands are the perfect instrument of a boundless vocation that gives him not a moment's peace. Obregón has been painting since before he had the use of reason, at all hours, wherever he is, with whatever is at hand. One night, back in the days of the drowned man, we had gone to drink mullein in a sailors' canteen still only half constructed. The tables were piled up in the corners, among bags of cement and lumps of lime, and the carpentry workbenches, to make the doors. Obregón was lost in thought for a long time, unhinged by the smell of turpentine, until he climbed up on a table with a can of paint, and in a single masterly broad stroke painted a green unicorn on the bare wall. It was not easy to convince the owner that this unique brushstroke was worth much more than the house itself. But we did.

The nameless canteen was called El Unicornio from that night on, and it was an attraction for gringo tourists and idiots from Bogotá until it was blown away by the inexorable winds that take everything away in time.

On another occasion, Obregón broke both his legs in a traffic accident, and during two weeks in hospital sculpted his totemic animals in the plaster of his casts with a scalpel a nurse lent him. The masterwork was not his, however, but what the surgeon had to do to remove the two sculpted legs, which are now in a private collection in the United States. A journalist who visited him at home asked him with annoyance what was wrong with his spaniel puppy that didn't calm down for an instant, and Obregón answered, "She's nervous because she knows I'm going to paint her." He did paint her, of course, as he paints everything he comes across, because he thinks that everything that exists in the world is there for him to paint. In his viceroy's house in Cartagena de Indias, where the whole of the Caribbean Sea pours in through a single window, one finds his daily life as well as another painted life everywhere: on the lamps, on the toilet seat, on the glass of the mirrors, on a cardboard box in the fridge. Many things that in other artists are defects are legitimate virtues in him, such as sentimentalism, such as symbols, such as lyrical raptures, such as patriotic fervor. Even some of his failures live on, like that woman's head that was burned in the kiln, but which Obregón still keeps in the best spot in his house, with one side eaten away and a queen's tiara on her forehead. It's not possible to think that failure was not desired and calculated when one discovers in the face without eyes the inconsolable sadness of the woman who never arrived.

Sometimes, when there are friends at his house, Obregón goes into the kitchen. It's a pleasure to watch him setting out on the table the blue bream, the pig's snout with a carnation in its nose, the rack of veal ribs with the trace of the heart still visible, green plantains from Arjona, yucca from San Jacinto, yams from Turbaco. It's a pleasure to watch how he prepares everything, how he cuts and distributes according to their shapes and colors, and how he puts it all to boil in big pots of water with the same charm he paints with. "It's like putting the whole landscape into the stew," he says. Then, as it boils, he tastes the broth with a wooden spoon and empties into it bottles and bottles and bottles of Tres Esquinas rum, which gradually replaces the water in the pot as it evaporates. In the end, we understand why we had to wait so long and as ceremoniously as for the supreme pontiff, and it's that this Stone Age *sancocho* stew that Obregón serves in achiote leaves is nothing to do with cuisine, but is an edible painting. He does everything like this, the way he paints, because he doesn't know how to do anything any other way. It's not that he only lives to paint. No: it's that he's only living when he paints. Always barefoot, in a cotton shirt he must have previously used to clean his brushes and trousers he's cut off himself with a butcher's knife, and with the kind of bricklayer's rigor that God would have liked his priests to have.

October 20, 1982, *El País,* Madrid

# Literature Without Pain

Not long ago I indulged in the frivolity of telling a group of students that you can learn universal literature in one afternoon. A young woman in the group—a fanatic of belles lettres and clandestine author of verses—immediately asked me to be more specific: "When can we come over so you can teach us?" So they came over the following Friday and we talked about literature until six, but we couldn't get past German romanticism, because they too indulged in a frivolity: leaving to go to a wedding. I told them, of course, that one of the conditions of learning all of literature in one afternoon was not accepting a wedding invitation for the same time, since for getting married and being happy there is much more time available than for learning poetry. It had all started and continued and finished as a joke, but in the end I was left with the same impression as they were: if we hadn't learned all of literature in three hours, at least we'd gotten a pretty acceptable notion of it without having to read Jean-Paul Sartre.

When you hear a record or read a book that dazzles you, the natural impulse is to look for someone to share it with. This happened to me when I discovered by chance Béla Bartók's *Quintet for String Quartet and Piano,* which was not so popular then, and it happened to me again when I heard on the car radio the very beautiful and rare *Concerto Gregoriano for Violin and Orchestra* by Ottorino Respighi. They were both very difficult to find, and my closest music-loving friends had never heard of them, so I went all over the place trying to find those records so we could listen to them together. Something similar has been happening to me for many years with Juan Rulfo's novel *Pedro Páramo*, an entire edition of which I think I've bought just to always have enough copies for my friends to take with them. The only condition is that we meet as soon as possible to talk about that beloved book.

Of course, the first thing I explained to my good students was my idea, perhaps too personal and simplistic, of teaching literature. In fact, I have always believed that a good literature course should not be anything more than a guide to the good books that people should read. Each era does not have as many essential books as teachers who enjoy terrorizing their pupils claim, and you can speak of all of them in a single afternoon, as long as nobody has an unavoidable commitment to attend a wedding. Reading these essential books with pleasure and good judgment is another matter for many afternoons of life, but if the students are lucky enough to be able to do so they'll end up knowing as much about literature as the wisest of their teachers. The next step is more frightening: specialization. And a step farther is the most detestable one a person can take in this life: erudition. But if what students want is to excel at visits, they don't have to pass through any of these three purgatories, but simply buy the two volumes of a providential work called *Mil libros—A Thousand Books*. Luis Nueda and Don Antonio Espina wrote it back in 1940, and there, in alphabetical order, are summaries of more than a thousand basic books of universal literature, with their plots and interpretations, and impressive notes on their authors and their times. There are many more books, of course, than the ones I'd need for my afternoon class, but they have the advantage that you don't have to read them. Nor do you have to be embarrassed: I have those two savior volumes on my desk where I write, I've had them for many years, and I have saved myself from grave predicaments in the paradise of intellectuals, and by having them and knowing them I can assure you that those who pontificate at social occasions have them too and use them, as do the newspaper columnists.

Luckily, the books of a lifetime are not so many. Not long ago, the Bogotá magazine *Pluma* asked a group of writers which books had been most significant for them. They said to name only five, without including the obvious ones, such as the Bible, *The Odyssey,* or *Don Quixote.* My final list was this: *A Thousand and One Nights, Oedipus Rex* by Sophocles, *Moby-Dick, Floresta de lírica española,* which is an anthology by Don José Manuel Blecua that reads like a detective novel, and a dictionary of the Spanish language that is not, obviously, that of the Royal Academy. The list is debatable, of course, like all lists, and offers subjects for many hours of conversation, but my reasons are simple and sincere: if I had only read these five books—as well as the obvious ones, of course—I would have read enough to write all that I have written. That is, a list for professional purposes. However, I did not arrive at *Moby-Dick* by an easy route. At first, I had in its place Alexander Dumas's *The Count of Monte Cristo,* which, to my mind, is a perfect novel, but only for structural reasons, and that aspect was already more than satisfied by *Oedipus Rex.* Later I thought of Tolstoy's *War and Peace,* which in my opinion is the best novel ever written in the history of the genre, but actually since it is, it seemed fair to omit it as one of the obvious books. *Moby-Dick,* on the other hand, whose anarchic structure is one of the most beautiful disasters of literature, instilled me with a mythic impulse that I no doubt needed in order to write.

In any case, the one-afternoon literature course as much as the survey of five books leads one to think, once more, of so many unforgettable works that recent generations have forgotten. Three of them, a little more than twenty years ago, were first rate: *The Magic Mountain* by Thomas Mann, *The Story of San Michele* by Axel Munthe, and *Le Grande Meaulnes* by Alain Fournier. I wonder how many of today's students of literature, even the most diligent, have even taken the trouble to wonder what might be inside these three marginalized books. One has the impression they had a marvelous, though momentary, destiny, like some by Eça de Queiroz and Anatole France, and like *Point Counter Point* by Aldous Huxley, which was a sort of epidemic in the blue years of our adolescence; or like *The Goose Man* by Jakob

Wassermann, which I might owe more to nostalgia than to poetry; or like *The Counterfeiters* by André Gide, who might have been even falser, even more counterfeit, than their own author suspected. There is only one surprising case in this rest home for retired books, and that's Hermann Hesse, who was a sort of dazzling explosion when they gave him the Nobel Prize in 1946, and then he plummeted into oblivion. But in recent years his books have been rescued with as much strength as before by a generation that maybe finds in them a metaphysics that corresponds to their own doubts.

Clearly none of this is worrying, but just a salon enigma. The truth is that there shouldn't be any compulsory books, or books read as penance, and the healthy way is to stop reading on the page when it becomes unbearable. However, for masochists who prefer to carry on in spite of everything, there is a correct formula: put the unreadable books in the bathroom. Maybe several years of good digestion can bring Milton's *Paradise Lost* to a happy conclusion.

December 8, 1982, *El País*, Madrid

# From Paris, with Love

I came to Paris for the first time one freezing December night in 1955. I arrived by train from Rome to a station decked out with Christmas lights, and the first thing that caught my attention were the couples who kissed each other everywhere. On the train, in the metro, in cafés, on elevators, the first postwar generation threw themselves with all their energy into the public consumption of love, which was still the only cheap pleasure after the disaster. They kissed in the middle of the street, with no worries about hindering pedestrians, who moved aside without looking at them or paying any attention, as we do with stray dogs that hang onto each other, making puppies in the middle of the town square. Those outdoor kisses were not frequent in Rome—which was the first European city I'd lived in—nor, of course, in the misty and prudish Bogotá of those days, where it was even difficult to kiss in bedrooms.

This was in the dark days of the war in Algeria. In the background of the nostalgic accordion music on the corners, beyond the street smell of chestnuts roasting in the braziers, repression was an insatiable specter. All of a sudden, the police would block off the exit of a café or of one of the North African bars on the Boulevard Saint-Michel and violently drag away anyone who didn't have a Christian face. One of those, inevitably, was me. No explanations worked: not just our faces, but also the accent with which we spoke French, were reasons for our undoing. The first time they put me in the cage with the Algerians, at the Saint-Germain-des-Prés police station, I felt humiliated. It was a Latin American prejudice: jail was something to be ashamed of then, because as children we didn't have a very clear distinction between political and common crimes, and our conservative adults took care of inculcating that confusion and keeping us in it. My situation was even more dangerous, because, even though the police dragged me away because they thought I was Algerian, once inside the cell the Algerians distrusted me when they realized that, despite my face of a door-to-door fabric salesman, I did not understand a single word they said. However, since they and I continued to be such assiduous visitors to the nocturnal lockups, we ended up reaching an understanding. One night, one of them said if I was going to be an innocent prisoner wouldn't it be better to be a guilty one, and put me to work for the Algerian National Liberation Front. He was Ahmed Tebbal, a doctor, who was one of my best friends in Paris during those days, but he died of a different war death after the independence of his country. Twenty-five years later, when I was invited to the celebration of that anniversary in Algeria, I declared to a journalist something that seemed hard to believe: the Algerian Revolution is the only one for which I've actually been imprisoned.

Nevertheless, Paris back then was not only a city of the Algerian War. It was also the place for the most generalized exile of Latin Americans in a long time. In effect, Juan Domingo Perón—who was not the same then as in later years—was in power in Argentina, General Ordía was in Peru, General Rojas Pinilla was in Colombia, General Pérez Jiménez was in Venezuela, General Anastasio Somoza was in Nicaragua, General Rafael Leónidas Trujillo was in Santo Domingo, General Fulgencio Batista was in Cuba. We were so many fugitives of so many simultaneous patriarchs that the poet Nicolás Guillén would lean out over his balcony of the Hotel Grand Saint-Michel, on Rue Cujas, every morning and shout out the news from Latin America in Spanish. One morning he shouted, "The man has fallen." Only one man had fallen, of course, but we all woke up with the illusion that the fallen general was the one from our own country.

When I arrived in Paris, I was nothing but a raw Caribbean. I am most grateful to that city, with which I have many old grudges, and many even older loves, for having given me a new and resolute perspective on Latin America. The vision of the whole, which we didn't have in any of our countries, became very clear here around a safe table, and one ended up realizing that, in spite of being from different countries, we were all crew members of the same boat. It was possible to travel all around the continent and meet its writers, its artists, its disgraced or budding politicians, just by making rounds of the crowded cafés of Saint-Germain-des-Prés. Some didn't arrive, as happened to me with Julio Cortázar—whom I already admired for the wonderful stories of *Bestiario*—and for whom I waited for almost a year in the Old Navy café, where someone had told me he often went. I finally met him fifteen years later, also in Paris, and he was still as I'd imagined him since long ago: the tallest man in the world, who never decided to grow old. The faithful copy of that unforgettable Latin American who, in one of his short stories, liked to walk through the misty dawns to go and watch the guillotine executions.

We breathed in the songs of Brassens in the air. The lovely Tachia Quintana, a bold Basque woman whom we Latin Americans from all over had adopted as one of our own exiles, performed the miracle of making a succulent paella for ten on a tiny spirit stove. Paul Coulaud, another of our converts, had found a name for that life: *la misère dorée,* golden misery. I didn't have a very clear appreciation of my situation until one night when I found myself near the Jardin de Luxembourg without having eaten a chestnut all day and with no place to sleep. I was wandering the boulevards for hours, in the hope that a police patrol sweeping the streets for Arabs would pick me up so I could sleep in the warm cell, but no matter where I looked I couldn't find one. At dawn, when the palaces along the Seine began to show their silhouettes in the thick fog, I headed over to the Îsle de la Cité with long, decisive strides and with the face of an honest worker who's just got up to go to his factory. As I was crossing the Saint-Michel bridge, I sensed that I was not alone in the fog because I could clearly hear the footsteps of someone approaching from the opposite direction. I saw him take shape in the fog, on the same sidewalk and with the same rhythm as me, and I saw up close his red and black plaid jacket, and in the instant our paths crossed at the middle of the bridge I saw his unruly hair, his Turk's moustache, his sad countenance of backdated hunger and sleepless nights, and I saw his eyes brimming with tears. My heart froze, because that man seemed to be me, on my way back.

That's my most intense memory of those times, and I've remembered it with more force than ever now that I've returned to Paris on my way back from Stockholm. The city has not changed since then. In 1968, when I was lured by my curiosity to see what had happened after that marvelous explosion of May, I found that lovers were not kissing in public, and they'd replaced the cobblestones in the streets, and they'd erased the most beautiful graffiti ever written on walls: "Imagination to power," "Beneath the pavement, the beach," "Make love on top of the others." Yesterday, after walking around the places that were once mine, I could only perceive one novelty: some municipal workers dressed in green, who traveled the streets on green motorcycles and carried mechanical hands like space explorers to collect from the street the shit that a million captive dogs expel every twenty-four hours in the loveliest city on earth.

December 29, 1982, *El País*, Madrid

# Return to Mexico

I once said in an interview, "Almost the only memory left to me of Mexico City, where I have so many beloved friends, is the incredible afternoon when the sun was shining and rain was falling in Chapultepec Forest, and I was so fascinated by that prodigious weather that my sense of direction was disturbed and I walked around and around in the rain, without finding a way out."

Ten years after that declaration I have returned to look for that enchanted forest and I found it rotten from the air pollution and looking like it hasn't rained on those wilted trees since that day. This experience revealed to me how much of my life and that of my family has been spent in this Luciferian city, which is today one of the most extensive and populous in the world, and how much we have changed together, we and the city, since we arrived without an address or a dime in our pockets, on July 2, 1961, at the dusty central railway station.

I'll never forget the date, even if it wasn't stamped on a useless passport, because the next day a friend woke me up very early in the morning by phoning to tell me that Hemingway had died. Sure enough, he had blown his head off with a rifle shot through the roof of his mouth, and that atrocity remained forever in my mind as the start of a new era. Mercedes and I, who had been married for two years, and Rodrigo, who wasn't yet a year old, had been living for the previous months in a hotel room in Manhattan. I was working as a correspondent for a Cuban news agency in New York, and I'd never known a more suitable place to be murdered. It was a sordid and solitary office, in an old building of the Rockefeller Center, with a room full of teletypes and an editorial room with a single window that looked out over an abysmal courtyard, always sad and smelling of frozen soot, and from the bottom of which rose the din at all hours of rats fighting over leftovers in the garbage cans. When that place became unbearable, we put Rodrigo in a basket and left on the first bus going south. All our capital in the world amounted to three hundred dollars, and another hundred that Plinio Apuleyo Mendoza sent us from Bogotá to the Colombian consulate in New Orleans. It was a lovely bit of madness: we were trying to get to Colombia through the cotton plantations and black towns of the United States, the only guide we brought being my recent memory of the novels of William Faulkner.

As a literary experience, all that was fascinating, but in real life— even being so young—it was crazy. Twelve days on buses along secondary, sweltering, and sad roads, eating in grotty diners and sleeping in even worse hotels. In department stores in the cities of the south we encountered the ignominy of discrimination for the first time: there were two separate public water fountains, one for whites and the other for negros, with a sign marking each one. In Alabama we spent a whole night looking for a hotel room, and in every one they told us they were full, until one night porter discovered by chance that we weren't Mexican. However, as usual, what most tired us were not the interminable days under the burning June heat or the bad nights in cheap hotels, but the bad food. Tired of cardboard hamburgers and malted milks, we ended up sharing the baby's jars of stewed fruit and vegetables. At the end of that heroic voyage we had managed once more to confront reality and fiction. The immaculate parthenons in the middle of the cotton fields, farmers taking siestas under the eaves of roadside stalls, the shacks of black workers surviving in misery, the white heirs to Uncle Gavin Stevens, who walked to church on Sunday with their languid wives dressed in muslin: the terrible life of Yoknapatawpha

County had paraded before our eyes through the window of a bus, and was as true and as human as in the novels of the old master.

However, all the emotion of that experience went all to hell when we reached the Mexican border, dusty and dirty Laredo that was already familiar from so many movies about smugglers. The first thing we did was go into a cheap restaurant for a hot meal. The first thing they served, instead of soup, was a dish of tender, yellow rice, prepared in a different way from on the Caribbean coast. "Praise the Lord," Mercedes exclaimed. "I'd stay here forever, if only to keep eating this rice." She could never have imagined to what extent her desire to stay would be fulfilled. Not for that plate of fried rice, though, because destiny would play a very funny joke on us: the rice we eat at home we have brought from Colombia, almost as contraband, in the suitcases of friends who come to visit, because we've learned to survive without our childhood foods, except for that patriotic rice the snowy grains of which can be counted one by one on the plate.

We arrived in Mexico City on a mauve evening, with our last twenty dollars and nothing in the future. We only had four friends here. One of them was the poet Álvaro Mutis, who had already had some hard years in Mexico, but hadn't yet reached his soft ones. Another was Luis Vicens, one of the great Catalans who had come from Colombia a short while before us, fascinated by Mexican cultural life. Another was the sculptor Rodrigo Arenas Betancur, who was planting monumental heads all across this interminable country. The fourth was the writer Juan García Ponce, who had been to Colombia as a jury member for a painting prize, but we barely remembered each other, due to the dense state of intoxication we'd both been in the night we met for the first time. He was the one who phoned me as soon as he heard of my arrival, and shouted with his florid way with words, "That bastard Hemingway blew his fucking brains out with a shotgun." That was the exact moment—and not at six o'clock the previous evening—that I truly arrived in Mexico City, without really knowing why, or how, or for how long. That was twenty-one years ago now and I still don't know, but here we are. As I said on a recent memorable occasion, I've written my books here, I've raised my children here, and I've planted my trees here.

I've revived this past—rarified by nostalgia, it's true—now that I've returned to Mexico like so many times before, and for the first time I've found myself in a different city. There are no courting couples left in the Chapultepec Forest, and nobody seems to believe in the radiant sun of January, because it's such a rarity these days. Never, ever, have I found so much uncertainty in the hearts of my friends. Can this be possible?

January 26, 1983, *El País*, Madrid

# Okay, We'll Talk About Literature

Jorge Luis Borges said in a long-ago interview that the problem with young writers then was that at the moment of writing they were thinking of success or failure. Whereas, when he was starting out he only thought of writing for himself. "When I published my first book," he said, "in 1923, I had three hundred copies printed and I distributed them among my friends, except for a hundred copies, which I took to the magazine *Nosotros*." One of the editors of the publication, Alfredo Bianchi, looked at Borges in terror and said, "But you don't expect me to sell all those books?" "Of course not," Borges answered, "in spite of having written them, I'm not completely crazy." Anyway, the author of the interview, Alex J. Zisman, who was then a Peruvian student in London, told in an aside that Borges had suggested to Bianchi that he could slip copies into the pockets of the overcoats people left hanging in the office closet, and thus get some reviews published.

Thinking of this episode, I remembered another perhaps too well known, about the wife of the then famous North American writer Sherwood Anderson finding the young William Faulkner writing in pencil leaning on an old wheelbarrow. "What are you writing?" she asked him. Faulkner, without looking up, answered, "A novel." Mrs. Anderson only managed to exclaim, "My God!" Nonetheless, a few days later Sherwood Anderson sent someone to tell Faulkner that he was prepared to take the novel to a publisher, on the condition that he didn't have to read it. The book must have been *Soldiers' Pay,* which came out in 1926—in other words, three years after Borges's first book—and Faulkner had published four more before he was considered a recognized author whose books were accepted by publishers without too much of a runaround. Faulkner himself once declared that after those first five books he felt forced to write a sensationalist novel, since the previous ones hadn't earned enough money to feed his family. That obligatory book was *Sanctuary,* and it's worth noting, because this reveals very well what Faulkner's idea of a sensationalist novel was.

I've remembered these episodes of the origins of great writers in the course of an almost four-hour-long conversation I had yesterday with Ron Sheppard, one of the literary writers for *Time* magazine, who is preparing a piece on Latin American literature. Two things about that interview pleased me. The first was that Sheppard only spoke to me and only made me speak about literature, and demonstrated, without the least sign of pedantry, that he knows very well what it is. The second is that he had read all my books with close attention and had studied them very well, not only individually, but in order and as a whole, and he'd also taken the trouble to read numerous interviews with me so he wouldn't fall back on the same old questions as ever. This last point doesn't interest me so much for flattering my vanity—something that, in any case, cannot nor should not be discarded when talking with any writer, even with those who seem most modest—rather because it allowed me to better explain, with my own experience, my personal conceptions of the job of writing. Every interviewed writer discovers immediately—by any tiny carelessness—if interviewers have not read a book they're talking about, and from that instant, and maybe without them noticing it, place them in a disadvantageous situation. On the other hand, I have a very fond memory of a very young Spanish journalist, who conducted a very meticulous interview about my life believing that I was the author of the song of the yellow butterflies, which was playing everywhere at the time, but who had not the slightest idea that the music had been inspired by a book and that, moreover, I was the one who'd written it.

Sheppard didn't ask any concrete question, or use a tape recorder, but every once in a while he took very brief notes in a school exercise book, nor did he care what prizes I'd been given before or now, nor did he try to find out what my engagement was as a writer, or how many books I'd sold, or how much money I'd earned. I'm not going to give a summary of our conversation, because everything we talked about now belongs to him and not to me. But I haven't been able to resist the temptation to point out the fact as an encouraging event in the troubled waters of my private life today, when I do nothing but answer the same questions several times a day with the same answers as ever. And even worse: the same questions, which have less to do every day with my job as a writer. Sheppard, on the other hand, and as naturally as he breathed, moved without stumbling through the densest mysteries of literary creation, and when he said goodbye he left me drenched in nostalgia for the times when life was simpler and one enjoyed the pleasure of wasting hours and hours talking of nothing but literature.

However, none of what we talked about grabbed my attention as intensely as the Borges quote: "Now, writers think of failure and success." One way or another, I've said the same thing to so many young writers I meet in these worlds. Not all of them, fortunately, have I seen trying to finish a novel hastily and carelessly in time to enter it in a contest. I have seen them plummet into chasms of demoralization after a critical review, or after a rejection letter from a publisher. I once heard Mario Vargas Llosa say something that disconcerted me from that start: "At the moment he sits down to write, every writer decides if he's going to be a good writer or a bad writer." Nevertheless, several years later a twenty-three-year-old kid arrived at my house in Mexico who had just published his first novel six months earlier and that night felt triumphant because he'd just submitted his second novel to his editor. I expressed my perplexity at the haste with which he was conducting his premature career, and he answered with a cynicism I still want to remember as involuntary: "You have to think a lot before writing because everyone reads everything you write. But I can write very fast, because very few people read me." Then I understood, like a dazzling revelation, Vargas Llosa's phrase: that kid had decided to be a bad writer, as, indeed, he was until he got a good job at a used-car dealership, and stopped wasting his time writing. However—I think now—maybe his fate would have been different if before learning how to write he'd learned how to talk about literature. These days there is a fashionable phrase: "We want fewer deeds and more words." It is a phrase, of course, charged with great political treachery. But it could serve writers as well.

A few months ago I said to Jomi García Ascot that the only thing better than music is talking about music, and last night I was about to say the same thing about literature. But then I thought more carefully. Actually, the only thing better than talking about literature is doing it well.

February 9, 1983, *El País*, Madrid

# That News Board

From the third decade of this century, and for about ten years, a newspaper existed in Bogotá that perhaps had few antecedents in the world. It was a board like we had in schools back then, where the latest news would be written in chalk, and it was hung twice a day over the railings of *El Espectador*'s balcony. That intersection of Avenida Jiménez de Quesada and Carrera Séptima—known for many years as the best street corner in Colombia—was the busiest place in the city, especially at the times when the news board appeared: twelve noon and five in the afternoon. It would become difficult, if not impossible, for the streetcars to get through the hindrance of the impatiently waiting crowd.

Those street readers also had a possibility we don't have nowadays, and that was to applaud the news they thought good, to whistle disapprovingly at news that didn't completely satisfy them and throw stones against the board when the news struck them as contrary to their interests. It was a form of active and immediate participation, by which *El Espectador*—the evening paper that sponsored the board—had a thermometer more efficient than any other to measure the fever of public opinion.

Television did not yet exist, and there were very full radio news bulletins, but at fixed hours, so before going to eat lunch or dinner, one might stand waiting for the appearance of the board in order to arrive home with a more complete vision of the world. One afternoon we learned—with a murmur of astonishment—that Carlos Gardel had died in Medellín, in an airplane crash. When there was very big news, like that one, the board would change several times outside of its usual hours, to feed with extraordinary bulletins the public's apprehension. This almost always happened during elections, and did so in an exemplary and unforgettable way during Enrique Concha Venegas's famous flight between Lima and Bogotá, the incidents of which we saw reflected, hour after hour, on the news balcony. On April 9, 1948—at one in the afternoon—the popular leader Jorge Eliécer Gaitán was struck down by three well-aimed bullets. Never, in the stormy history of the chalkboard, had such big news happened so close by. But it couldn't register it because *El Espectador* had moved its offices and modernized informative systems and habits, and only a few old-fashioned nostalgic guys remembered when we knew it was twelve noon or five in the afternoon because we saw the news board appear on the balcony.

Nobody remembers now at *El Espectador* whose original idea that direct and alarming form of modern journalism was in that remote and lugubrious city as Bogotá then was. But we know that the one who drafted the headlines, in general terms, was a kid who was barely twenty years old and would go on to be, without doubt, one of Colombia's best journalists without having gone beyond primary school. Today—after fifty years in the profession—all his compatriots know his name was, and still is, José Salgar.

The other night, at an in-house tribute to him at the newspaper, José Salgar said, more serious than joking, that due to that anniversary he'd received in life all the praise usually kept for the dead. Maybe he hadn't heard that the most surprising thing in his journalistic life is not having completed half a century—something that has happened to many old men—but the reverse: having started at the same newspaper at the age of twelve, and when he'd already been looking for work as a journalist for almost two years. In fact, every time he walked home from school, back then in 1939, José Salgar dawdled in front of the windows of the *Mundo al Día* watching the pedal presses printing the variety newspaper, which was in great demand at the time, the most read section being one of pure journalism. It was called "I Saw It with My Own Eyes," and it was readers' own experiences told in their own words. For every piece they published, *Mundo al Día* paid five centavos, at a time when almost everything cost five centavos: the newspaper, a cup of coffee, a shoeshine, a streetcar ride, a soda, a packet of cigarettes, a child's cinema ticket, and many other primary and secondary necessities. So anyway, José Salgar, from the time he turned ten, began sending in his written experiences, not so much for the five centavos as to see them in print, and he never succeeded. Fortunately, since if they had he would have been celebrating fifty years of journalism two years ago, which would have been almost abusive.

He began in order: at the lowest rung. A friend of his family who worked in *El Espectador*'s printing works took him along to work with him on a shift that began at four in the morning. José Salgar was assigned the tough task of melting the metal bars for the linotype, and his seriousness caught the attention of a star linotypist—the kind of guy they don't make anymore—who, in turn, caught the attention of his workmates for two distinguished virtues: because he looked like a twin brother of the president of the Republic, Don Marco Fidel Suárez, and because he was as knowledgeable as his lookalike on the secrets of the Spanish language, to such an extent that he was a candidate for the Academia de la Lengua. After six months of melting lead for the linotypes, José Salgar was sent to a cramming school by the editor in chief—Alberto Galindo—even if it was just to learn the elemental rules of spelling, and was promoted to office messenger. From then on he worked his way up from the inside, until becoming what he is today, deputy director of the newspaper and its most senior employee. In the times when he started to write the news boards a street photographer took his picture in a black suit with wide lapels and a hat with a tilted brim, in the style of the time imposed by Carlos Gardel. In photos of him these days he doesn't resemble anyone but himself.

When I joined the staff of *El Espectador*—in 1953—José Salgar was the heartless managing editor who ordered me, as if it were the golden rule of journalism, "Wring the swan's neck," meaning to stick to the facts. For a novice from the provinces who was ready to get himself killed for literature, that order was not much short of an insult. But maybe José Salgar's greatest merit has been to know how to give orders without pain, because he doesn't put on a boss's face when he gives them, but that of a subordinate. I don't know if I did what he told me to or not, but instead of feeling offended I thanked him for the advice, and since then—and still today—we've been accomplices.

Maybe what we're most grateful to each other for is that when we're working together we don't stop doing so even in our time off. I remember that we didn't leave each other's side for a minute during those three historic weeks when Pope Pius XII got the hiccups that wouldn't go away, and José Salgar and I declared ourselves on permanent watch, waiting for either of the two endings to the news: either the pope cured his hiccups or he died. On Sundays we drove out to the countryside on the plateau roads, with the radio on, to follow without pause the rhythm of the pope's hiccups, but without going too far away, so we could get back to the office as soon as we heard the outcome. I was remembering those times one night last week when we attended his retirement dinner, and I think I hadn't realized till then that maybe the sleepless feel of the job came to José Salgar from the incurable custom of the news board.

September 21, 1983, *El Espectador,* Madrid

# Return to the Seed

U nlike most good and bad writers of all eras, I've never idealized the town where I was born and where I was raised until
the age of eight. My memories of that time—how many times
I've said it—are the clearest and most real I happen to have, to the
extreme that not only can I evoke as if it were yesterday the appearance
of each one of the houses that are still there, but I can even discover in a
wall a crack that didn't exist during my childhood. A town's trees tend
to last longer than human beings, and I've always had the impression
that they remember us too, maybe better than we remember them.

I was thinking all this, and much more, as I walked the dusty,
scorched streets of Aracataca, the small town where I was born and
where I returned a few days ago sixteen years after my last visit. A bit
overwhelmed by reunions with so many childhood friends, bewildered
by a troop of children among whom I seemed to recognize myself
when the circus came to town, I had, nevertheless, enough serenity to
be surprised that nothing had changed in the house of General José
Rosario Durán—where now, of course, there was no one left from his
illustrious family; that despite the freshly painted strips the plazas were
still the same, with their thirsty dust and almond trees as sad as they'd
always been, and that the church had been painted and repainted many
times in half a century, but the dial of the clock on the tower is the

same. "And that's nothing," someone specified. "The man who repairs it is still the same one."

Much—I would say too much—has been written on the affinities between Macondo and Aracataca. The truth is that each time I return to the real town I find it resembles the fictional one less, except for certain external elements, like the overpowering heat at two in the afternoon, its white, scorching dust, and the almond trees that are still there on some street corners. There is a geographical similarity that is obvious, but which doesn't go much further. For me there is more poetry in the history of *animes* than in all that I have tried to leave in my books. The same word—*animes*—is a mystery that has pursued me since those times. The dictionary of the Royal Academy says that the *anime* is a plant and its resin ("elemi," in English). In the same way, although with many more precisions, Mario Alario di Filippo's excellent lexicon of Colombianisms defines this word. Father Pedro María Revollo, in his *Costeñismos colombianos*, doesn't even mention it. Meanwhile, Sundenheim, in his *Vocabulario costeño*, published in 1922 and seemingly forgotten forever, devotes a very ample note of which I'll transcribe the part that most interests us: "The *anime*, among us, is a sort of benevolent *duende* who helps its protégés in difficult and critical moments, and thus when someone is said to have *animes* we are given to understand they count on a person or mysterious force that has provided them its help." As we can see, Sundenheim identified them with magical creatures, *duendes*, and more precisely, with those described by Michelet.

The *animes* of Aracataca were something else: minuscule beings, no more than an inch high, that lived in the bottom of the large earthenware jars. Sometimes they were confused with *gusarapos*, which some people called *sarapicos*, and which were really mosquito larvae frolicking in the depths of the drinking water. But those who knew did not confuse them: *animes* had the ability to escape their natural refuge, even if the jar was well sealed, and they enjoyed getting up to all sorts of mischief in the house. That's all they were: naughty, but benevolent spirits, who curdled the milk, changed the color of children's eyes, rusted the locks, or provoked twisted dreams. However, there were times when their moods would get deranged, for reasons that were never understood, and they would take to stoning the house where they lived. I met them at the house of Don Antonio Daconte, an Italian emigrant who brought great novelties to Aracataca: silent films, the billiards hall, bicycles for rent, gramophones, the first radio receivers. One night word went round town that the *animes* were stoning Don Antonio Daconte's house, and everybody went to see. Contrary to what people might think, it was not a horrific spectacle, but rather a joyful party that in any case did not leave a single window intact. You couldn't see who was throwing them, but stones came from every direction and had the magic virtue of not hitting any people but striking their exact objectives: anything made of glass. A long time after that enchanted night, we children carried on sneaking into Don Antonio Daconte's house to take the lid off the water jar and see the *animes*—quiet and almost transparent—getting bored at the bottom of the water.

What might have been the most famous house in town was next door to that of my grandparents on a corner like so many others, and known as *the house of the dead*. In it lived the parish priest who baptized our whole generation. Francisco C. Angarita, who was famous for his tremendous moralizing sermons. Many good and bad things were murmured about Father Angarita, whose fits of rage were fearful; but just a few years ago I found out that he had taken a very definite and consistent position during the strike and massacre of the banana workers.

I often heard it said that *the house of the dead* was called that because people saw the ghost of someone who during a session of spiritualism said his name was Alfonso Mora wandering there at night. Father Angarita told the tale with such realism that your hair would stand on end. He described the apparition as a heavyset man, with his shirtsleeves rolled up to the elbows, his hair short and tightly curled, and the perfect luminous teeth of a black man. Every night, at the stroke of midnight, after walking through the house, he disappeared under the calabash tree that grew in the middle of the courtyard. The area around the tree, of course, had been excavated many times in search of buried treasure. One day, in bright sunlight, I went next door in pursuit of a rabbit, and tried to catch it in the outhouse, where it had hidden. I pushed open the door, but instead of the rabbit, I saw the man crouched in the latrine, with a look of pensive sadness we all have in those circumstances. I recognized him immediately, not only by his sleeves rolled up to his elbows, but also by his beautiful teeth that shone in the darkness.

These and many other things I remembered a few days ago in that scorching town, while old and new friends, and those who were just beginning to be friends, seemed to be truly pleased that we were together again after so long. It was the same source of poetry whose drumroll of a name I've heard resonate in half the world, in almost every language, and that, nonetheless, seems to exist more in memory than in reality. It is difficult to imagine another place more forgotten, more abandoned, more apart from God's ways. How could one not feel one's soul twisted by a sense of upheaval?

December 21, 1983, *El País*, Madrid

# How Do You Write a Novel?

This, without doubt, is one of the questions people most often ask novelists. Depending on who's asking, you always have a satisfactory answer. Even more: it's useful to try to answer, because not only is there pleasure in variety, as they say, but also within it is the possibility of finding the truth. Because one thing is certain: I believe that those who most often ask themselves the question of how you write a novel are novelists themselves. And we also give ourselves a different answer every time.

I'm referring, of course, to writers who believe that literature is an art destined to improve the world. The others, the ones who believe that literature is an art destined to improve their bank accounts, have formulas for writing that are not only accurate, but can be resolved as precisely as if they were mathematical formulas. Editors know this. One of them amused himself recently explaining to me how easy it was for his publishing house to win the National Literature Prize. In the first place, they had to analyze the members of the jury, their personal history, their work, their literary tastes. The editor thought that the sum of all those elements would end up supplying an average of the general jury taste. "That's what computers are for," he said. Once they'd established what kind of book had the best possibilities of being awarded the prize, they had to proceed with a method contrary to what we normally use in life: instead of looking where that book was, they had to investigate which author, good or bad, was best equipped to fabricate it. All the rest was a question of signing a contract to get that author to sit down and write to measure the book that will win next year's National Literature Prize. The alarming thing is that the editor had submitted this game into the mill of computers, and they had given him an eighty-six percent chance of accuracy.

So the problem is not how to write a novel—or a short story—but how to write one seriously, even if afterward it doesn't win any prizes or sell any copies. That is the answer that does not exist, and if anyone is in a position to know that it's the same guy who's writing this column with the secret aim of finding his own solution to the enigma. For I have returned to my study in Mexico, where a year ago I left several unfinished short stories and the beginnings of a novel, and I feel as if I can't find the thread to unravel the ball. With the stories, there were no problems: they're in the garbage. After reading them at the healthy distance of a year later, I venture to swear—and maybe it's true—that it wasn't me who wrote them. They were part of an old project of sixty or more short stories on the lives of Latin Americans in Europe, and their principal defect was the basis for tearing them up: not even I believed them.

I will not be so arrogant as to say my hand didn't shake as I tore them to shreds and then dispersed the strips to keep them from being reconstructed. I trembled, and not just my hand, since I have a memory about ripping up paper that might seem encouraging but I find depressing. It's a memory that goes back to July of 1955, the eve of my trip to Europe as *El Espectador*'s special envoy, when the poet Jorge Gaitán Durán arrived at my room in Bogotá to ask me to leave him something to publish in the magazine *Mito*. I had just gone through my papers, had put the ones I thought worth keeping away safely and had ripped up the ones I thought beyond recovery. Gaitán Durán, with his insatiable voracity for literature, and most of all at the possibility of discovering hidden values, began to go through the wastepaper basket, and all of a sudden he found something that caught his attention. "But this is very publishable," he said. I explained why I'd thrown it away: it was a whole chapter that had been cut from my first novel, *Leaf Storm*—already published by then—and it could have no other honest destination than the garbage can. Gaitán Durán did not agree. He thought that in reality the text would have been superfluous to the novel, but had a different value on its own. More to try to please him than because he'd convinced me, I authorized him to tape the torn strips back together and publish the chapter as if it were a story.

"What title shall we give it?" he asked, using a plural that had rarely been as appropriate as in that case. "I don't know," I said. "Because it is nothing more than Isabel's monologue as she watches it rain in Macondo." Gaitán Durán wrote across the top of the first page almost as I was saying it: "Monologue of Isabel Watching It Rain in Macondo." That's how one of my stories that has received the most praise from critics and, especially, from readers came to be published. However, that experience did not prevent me from continuing to rip up manuscripts I didn't think were publishable, but rather taught me that it's necessary to tear them in such a way that they can never be pieced back together.

Tearing up stories is inevitable, because writing them is like pouring concrete. Whereas writing a novel is like laying bricks. What this means is that if a story doesn't set in the first attempt it's best not to insist. A novel is easier: you start over again. This is what has happened now. Neither the tone nor the style nor the personalities of the characters were right for the novel I'd left half finished. But here too the explanation is singular: not even I believed it. Trying to find the solution, I reread two books I supposed would be useful. The first was *Sentimental Education,* by Flaubert, whom I hadn't read since my remote insomnias of university, and only served now to avoid some analogies that would have been suspicious. But it did not resolve my problem. The other book I read again was Yasunari Kawabata's *The House of the Sleeping Beauties,* which had struck me to my core three years ago and continues to be a beautiful book. But this time it was of no use, because I was looking for clues about the sexual behavior of the elderly, but what I found in the book was that elderly Japanese sex, which seems to be as odd as everything Japanese, has nothing to do with the sexual behavior of elderly Caribbeans. When I told of my worries at the table, one of my sons—the one with more common sense—said, "Wait a few more years and you'll find out firsthand." But the other, who is an artist, was more concrete: "Go back and reread *The Sorrows of Young Werther*," he said, without the slightest trace of mockery in his voice. I tried, in effect, not only because I am a very obedient father, but also because I sincerely thought Goethe's famous novel could be useful to me. But the truth is that on this occasion I did not end up weeping at his miserable burial, as happened the first time, but rather I didn't get past the eighth letter, which is the one where the suffering young man tells his friend Wilhelm how he's starting to feel happy in his solitary cabin. This is where I find myself, so it's not a rare occurrence that I have to bite my tongue to keep from asking everyone I meet: "Tell me something, brother: how the hell do you write a novel?"

## HELP

I once read a book, or saw a film, or someone told me about a real event, with the following plot: a navy officer smuggles his lover into his cabin aboard a warship, and they experience a boundless love within that oppressive enclosure, without anyone discovering her for several years. I beg anyone who knows the author of this lovely story to let me know urgently, as I've asked so many people who don't know that I'm starting to suspect that maybe I made it up myself and now I don't remember. Thank you.

January 25, 1984, *El País*, Madrid

A NOTE ON THE TYPE

This book was set in a modern adaptation of a type designed by the first William Caslon (1692–1766). The Caslon face, an artistic, easily read type, has enjoyed more than two centuries of popularity in the English-speaking world. This version, with its even balance and honest letterforms, was designed by Carol Twombly for the Adobe Corporation and released in 1990.

Composed by North Market Street Graphics,
Lancaster, Pennsylvania

Printed and bound by Berryville Graphics,
Berryville, Virginia

Designed by Cassandra J. Pappas